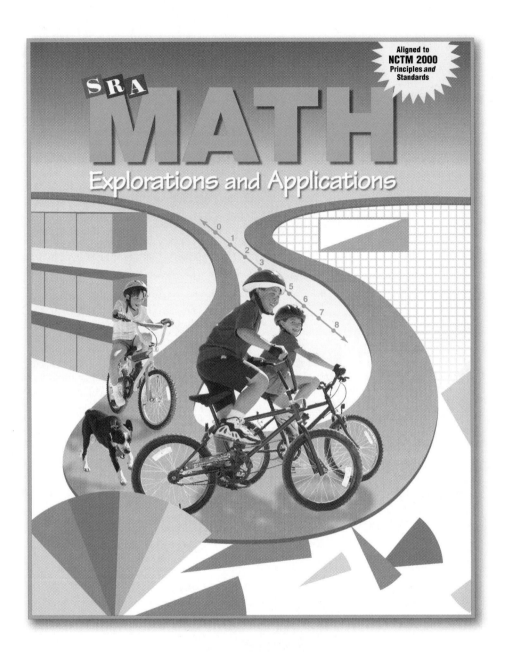

SRA MATH
Explorations and Applications

Stephen S. Willoughby
Carl Bereiter
Peter Hilton
Joseph H. Rubinstein

Co-author of Thinking Story® selections Marlene Scardamalia

A Division of The **McGraw·Hill** *Companies*

Columbus, Ohio
Chicago, Illinois

Table of Contents i, PhotoEdit; ii, iii, SuperStock; iv, Jack Zehrt/FPG.

Unit 1 3, PhotoEdit; 4, 5, SuperStock;; 9, 10, 19, ©Fotosmith; 20, PhotoDisc; 21, 22, ©FOTOfactory; 23, SuperStock; 25, ©FOTOfactory; 26, ©Fotosmith; 28, SuperStock; 30, ©FOTOfactory; 38, PhotoDisc; 40-44, ©FOTOfactory; 46, SuperStock; 47, ©Fotosmith; 48-54, ©FOTOfactory; 55, ©Fotosmith; 58, SuperStock; 59 (l), PhotoDisc, (r), William Rosenthal; 61, William Rosenthal; 62 (t), SuperStock, (b), ©FOTOfactory; 63, SuperStock; 66-67, 70, ©FOTOfactory; 72 (l, c, cr, r), PhotoDisc, (cl), SuperStock; 73, ©Fotosmith; 76, PhotoDisc; 82, ©Fotosmith; 87, 88, 93, 99, SuperStock; 103, David Young Wolff/PhotoEdit; 120, Aaron Haupt; 122, 125.

Unit 2 127, SuperStock; 129, PhotoDisc; 135, ©FOTOfactory; 139, SRA; 140 (t), SuperStock, (b), PhotoDisc; 144, 145, SuperStock; 146, PhotoDisc; 149, 152, ©FOTOfactory; 155, 156, 160, SuperStock; 162 (t), PhotoDisc, (b), SuperStock; 168, SuperStock; 173, PhotoDisc; 174, ©Fotosmith; 178, Aaron Haupt; 179, 181, PhotoDisc; 182, ©FOTOfactory; 183, SuperStock; 193, ©Fotosmith; 194, SuperStock; 195, Aaron Haupt; 196 (t), Rob Downey, (b), PhotoDisc; 197, SuperStock; 199, ©Fotosmith; 200, 201, SuperStock; 203, 204, PhotoDisc; 216, Dennis MacDonald/PhotoEdit; 221 (t), ©FOTOfactory, (b), SuperStock.

Unit 3 227, SuperStock; 230, 231, 233, 235, PhotoDisc; 239, ©Fotosmith; 240, ©FOTOfactory; 242 (tl, tr, br, cr), PhotoDisc, (bl, cl), ©FOTOfactory; 243 (t), William Rosenthal, (tc, cb), ©FOTOfactory, (tb), Renee Lynn/Photo Researchers, Inc., (ct), A. Schmidecker/FPG, (bc), Carroll Segher/Photo Researchers, Inc., (b), SuperStock, (bt), Jan Halaska/Photo Researchers, Inc.; 244 (tl, ct), William Rosenthal, (cb, b), ©FOTOfactory, (tr), Rob Downey; 245, PhotoDisc; 248 (tl), Visuals Unlimited, (tr, cl, cr, br), PhotoDisc, (bl), SuperStock; 249 (t), William Rosenthal, (tc, cb), ©FOTOfactory, (tb), Renee Lynn/Photo Researchers, Inc., (ct), A. Schmidecker/FPG, (bt), Jan Halaska/Photo Researchers, Inc., (bc), Carroll Segher/Photo Researchers, Inc., (b), SuperStock; 250 (tl), Frank Siteman/PhotoEdit, (tr, ct), Rob Downey, (cb, b), PhotoDisc; 251, 253, PhotoDisc; 254, ©FOTOfactory; 255, PhotoDisc; 257, ©Fotosmith; 258, ©FOTOfactory; 259, ©Fotosmith; 261, ©FOTOfactory; 265, PhotoDisc; 267, ©Fotosmith; 268, PhotoDisc; 274, ©FOTOfactory; 275, 276, ©Fotosmith; 277, 278, 279, ©FOTOfactory; 280, ©Fotosmith; 281, 282, PhotoDisc; 284, ©Fotosmith; 287 (t), SuperStock, (b), Tom Prettyman/PhotoEdit; 289, 291, ©Fotosmith; 292, SuperStock; 293, PhotoDisc; 294 (t), SuperStock, (b), Mary Kate Denny/PhotoEdit; 297, ©Fotosmith; 303, PhotoDisc; 307, ©Fotosmith; 308, ©FOTOfactory; 315, PhotoDisc; 321, ©Fotosmith; 323, Tony Freeman/PhotoEdit; 326 (t), PhotoDisc, (b), SuperStock; 331, SuperStock; 332, ©FOTOfactory; 334, ©Fotosmith.

Unit 4 339, Jack Zehrt/FPG; 344 (tl, tr, cl), Rob Downey, (cr), PhotoDisc, (b), ©FOTOfactory; 345 (t, tc, tb, c, b), PhotoDisc, (bt), Visuals Unlimited; 346, ©FOTOfactory; 347, PhotoDisc; 347, Rob Downey; 348 (t), Tony Freeman/Photoedit, (tc, c, bt,b), PhotoDisc, (ct), Myrleen Ferguson/PhotoEdit; 350, Tony Freeman/PhotoEdit; 356, ©Fotosmith; 362, ©FOTOfactory; 363, PhotoDisc; 364, ©Fotosmith; 367, Gary A. Conner/PhotoEdit; 373, 381, PhotoDisc; 382 (tl, tr), ©FOTOfactory, (bl), PhotoDisc, (br), Michael Newman/PhotoEdit; 383, 384, ©FOTOfactory; 388, ©Fotosmith; 389, PhotoDisc; 390 (tr), SuperStock, (c, br), PhotoDisc; 391, PhotoDisc; 398 (t), Myrleen Ferguson/PhotoEdit, (b), ©FOTOfactory; 399, PhotoDisc; 402, ©Fotosmith; 403, PhotoDisc; 404 (l), PhotoDisc, (r), ©FOTOfactory; 405, ©Fotosmith; 407, 410, PhotoDisc; 412 (t), ©FOTOfactory, (b), PhotoDisc; 414 (t), William Rosenthal, (b), Michael Newman/PhotoEdit; 419, ©FOTOfactory; 425, 429, 431, 440, PhotoDisc; 441 (t), PhotoDisc, (b), SuperStock; 442, PhotoDisc; 443, PhotoDisc; 460, Rob Downey; 467 (l), Rob Downey, (r), PhotoDisc; 470, PhotoDisc; 473 (l), PhotoDisc, (r), ©FOTOfactory; 476 (l), PhotoDisc, (c, r), Rob Downey.

www.sra4kids.com

SRA/McGraw-Hill

A Division of The McGraw·Hill Companies

Printed in the United States of America.

Send all inquiries to:
SRA/McGraw-Hill
P. O. Box 812960
Chicago, IL 60681

ISBN 0–07–579600–7

1 2 3 4 5 6 7 8 9 VHP 05 04 03 02

Contents

Contents

UNIT 2 · Multiplication and Division — 126

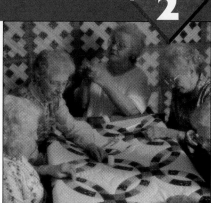

LESSON

Contents

Resources

Addition and Subtraction

NUMBER RELATIONSHIPS

- rounding and estimating
- odds and evens
- equalities and inequalities
- perimeter
- time

SCHOOL TO WORK CONNECTION

Letter carriers use math . . .

The letter carrier usually organizes the mail into two piles: batches going to even-numbered addresses and batches going to odd-numbered addresses. This way the carrier can go down one side of your street, cross at the end of the street, and go up the other side.

Counting and Estimating

How many books are on a shelf?

My estimate was 120 books.
I counted 135 books.

Estimate.

◆ What things will you estimate?

◆ How many did you estimate?

Check your estimate.

◆ How many did you count?

Talk about the Thinking Story "The Fur-Lined Letter."

In your Math Journal tell how you made your estimate. What would you do differently next time to improve your accuracy?

Find the numbers that are written twice.

1 Start counting from 8.

8 12 10 11 9 16 14 18 11 13 15 17 13

2 Start counting from 47.

49 51 47 52 56 55 50 53 57 48 50 52 54

3 Start counting from 96.

105 97 102 96 101 106 99 103 100 104 99 106 98

4 Start counting from 379.

387 381 388 382 386 379 383 385 380 383 382 384

5 Start counting from 212.

212 216 214 215 213 220 218 222 215 217
219 221 218

6 Start counting from 77.

79 81 77 82 86 85 80 83 87
78 80 82 84

7 Start counting from 32.

35 43 32 40 33 38 34 41 38 36
39 42 37 35

LESSON 2

Counting to 1000

How many buttons? Show the number with your Number Wheel. Then write it.

1 One hundred thirty-two

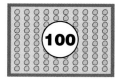 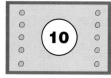   

Show.   Then write. ■

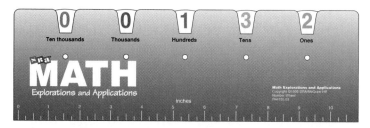

2 Twenty-seven

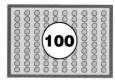 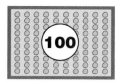 

Show.   Then write. ■

3 Two hundred five

Show.   Then write. ■

4 One hundred forty

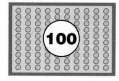    

Show.   Then write. ■

Count up or down. Fill in the missing numbers.

5 | 7 | 8 | ■ | ■ | ■ | 12 | ■ | 14 |

6 | 17 | 16 | 15 | ■ | ■ | ■ | ■ | 10 |

7 | 86 | 87 | ■ | ■ | ■ | 91 | ■ | 93 |

8 | 431 | 432 | ■ | ■ | ■ | 436 | ■ | 438 |

9 | 807 | 808 | ■ | ■ | ■ | ■ | ■ | 814 |

10 | 707 | 706 | ■ | ■ | ■ | 702 | ■ | 700 |

11 | ■ | ■ | 421 | 422 | ■ | ■ | ■ | 426 |

12 | 589 | ■ | 591 | ■ | ■ | 594 | ■ | 596 |

13 | ■ | ■ | 600 | 601 | 602 | ■ | ■ | 605 |

14 | ■ | 311 | 312 | ■ | ■ | ■ | ■ | 317 |

15 | 278 | ■ | ■ | ■ | 282 | 283 | ■ | 285 |

16 | 57 | 58 | ■ | ■ | 61 | ■ | ■ | 64 |

GAME

◆ **LESSON 2 Counting to 1000**

COOPERATIVE LEARNING

Roll a Number Game

Players:	Whole group or two, three, or four
Materials:	One 0–5 cube (red)
Object:	To make the greatest three-digit number
Math Focus:	Place value and mathematical reasoning

RULES

1. Draw blanks for a three-digit number on your paper, like this:

   ___ ___ ___

2. The first player rolls the cube once.

3. Write that number in one of the three blanks you made.

4. Take turns rolling the cube two more times and writing the number in the blanks.

5. After all three rolls, each player will have made a three-digit number. The player who makes the greatest three-digit number is the winner of the round.

SAMPLE GAME

Number Rolled	Amy's Number	Jack's Number	Toby's Number
First roll: 3	3 ___ ___	___ ___ 3	___ 3 ___
Second roll: 1	3 ___ 1	___ 1 3	___ 3 1
Third roll: 5	3 5 1	5 1 3	5 3 1

Toby won this round.

5	7	9
hundreds	tens	ones

When we read 579 we say "five hundred seventy-nine."
The 5 is in the hundreds place.
The 7 is in the tens place.
The 9 is in the ones place.
The number 579 stands for 5 hundreds, 7 tens, 9 ones.

Write each as some number of hundreds, tens, and ones. For example, 73 is 0 hundreds, 7 tens, 3 ones.

17 543   18 804   19 760   20 123

21 86   22 806   23 860   24 111

25 3   26 300   27 429   28 544

Write the standard number for each. For example, for seven hundreds, eight tens, nine ones you would write 789.

29 one hundred, two tens, three ones

30 zero hundreds, zero tens, seven ones

31 zero hundreds, seven tens, zero ones

32 seven hundreds, zero tens, zero ones

33 one hundred, five tens, nine ones

34 three hundreds, three tens, three ones

35 zero hundreds, two tens, nine ones

36 eight hundreds, zero tens, seven ones

37 six hundreds, five tens, five ones

38 In the number 159, which digit stands for the greatest number? Which digit stands for the least number?

LESSON 3

Measuring and Graphing

Each student in Brittany's class measured the length of the room in shoe units. Brittany made a graph of the results. Use a computer or other means to make a graph for your class.

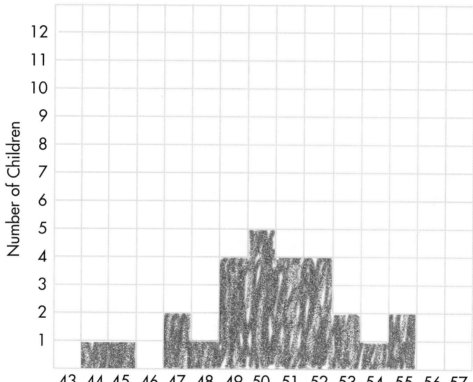

Play the "Animal Data" game.

Use the graph on page **10** to answer questions **1–7.**

❶ How many students counted 45 shoe units as the length of the room? How many students counted 55 shoe units? Which students do you think had longer shoes?

❷ How many students measured the length of the room as 56 shoe units?

❸ How many students measured the length of the room as 52 shoe units?

❹ How many students measured the length of the room as 51 shoe units?

❺ How many students measured the length of the room as 49 shoe units?

❻ How many students measured the length of the room as 48 shoe units?

❼ How many students measured the length of the room as 47 shoe units?

Make a bar graph to answer questions 8–10 for your class and classroom.

❽ What was the greatest number of shoe units anybody measured for the length of the room?

❾ What was the least number of shoe units anybody measured for the length of the room?

❿ What was the most common number of shoe units for the measure of the length of the room?

In your Math Journal explain why different people got different numbers of shoe units as the length of the room.

LESSON
4

Counting to 10,000

Count up or down. Fill in the missing numbers.

1 (997 | 998 | ■ | ■ | ■ | ■ | 1003)

2 (2076 | 2077 | ■ | ■ | ■ | ■ | 2082)

3 (6543 | 6542 | ■ | ■ | ■ | ■ | 6537)

4 (4096 | 4097 | ■ | ■ | ■ | ■ | 4102)

5 (■ | ■ | 7238 | 7239 | ■ | ■ | 7242)

6 (■ | ■ | 1010 | 1011 | ■ | ■ | 1014)

7 (9995 | 9996 | ■ | ■ | ■ | ■ | 10,001)

8 (3111 | ■ | ■ | ■ | ■ | ■ | 3117)

9 (■ | ■ | ■ | 5008 | 5009 | ■ | 5011)

10 (■ | 825 | 826 | ■ | ■ | ■ | 830)

11 (2001 | ■ | ■ | ■ | ■ | ■ | 2007)

COOPERATIVE LEARNING

Counting and Writing Numbers Game

GAME

Players:	Two
Materials:	Pencil, paper
Object:	To say and write the ending number
Math Focus:	Counting numbers, writing numbers, and mathematical reasoning

RULES

1. The first player chooses a starting and an ending number. Each must be more than 1000 and less than 10,000. He or she counts one, two, or three from the starting number. For example, if the starting number is 1351, the first player could write:

    1351, 1352   1351, 1352, 1353   1351, 1352, 1353, 1354

2. The second player starts where the first player leaves off. He or she writes the next one, two, or three numbers. If the first player stops at 1353, the second player could write:

    1354   1354, 1355   1354, 1355, 1356

3. Players take turns counting and writing one, two, or three numbers.

4. The player who finishes on the ending number wins the round.

MATH JOURNAL

In your Math Journal explain what you would do if it were your turn to start counting from 2625 and the ending number was 2630.

Place Values

The chart shows the number of thousands, hundreds, tens, and ones in each number. Write the number on your paper.

	Thousands	Hundreds	Tens	Ones
1	7	5	4	3
2	0	4	0	4
3	6	5	4	3
4	0	0	1	0
5	1	2	3	4
6	0	0	0	1

7 In the number 1234, what does the 2 stand for? What does the 3 stand for? Which of the digits, 1, 2, 3, or 4, stands for the greatest number?

8 In the number 10, how many thousands are there? How many hundreds are there? How many tens are there? How many ones are there?

9 In the number 498, how many thousands are there? How many hundreds are there? How many tens are there? How many ones are there?

10 In the number 2001, what do the 0s stand for?

11 In the number 21, what does the 2 stand for? In which number does the 2 stand for a greater number, 2001 or 21?

12 In the number 444, which digit in which place stands for the least number?

Solve.

13 Use the digits 4 and 5 once. What is the greatest number you could make?

14 Use the digits 4 and 5 once. What is the least number you could make?

15 Are there any other two-digit numbers you can make using a 4 and 5 once each?

16 Use the digits 2, 4, and 6 once. What is the greatest number you could make?

17 Use the digits 2, 4, and 6 once. What is the least number you could make?

18 Are there any other three-digit numbers you can make using a 2, 4, and 6 once each? How many can you make all together? Write them all on your paper. Include the numbers you showed for questions 16 and 17.

19 How many four-digit numbers can you make using each of the digits 9, 8, 7, and 6 once each? Which is greatest? Which is least?

20 Make a three-digit number in which all three digits are the same and the sum of the digits is 12.

21 Make a four-digit number in which all four digits are the same and the sum of the digits is 12.

22 Make a two-digit number in which both digits are the same and the sum of the digits is 12.

23 Make a list of three-digit numbers in which the first digit is 1 and the sum of the digits is 6. How many numbers like this are there?

24 Make a list of three-digit numbers in which the first digit is 2 and the sum of the digits is 6. How many numbers like this are there?

25 Make a list of three-digit numbers in which the first digit is 3 and the sum of the digits is 6. How many numbers like this are there?

LESSON
6

Reviewing Basic Facts

Add. Solve for _n_.

ALGEBRA
READINESS

① $3 + 1 = n$　　**②** $8 + 2 = n$　　**③** $3 + 8 = n$

④ $2 + 7 = n$　　**⑤** $9 + 9 = n$　　**⑥** $8 + 1 = n$

⑦ $2 + 8 = n$　　**⑧** $1 + 7 = n$　　**⑨** $9 + 4 = n$

⑩ $8 + 5 = n$　　**⑪** $7 + 10 = n$　　**⑫** $3 + 10 = n$

⑬ $4 + 10 = n$　　**⑭** $10 + 9 = n$　　**⑮** $7 + 6 = n$

⑯ $8 + 3 = n$　　**⑰** $7 + 8 = n$　　**⑱** $7 + 1 = n$

⑲　　$\begin{array}{r} 7 \\ + 8 \\ \hline \end{array}$　　**⑳**　　$\begin{array}{r} 6 \\ + 5 \\ \hline \end{array}$　　**㉑**　　$\begin{array}{r} 8 \\ + 1 \\ \hline \end{array}$

㉒　　$\begin{array}{r} 9 \\ + 3 \\ \hline \end{array}$　　**㉓**　　$\begin{array}{r} 4 \\ + 7 \\ \hline \end{array}$　　**㉔**　　$\begin{array}{r} 10 \\ + 3 \\ \hline \end{array}$

GAME

Play the "Addition Table" game.

Subtract.

㉕ $\begin{array}{r} 8 \\ -\ 1 \\ \hline \end{array}$ ㉖ $\begin{array}{r} 20 \\ -\ 10 \\ \hline \end{array}$ ㉗ $\begin{array}{r} 10 \\ -\ 2 \\ \hline \end{array}$ ㉘ $\begin{array}{r} 17 \\ -\ 10 \\ \hline \end{array}$

㉙ $\begin{array}{r} 9 \\ -\ 3 \\ \hline \end{array}$ ㉚ $\begin{array}{r} 14 \\ -\ 9 \\ \hline \end{array}$ ㉛ $\begin{array}{r} 18 \\ -\ 9 \\ \hline \end{array}$ ㉜ $\begin{array}{r} 7 \\ -\ 6 \\ \hline \end{array}$

㉝ $\begin{array}{r} 12 \\ -\ 4 \\ \hline \end{array}$ ㉞ $\begin{array}{r} 15 \\ -\ 3 \\ \hline \end{array}$ ㉟ $\begin{array}{r} 13 \\ -\ 9 \\ \hline \end{array}$ ㊱ $\begin{array}{r} 11 \\ -\ 10 \\ \hline \end{array}$

㊲ 8 − 5 = ■ ㊳ 20 − 9 = ■

㊴ 14 − 8 = ■ ㊵ 17 − 5 = ■

㊶ 13 − 6 = ■ ㊷ 19 − 10 = ■

㊸ 7 − 2 = ■ ㊹ 10 − 3 = ■

㊺ 11 − 8 = ■ ㊻ 13 − 4 = ■

㊼ 16 − 7 = ■ ㊽ 14 − 6 = ■

㊾ 10 − 3 = ■ ㊿ 12 − 7 = ■

(51) 15 − 8 = ■ (52) 15 − 7 = ■

◆ **LESSON 6** Reviewing Basic Facts

Add or subtract. Watch the signs.

(53) $8 + 7 = $ ■   (54) $8 - 7 = $ ■   (55) $5 + 11 = $ ■

(56) $9 + 5 = $ ■   (57) $9 - 5 = $ ■   (58) $17 - 7 = $ ■

(59) $13 - 8 = $ ■   (60) $13 - 5 = $ ■   (61) $14 + 3 = $ ■

(62) $19 - 10 = $ ■   (63) $10 + 9 = $ ■   (64) $9 + 9 = $ ■

(65) $6 + 7 = $ ■   (66) $13 - 6 = $ ■   (67) $16 - 9 = $ ■

(68) $18 + 0 = $ ■   (69) $18 - 0 = $ ■   (70) $11 + 7 = $ ■

(71) $12 - 6 = $ ■   (72) $12 + 6 = $ ■   (73) $7 + 7 = $ ■

(74) $\begin{array}{r} 10 \\ + 7 \\ \hline \end{array}$ (75) $\begin{array}{r} 4 \\ + 8 \\ \hline \end{array}$ (76) $\begin{array}{r} 17 \\ - 9 \\ \hline \end{array}$ (77) $\begin{array}{r} 13 \\ - 7 \\ \hline \end{array}$

(78) $\begin{array}{r} 17 \\ - 8 \\ \hline \end{array}$ (79) $\begin{array}{r} 9 \\ + 8 \\ \hline \end{array}$ (80) $\begin{array}{r} 8 \\ + 9 \\ \hline \end{array}$ (81) $\begin{array}{r} 4 \\ + 14 \\ \hline \end{array}$

(82) $\begin{array}{r} 16 \\ + 2 \\ \hline \end{array}$ (83) $\begin{array}{r} 7 \\ - 1 \\ \hline \end{array}$ (84) $\begin{array}{r} 12 \\ - 11 \\ \hline \end{array}$ (85) $\begin{array}{r} 11 \\ + 1 \\ \hline \end{array}$

(86) $\begin{array}{r} 19 \\ - 0 \\ \hline \end{array}$ (87) $\begin{array}{r} 16 \\ - 7 \\ \hline \end{array}$ (88) $\begin{array}{r} 8 \\ + 10 \\ \hline \end{array}$ (89) $\begin{array}{r} 13 \\ + 5 \\ \hline \end{array}$

Roll a 15 Game

GAME

Players:	Two
Materials:	Two 0–5 cubes (red), two 5–10 cubes (blue)
Object:	To get the sum closer to 15
Math Focus:	Addition, subtraction, and mathematical reasoning

RULES

1. Take turns rolling the cubes one at a time.

2. Add the numbers as you roll. The sum of all the numbers you roll should be as close to 15 as possible.

3. You may stop after two, three, or four rolls.

If you rolled:	The sum would be:
7 and **1** and **4** and **7**	19
8 and **5**	13
4 and **4** and **8**	16
9 and **3** and **3**	15
5 and **10**	15

4. The player with the sum closer to 15 wins the round. (The best score is 15; the next best score is 14 or 16; and so on.)

MATH JOURNAL

Imagine that after two rolls your sum is 7. In your Math Journal tell what you would do on your next turns. What cube, if any, would you roll? Why?

Missing Terms

ACT IT OUT

Use play money or manipulatives to act out the stories.

ALGEBRA READINESS

1. Roberta has 8¢. She wants to buy a cup of lemonade that costs 10¢. How much more money does she need?   8 + ■ = 10

2. Helen has 5¢. She wants to buy a cup of lemonade for 10¢. How much more money does she need? 5 + ■ = 10

3. Angela has 2¢. She wants to buy a sticker that costs 12¢. How much more money does she need? 2 + ■ = 12

4. Amy had 10¢. She bought a piece of gum. Now she has 2¢. How much did she spend?   10 − ■ = 2

5 Amy borrowed 10¢ from James. Now she has 15¢.
How much money did she start with? $15 - 10 = $ ▨

6 Coco, the gorilla, had 13 bananas. He ate some.
Now he has seven bananas. How many did he eat?
$13 - $ ▨ $ = 7$

7 Alicia spent 15¢. She has 5¢ left. How much money
did she start with? ▨ $ - 15 = 5$

8 Lauren gave her friend three marbles. Lauren now has
seven marbles left. How many did she start with?
▨ $ - 3 = 7$

9 If Lauren had nine marbles after giving three marbles
to her friend, how many did she start with?
▨ $ - 3 = 9$

◆ **LESSON 7** Missing Terms

Solve these problems. Watch the signs.

ALGEBRA READINESS

(10) $4 + \blacksquare = 9$

(11) $\blacksquare + 5 = 9$

(12) $8 + \blacksquare = 15$

(13) $9 + \blacksquare = 15$

(14) $4 + \blacksquare = 11$

(15) $\blacksquare + 8 = 11$

(16) $14 - \blacksquare = 4$

(17) $\blacksquare - 3 = 10$

(18) $18 - \blacksquare = 8$

(19) $\blacksquare - 7 = 6$

(20) $\blacksquare - 4 = 4$

(21) $7 - \blacksquare = 3$

(22) Irvin rode his bicycle to Judy's house. Then he rode 3 more miles, for a total of 8 miles. How many miles did he ride to Judy's house?

(23) Narumi wrote some letters in the morning. Then she wrote five letters in the afternoon. If she wrote nine letters all together, how many letters did she write in the morning?

COOPERATIVE LEARNING

Do the "Missing Term Puzzle" activity.

GAME

Play the "Space" game.

Match the equation with the problem. Then solve.

24 Twelve people will be at the party. Five have arrived. How many more are expected?

25 There are ten chairs. There are 12 people. How many more chairs are needed?

26 Twelve people were at the party. Some went home. There are still six people at the party. How many people have left?

27 John got many presents. He has opened 12 of them. He still has six to open. How many presents did he get?

28 The day after the party John wrote thank-you cards to his 12 guests. He wrote seven cards, then he took a break. How many cards does he still have to write?

29 John had to borrow some chairs so that he would have ten chairs for the party. He owns four chairs. How many chairs did John have to borrow?

a. $10 + \blacksquare = 12$

b. $12 + 6 = \blacksquare$

c. $12 - \blacksquare = 6$

d. $5 + \blacksquare = 12$

e. $4 + \blacksquare = 10$

f. $7 + \blacksquare = 12$

Basic Facts

Solve these problems. Watch the signs.

1 $9 + 4 = \blacksquare$ **2** $4 + 9 = \blacksquare$ **3** $13 - 4 = \blacksquare$

4 $18 - 7 = \blacksquare$ **5** $9 + 9 = \blacksquare$ **6** $16 - 8 = \blacksquare$

7 $6 + 6 = \blacksquare$ **8** $6 + 7 = \blacksquare$ **9** $4 + 8 = \blacksquare$

10 $9 - 4 = \blacksquare$ **11** $11 - 4 = \blacksquare$ **12** $18 - 9 = \blacksquare$

13 $7 + 7 = \blacksquare$ **14** $7 + 8 = \blacksquare$ **15** $13 - 8 = \blacksquare$

16 $8 + 6 = \blacksquare$ **17** $12 - 7 = \blacksquare$ **18** $11 + 4 = \blacksquare$

19 $14 - 3 = \blacksquare$ **20** $8 - 2 = \blacksquare$ **21** $4 + 6 = \blacksquare$

22 $9 + 7 = \blacksquare$ **23** $14 - 4 = \blacksquare$ **24** $6 + 9 = \blacksquare$

25 $13 - 7 = \blacksquare$ **26** $11 + 8 = \blacksquare$ **27** $12 - 9 = \blacksquare$

28 $15 - 8 = \blacksquare$ **29** $3 + 9 = \blacksquare$ **30** $4 + 7 = \blacksquare$

Solve these problems. Watch the signs.

㉛ 20 − 10 = ■ ㉜ 18 − 10 = ■ ㉝ 10 − 7 = ■

㉞ 13 − 10 = ■ ㉟ 18 − 8 = ■ ㊱ 8 + 8 = ■

㊲ 5 + 5 = ■ ㊳ 10 − 8 = ■ ㊴ 0 + 7 = ■

㊵ 9 + 8 = ■ ㊶ 15 − 8 = ■ ㊷ 10 − 4 = ■

㊸ 11 − 3 = ■ ㊹ 16 − 9 = ■ ㊺ 12 − 4 = ■

㊻ 19 − 10 = ■ ㊼ 17 − 10 = ■ ㊽ 13 − 9 = ■

㊾ 16 − 6 = ■ ㊿ 15 − 5 = ■ (51) 5 + 5 = ■

PROBLEM SOLVING

Solve.

(52) Tara gave four dolls to Susan. Tara has four dolls left. How many did she start with?

(53) Calvin had 14 marbles. He lost some, and now he has four marbles. How many marbles did he lose?

COOPERATIVE LEARNING

Roll 20 to 5 Game

Players:	Two or more
Materials:	Two 0–5 cubes (red), two 5–10 cubes (blue)
Object:	To score closer to 5
Math Focus:	Subtraction and mathematical reasoning

RULES

1. Take turns rolling the cubes one at a time. Subtract the first number rolled from 20. From that result subtract the next number rolled, and so on.

2. Make a difference (answer) as close to 5 as possible. (The best score is 5; the next best is 4 or 6; the next after that is 3 or 7; and so on.)

3. You may stop after two, three, or four rolls.

4. The player who scores closest to 5 is the winner.

In your Math Journal explain your strategy for playing this game. Tell how you decided when to stop rolling the Number Cubes.

Write the missing numbers. Be ready to explain your answers.

(54) 1, 2, 3, 4, ■, ■

(55) 4, 5, 6, ■, ■, 9, 10

(56) 2, 4, 6, 8, ■, 12

(57) 8, 10, 12, 14, ■, ■, 20

(58) 3, 6, 9, 12, ■, ■, 21

(59) 10, 9, 8, 7, ■, 5, ■, ■

(60) 10, 8, 6, ■, ■, 0

(61) 12, 15, 18, 21, ■, ■, 30

(62) 4, 8, 12, 16, ■, ■, 28

(63) 1, 3, 5, ■, ■, ■, 13

Add or subtract. Watch the signs.

(64) $15 - 7 = ■$

(65) $12 + 7 = ■$

(66) $8 + 8 = ■$

(67) $5 + 11 = ■$

(68) $6 + 4 = ■$

(69) $9 + 4 = ■$

(70) $9 - 4 = ■$

(71) $11 + 3 = ■$

(72) $15 - 4 = ■$

(73) $\begin{array}{r} 6 \\ +\ 9 \\ \hline \end{array}$

(74) $\begin{array}{r} 16 \\ +\ 3 \\ \hline \end{array}$

(75) $\begin{array}{r} 14 \\ -\ 7 \\ \hline \end{array}$

(76) $\begin{array}{r} 17 \\ -\ 8 \\ \hline \end{array}$

Applying Addition and Subtraction

Solve these problems.

1. The score is 6 to 3. The Tigers are winning. How many runs behind are the Cubs?

2. The game will last seven innings. The teams have played four innings so far. How many more innings will they play in this game?

3. The Tigers have 11 hits so far. The Cubs have seven hits. How many hits have there been in the game?

4. The umpire brought 12 balls to the game. Some were lost. There are nine balls left. How many were lost?

5. The Tigers have 14 players on their team. There are nine players in the field. How many players are not on the field?

6. The Cubs pitcher threw ten pitches last inning. She has thrown five more pitches than that this inning. How many pitches has she thrown so far this inning?

7. Each team has six infielders. Two of the infielders are the pitcher and the catcher. How many other infielders does each team have?

8. If the Tigers score two more runs in this game and the Cubs score four more, what will the final score be? Who will win the game?

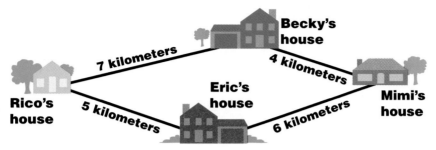

Solve these problems.

(9) How far is it from Eric's house to Mimi's house?

(10) How much farther is it from Becky's house to Rico's house than from Becky's house to Mimi's house?

(11) How far is it from Eric's house to Mimi's house and then to Becky's house?

(12) How far is it from Rico's house to Becky's house to Mimi's house?

(13) How far is it from Rico's house to Eric's house to Mimi's house?

(14) Becky left her house and walked 10 kilometers. She visited two friends. Whom did she visit?

(15) What is the shortest route from Eric's house to Becky's house? How long is that route?

(16) How far is it from Eric's house to Rico's house to Becky's house?

(17) How far is it from Rico's house to Eric's house to Mimi's house to Becky's house and back to Rico's house?

Talk about the Thinking Story "Swing Low, Sweet Willy (Part 1)."

In your Math Journal make up two more problems using the map.

LESSON 10

Adding and Subtracting Several Numbers

Solve these problems. Watch the signs.

1 $10 + 5 - 7 = $ ▪

2 $19 + 4 + 1 - 16 = $ ▪

3 $12 - 5 + 6 = $ ▪

4 $7 - 7 + 12 = $ ▪

5 $6 + 9 - 3 + 3 = $ ▪

6 $12 + 6 - 4 + 4 = $ ▪

7 $4 + 4 + 4 - 6 + 8 = $ ▪

8 $16 - 1 + 9 - 4 - 9 = $ ▪

9 $7 + 4 - 8 + 10 = $ ▪

10 $4 - 2 + 5 + 9 + 8 = $ ▪

11 $15 - 10 + 5 + 4 - 7 = $ ▪

12 $6 + 6 - 2 + 9 = $ ▪

13 $3 + 3 + 3 + 3 - 10 + 2 + 2 = $ ▪

14 $6 + 6 - 2 + 9 = $ ▪

15 $7 + 3 + 8 - 9 - 9 + 4 = $ ▪

16 $13 - 8 - 3 + 5 + 3 + 9 = $ ▪

17 $15 + 4 - 13 - 2 = $ ▪

FANTASTIC FACT

If you lined up **1 billion** one-dollar bills end-to-end, they would go around the world four times.

Solve these problems. Watch the signs.

⑱ $\begin{array}{r} 7 \\ +\ 8 \\ \hline \end{array}$	⑲ $\begin{array}{r} 5 \\ -\ 4 \\ \hline \end{array}$	⑳ $\begin{array}{r} 15 \\ -\ \ 6 \\ \hline \end{array}$	㉑ $\begin{array}{r} 17 \\ +\ \ 1 \\ \hline \end{array}$
㉒ $\begin{array}{r} 9 \\ +\ 8 \\ \hline \end{array}$	㉓ $\begin{array}{r} 7 \\ +\ 4 \\ \hline \end{array}$	㉔ $\begin{array}{r} 18 \\ -\ \ 9 \\ \hline \end{array}$	㉕ $\begin{array}{r} 1 \\ +\ 15 \\ \hline \end{array}$
㉖ $\begin{array}{r} 15 \\ -\ \ 6 \\ \hline \end{array}$	㉗ $\begin{array}{r} 14 \\ -\ \ 8 \\ \hline \end{array}$	㉘ $\begin{array}{r} 5 \\ +\ 7 \\ \hline \end{array}$	㉙ $\begin{array}{r} 15 \\ -\ \ 5 \\ \hline \end{array}$
㉚ $\begin{array}{r} 9 \\ +\ 9 \\ \hline \end{array}$	㉛ $\begin{array}{r} 10 \\ +\ 10 \\ \hline \end{array}$	㉜ $\begin{array}{r} 14 \\ -\ \ 4 \\ \hline \end{array}$	㉝ $\begin{array}{r} 1 \\ +\ 6 \\ \hline \end{array}$
㉞ $\begin{array}{r} 17 \\ -\ \ 7 \\ \hline \end{array}$	㉟ $\begin{array}{r} 13 \\ -\ 10 \\ \hline \end{array}$	㊱ $\begin{array}{r} 16 \\ -\ \ 6 \\ \hline \end{array}$	㊲ $\begin{array}{r} 20 \\ -\ 17 \\ \hline \end{array}$

㊳ $20 - 10 =$ ■	㊴ $17 - 8 =$ ■	㊵ $10 - 10 =$ ■
㊶ $5 + 9 =$ ■	㊷ $6 + 6 =$ ■	㊸ $3 + 3 =$ ■
㊹ $8 + 8 =$ ■	㊺ $4 + 9 =$ ■	㊻ $5 + 2 =$ ■
㊼ $2 + 8 =$ ■	㊽ $3 + 9 =$ ■	㊾ $17 - 4 =$ ■
㊿ $10 + 6 =$ ■	(51) $8 + 10 =$ ■	(52) $20 - 14 =$ ■

Odds and Evens

You can separate a set of six apples into two equal sets. Each set has three apples.

Can you separate a set of seven apples into two equal sets without cutting an apple?

The number of items in a set is **even** if you can separate the items into two equal sets. The number is **odd** if you cannot.

Count the number of items in each set. Write that number on your paper. Decide whether you can separate each set into two equal sets. You may use manipulatives to help. Write whether each set is *even* or *odd*.

❶

❷

❸

❹

❺

❻

❼

❽

 **Work with a friend. You may use manipulatives.**

9 Decide whether each number from 1 through 30 is even or odd. List all the even numbers in one row. List all the odd numbers in another row.

Even: 2, 4, 6, . . .

Odd: 1, 3, 5, . . .

10 Look at your lists. Is there an easy way to tell whether a number is even or odd by just looking at it? How?

Write the missing numbers on your paper.

11 2, 4, 6, ■, ■, ■, ■, ■, ■, ■, ■, ■, ■, ■, 30

12 1, 3, 5, ■, ■, ■, ■, ■, ■, ■, ■, ■, ■, ■, 29

Copy each list and circle the odd or even numbers.

13 Circle the even numbers: 4, 1, 2, 9, 11, 6, 5, 8, 20, 25

14 Circle the odd numbers: 15, 12, 18, 9, 13, 7, 29, 30, 1, 3

15 Circle the odd numbers: 30, 10, 16, 17, 21, 19, 26, 23

16 Circle the even numbers: 21, 22, 3, 8, 27, 2, 4, 6, 28, 20

 **In your Math Journal write something you know about even and odd numbers.**

◆ **LESSON 11 Odds and Evens**

Here is a model for adding 6 + 8.

17 If you add two even numbers, do you think the answer will be even or odd? Will that always be true? Explain.

Here is a model for adding 6 + 9.

18 If you add an even number and an odd number, do you think the answer will be even or odd? Will that always be true? Explain.

Here is a model for adding 7 + 9.

19 If you add two odd numbers, do you think the answer will be even or odd? Is that always true? Explain.

To check whether 9 − 5 = 4, you can add 4 and 5. Do you get 9?

Copy and complete these sentences.

20 When you subtract an even number from an even number, the answer is always ____.

21 When you subtract an even number from an odd number, the answer is always ____.

22 When you subtract an odd number from an even number, the answer is always ____.

23 When you subtract an odd number from an odd number, the answer is always ____.

You can use what you know about even and odd numbers to decide whether the answer to a problem should be even or odd. Sometimes this will help you find mistakes. Tell whether each of the following is true or false. Pick one false statement. Explain how you decided it was false using what you know about odds and evens.

Twelve of these equalities have errors. Write *T* for every equality that is true. Write *F* for every equation that is false.

24. $8 + 8 = 16$

25. $7 + 8 = 15$

26. $14 + 12 = 25$

27. $13 + 13 = 26$

28. $17 + 17 = 35$

29. $28 + 29 = 56$

30. $32 + 31 = 64$

31. $19 + 17 = 36$

32. $78 - 35 = 43$

33. $93 - 45 = 49$

34. $48 - 34 = 13$

35. $83 - 56 = 28$

36. $14 + 28 = 42$

37. $27 - 12 = 14$

38. $87 + 13 = 99$

39. $87 + 13 = 100$

40. $11 + 21 = 33$

41. $11 + 33 = 44$

42. $54 + 12 = 67$

43. $37 + 14 = 52$

Mid-Unit Review

Find the numbers that are written twice.

1 Start counting from 27.

29   31   27   32   36   35   30   33   37   28   30   32   34

2 Start counting from 789.

797   791   798   792   796   789   793   795   790   793   792   794

3 Start counting from 114.

118   114   121   115   123   117   124   119   118   122   116   123   120

4 Start counting from 171.

172   171   175   177   174   176   173   178   176   179   171

Write the number.

5 Two hundred thirty-nine   **6** Sixty-five

7 One hundred three   **8** Forty

9 Eighty-nine   **10** One hundred sixteen

11 One hundred ninety   **12** Seventeen

Count up or down. Fill in the missing numbers.

13

54	53	52				47

14

196	197				201		203

15

873	872	871				866

16

		2621	2622	2623			2626

17

		4039	4038	4037			4034

Use the number 1296.

(18) What number is in the hundreds place?
(19) What number is in the tens place?
(20) In what place is the number 1?
(21) In what place is the number 2?

Solve these problems. Watch the signs.

(22) 9
    + 8

(23) 7
    + 5

(24) 4
    + 8

(25) 6
    + 7

(26) 5
    + 6

(27) 10
    − 4

(28) 16
    − 8

(29) 13
    − 9

(30) 11
    − 3

(31) 14
    − 6

(32) 7 + 6 = ■

(33) 8 + 9 = ■

(34) 10 − 3 = ■

(35) 13 − 5 = ■

(36) 5 + ■ = 12

(37) ■ + 3 = 9

Answer the questions. Tell whether you could use addition, subtraction, or either to solve each problem.

(38) Marcy's cat has seven kittens. Five are white and the rest are gray. How many kittens are gray?

(39) Jake raked leaves one morning. He filled six bags of leaves. After lunch he filled five bags of leaves. How many bags did Jake fill?

(40) Lauren has 7¢. She wants to buy a cup of lemonade for 15¢. How much more money does she need?

Solve these problems. Watch the signs.

(41) 10 + 3 − 8 = ■

(42) 3 + 3 + 3 − 2 − 2 = ■

(43) 7 + 8 − 6 + 4 = ■

(44) 9 + 7 − 8 + 5 + 2 − 7 = ■

(45) 5 + 5 − 4 + 8 − 9 + 8 = ■

Adding and Subtracting

Solve these problems. Watch the signs.

1 7 + 8 = ■   **2** 19 − 10 = ■   **3** 4 + 4 = ■

4 3 + 7 = ■   **5** 8 − 2 = ■   **6** 14 − 8 = ■

7 17 − 9 = ■   **8** 9 + 7 = ■   **9** 6 + 6 = ■

10 11 − 4 = ■   **11** 3 − 3 = ■   **12** 9 + 9 = ■

13 15 − 9 = ■   **14** 13 − 4 = ■   **15** 3 + 9 = ■

16 8 − 7 = ■   **17** 1 + 8 = ■   **18** 16 − 7 = ■

19 6 + 7 = ■   **20** 10 + 5 = ■   **21** 4 + 13 = ■

Number correct ■

22 David had eight library books. He returned two of them. How many library books does he have now?

23 Kate brought six apples to school. She ate some for lunch. How many apples does she have now?

Abigail, Billy, Charles, Diego, and Emma held a contest. They wanted to see whose estimate came closest to the actual length and width of a book. They wrote their estimates in a table.

Name	Length of Book (in cm)	Width of Book (in cm)
Abigail	20	15
Billy	15	12
Charles	12	8
Diego	17	8
Emma	15	10

Solve these problems.

24 What is the greatest estimate for the length of the book? What is the difference between the greatest and the least estimates for the length?

25 What is the difference between the greatest and least estimates for the width of the book?

26 Did any two students have the same estimate for the length of the book? If so, which two?

After the students estimated, they measured the book carefully. The length of the book is 17 cm, and the width is 10 cm.

27 Which estimate of length differed the most from the actual length? What was the difference?

28 Which estimate of width differed the most from the actual width? What was the difference?

Make up your own questions about the table and write them in your Math Journal. Ask a classmate to answer them.

LESSON 13

Regrouping for Addition

3 tens and 12 = 42

Write the standard name for each of these. You may use manipulatives to help. The first two have been done for you.

1 2 tens and 8 = **28**

2 5 tens and 12 = **62**

3 6 tens and 15 = ■

4 4 tens and 0 = ■

5 7 tens and 16 = ■

6 0 tens and 14 = ■

7 8 tens and 3 = ■

8 8 tens and 13 = ■

9 4 tens and 10 = ■

10 3 tens and 0 = ■

11 3 tens and 7 = ■

12 3 tens and 17 = ■

13 6 tens and 17 = ■

14 11 tens = ■

15 13 tens = ■

16 17 tens = ■

2 hundreds and 14 tens = 340

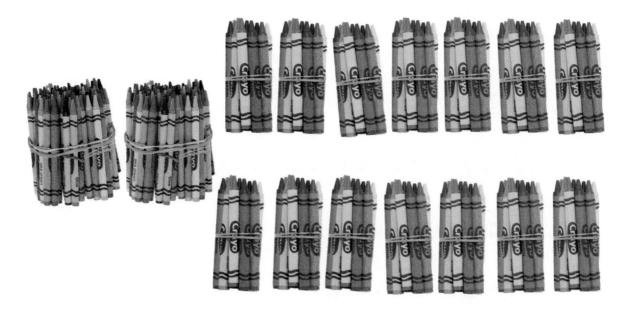

Write the standard name for each of these. You may use manipulatives to help. The first two have been done for you.

17 2 hundreds and 8 tens = **280**

18 5 hundreds and 12 tens = **620**

19 4 hundreds and 0 tens = ▦

20 4 hundreds and 10 tens = ▦

21 4 hundreds and 17 tens = ▦

22 1 hundred and 17 tens = ▦

23 0 hundreds and 17 tens = ▦

24 0 hundreds and 13 tens = ▦

25 8 hundreds and 18 tens = ▦

26 2 hundreds and 4 tens = ▦

27 7 hundreds and 0 tens = ▦

28 0 hundreds and 18 tens = ▦

29 0 hundreds and 3 tens = ▦

30 8 hundreds and 10 tens = ▦

31 9 hundreds and 9 tens = ▦

32 4 hundreds and 3 tens = ▦

33 7 hundreds and 16 tens = ▦

34 7 hundreds and 18 tens = ▦

◆ **LESSON 13   Regrouping for Addition**

Write the standard name for each of these. You may use manipulatives to help.

35 7 tens and 0 = ■

36 7 tens and 5 = ■

37 7 tens and 15 = ■

38 7 hundreds and 5 tens = ■

39 7 hundreds and 15 tens = ■

40 3 hundreds and 6 tens = ■

41 3 hundreds and 10 tens = ■

42 6 tens and 12 = ■

43 3 tens and 10 = ■

44 2 tens and 14 = ■

45 0 tens and 16 = ■

46 0 hundreds and 16 tens = ■

47 2 hundreds and 6 tens = ■

48 7 hundreds and 19 tens = ■

49 0 hundreds and 10 tens = ■

50 7 hundreds and 2 tens = ■

51 5 hundreds and 18 tens = ■

52 6 tens and 5 = ■

53 8 hundreds and 4 tens = ■

54 0 tens and 8 = ■

GAME   **Play the "Rummage Sale" game.**

Write the standard name for each. You may use manipulatives to help.

55 4 tens + 3 tens =

56 7 tens + 2 tens =

57 8 tens + 5 tens =

58 8 tens + 5 ones =

59 1 hundred + 7 tens =

60 7 tens + 2 hundreds =

61 4 hundreds + 5 hundreds =

62 4 tens + 5 tens =

63 3 hundreds + 5 hundreds =

64 3 hundreds + 5 tens =

65 6 tens + 4 hundreds =

66 6 hundreds + 4 tens =

67 3 hundreds + 5 tens + 7 ones =

68 2 hundreds + 3 tens + 4 ones =

69 4 ones + 3 tens + 2 hundreds =

70 3 tens + 2 hundreds + 4 ones =

71 5 hundreds + 6 tens + 1 one =

72 1 hundred + 8 tens + 8 ones =

Add.

73
```
   20
+  60
```

74
```
   200
+  600
```

75
```
   6
+  3
```

76
```
   600
+  300
```

77
```
   50
+  40
```

78
```
   500
+  400
```

79
```
   700
+  100
```

80
```
   7
+  1
```

Adding Two-Digit Numbers

25 + 47 = _?_

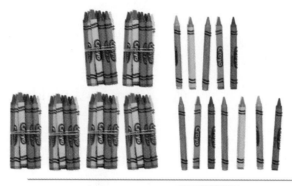

| 2 tens and 5 | 25 |
| + 4 tens and 7 | + 47 |

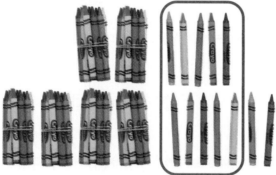

1 ten
2 tens and 5   1
+ 4 tens and 7   25
         2   + 47
               2

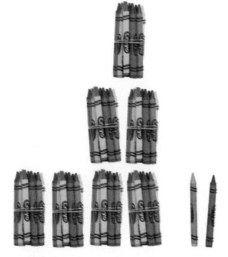

1 ten
2 tens and 5   1
+ 4 tens and 7   25
7 tens and 2   + 47
               72

Add.

1   45
     + 26

2   51
     + 39

3   29
     + 39

4   27
     + 54

Add. Use crayons or other manipulatives to help.

⑤   43
    + 28

⑥   57
    + 29

⑦   36
    + 51

⑧   36
    + 54

⑨   19
    + 38

⑩   25
    + 25

⑪   43
    + 20

⑫   43
    + 30

⑬   82
    + 9

⑭   16
    + 37

⑮   17
    + 37

⑯   45
    + 45

⑰   35
    + 45

⑱   34
    + 45

⑲   24
    + 18

⑳   76
    + 6

㉑   32
    + 42

㉒   29
    + 41

㉓   18
    + 18

㉔   53
    + 34

PROBLEM SOLVING

Solve.

㉕ Mr. Burgess counted 19 oranges on one of his trees and 28 oranges on another tree. How many oranges did he count on the trees all together?

㉖ Willy had 14 CDs to take back to the library. His mother gave him 16 more to return. How many CDs did Willy return all together?

◆ **LESSON 14** **Adding Two-Digit Numbers**

Solve.

Sam has 23 marbles. Zora has 34 marbles. Todd has 17 marbles. Peter has 18 marbles.

27 Who has the most marbles?

28 Who has the fewest marbles?

29 If Sam and Zora put all their marbles together, how many will they have?

30 If Peter and Sam put all their marbles together, how many will they have?

31 If Peter and Todd put all their marbles together, how many will they have?

32 If Sam, Zora, Todd, and Peter all put their marbles together, how many will they have?

33 If Sam and Todd put their marbles together, and Zora and Peter put their marbles together, which pair would have more marbles?

34 If Todd and Peter put their marbles together, how many more marbles would they have than Zora?

C∞PERATIVE LEARNING

Roll and Add Game

Players:	Two or three
Materials:	Two 0–5 cubes (red), two 5–10 cubes (blue)
Object:	To make the greatest sum
Math Focus:	Adding two-digit numbers and place value

RULES

1. Take turns rolling all four cubes. If you roll a 10, roll that cube again.

2. Use any combination of the numbers rolled to make two two-digit numbers. Find the sum of these numbers.

3. The player with the greatest sum is the winner.

OTHER WAYS TO PLAY THIS GAME

1. Find the least sum.

2. Try to make a sum of exactly 40 (or 50, 60, 70, and so on).

In your Math Journal explain how you played this game. How did you make the greatest sum?

LESSON 15

Regrouping for Subtraction

There is more than one way to write a number. For example, 42 can be written as 3 tens and 12.

Rewrite to show ten more ones.

❶ 27 = ■ tens and ■

❷ 80 = ■ tens and ■

❸ 68 = ■ tens and ■

❹ 70 = ■ tens and ■

❺ 21 = ■ tens and ■

❻ 51 = ■ tens and ■

❼ 52 = ■ tens and ■

❽ 62 = ■ tens and ■

❾ 16 = ■ tens and ■

❿ 12 = ■ tens and ■

Solve.

Jessica has four $10 bills and three $1 bills. She must pay Mr. Gómez $8.

⓫ How much money does Jessica have?

⓬ How can Jessica pay $8?

⓭ How much will Jessica have left?

This also works with greater numbers.

230 = 1 hundred and 13 tens

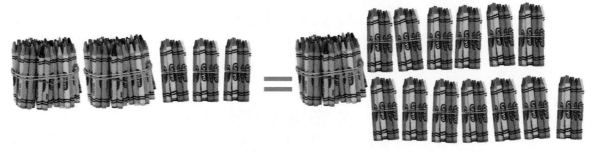

Rewrite to show ten more tens.

⑭ 420 = ■ hundreds and **12** tens   ⑮ 700 = ■ hundreds and **10** tens

⑯ 760 = ■ hundreds and ■ tens   ⑰ 160 = ■ hundreds and ■ tens

⑱ 240 = ■ hundreds and ■ tens   ⑲ 500 = ■ hundreds and ■ tens

⑳ 580 = ■ hundreds and ■ tens   ㉑ 980 = ■ hundreds and ■ tens

㉒ 120 = ■ hundreds and ■ tens   ㉓ 390 = ■ hundreds and ■ tens

㉔ 470 = ■ hundreds and ■ tens   ㉕ 600 = ■ hundreds and ■ tens

㉖ 530 = ■ hundreds and ■ tens   ㉗ 220 = ■ hundreds and ■ tens

Solve.

Mr. Taylor has one $100 bill and two $10 bills. He must pay
Ms. Kwan $30.

㉘ How can Mr. Taylor pay $30?

㉙ How much money will he have left?

◆ LESSON 15 Regrouping for Subtraction

Here's another example of how numbers can be rewritten.
205 = 20 tens and 5 = 19 tens and 15

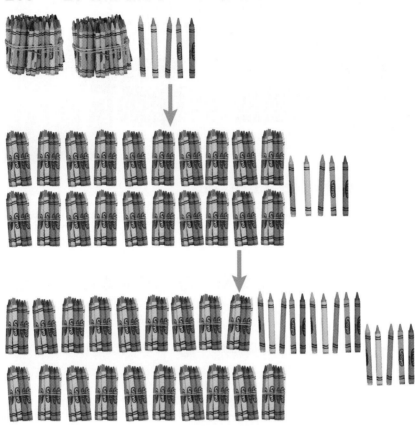

Rewrite to show no hundreds and then ten more ones.

30 307 = 30 tens and 7 = 29 tens and ■

31 600 = ■ tens and 0 = ■ tens and 10

32 604 = ■ tens and ■ = ■ tens and ■

33 809 = ■ tens and ■ = ■ tens and ■

34 700 = ■ tens and ■ = ■ tens and ■

35 707 = ■ tens and ■ = ■ tens and ■

If you counted to 100 every minute and kept counting for eight hours every day, five days a week, it would take more than a month to count to 1,000,000.

**Use play money to help you solve the problems.
Use $1, $5, $10, and $20 bills only.**

36 If you have a $1 bill, a $5 bill, a $10 bill, and a $20 bill, how much money do you have?

37 Mary has four bills worth a total of $17. Is this possible? If so, how?

38 Nigel has eight bills worth a total of $17. Is this possible? If so, how?

39 Aaron has ten bills worth a total of $17. Is this possible? If so, how?

40 Think of five ways you can make $17 with only $1 bills, $5 bills, $10 bills, and $20 bills. List them.

41 Think of five ways you can make $37 with only $1 bills, $5 bills, $10 bills, and $20 bills. List them.

42 Think of five ways you can make $40 with only $1 bills, $5 bills, $10 bills, and $20 bills. List them.

43 Think of five ways you can make $43 with only $1 bills, $5 bills, $10 bills, and $20 bills. List them.

If you earned $1 each second for 40 hours a week, it would take 134 years to earn 1 billion dollars.

LESSON 16

Subtracting Two-Digit Numbers

31 − 14 = __?__

3 tens and 1	31
− 1 ten and 4	− 14

2 11	2 11
3̶ tens and 1̶	3̶1̶
− 1 ten and 4	− 14

2 11	2 11
3̶ tens and 1̶	3̶1̶
− 1 ten and 4	− 14
7	**7**

2 11	2 11
3̶ tens and 1̶	3̶1̶
− 1 ten and 4	− 14
1 ten and 7	**17**

Subtract.

| ① 43
− 29 | ② 86
− 37 | ③ 87
− 37 | ④ 28
− 19 |

| ⑤ 38
− 19 | ⑥ 50
− 25 | ⑦ 75
− 50 | ⑧ 75
− 25 |

| ⑨ 61
− 47 | ⑩ 94
− 46 | ⑪ 90
− 45 | ⑫ 80
− 45 |

| ⑬ 72
− 38 | ⑭ 61
− 24 | ⑮ 44
− 36 | ⑯ 81
− 24 |

| ⑰ 66
− 17 | ⑱ 70
− 55 | ⑲ 38
− 29 | ⑳ 91
− 47 |

Solve.

㉑ There were 60 sweaters on the shelves in Mrs. Dunlap's store. She sold 29 of them. How many sweaters are left on the shelves?

㉒ Mr. Downes had 54 pencils in a can. He gave out 27 of them to the students in his class. How many pencils are left in the can?

㉓ There are 37 chairs around the swimming pool. People are sitting in 28 of them. How many empty chairs are there?

◆ **LESSON 16   Subtracting Two-Digit Numbers**

Solve.

㉔ Janet had 68 videos in her collection. She gave away 19 as presents. How many videos does she have in her collection now?

Michael has 23 stickers. Jill has 34 stickers. Adam has 17 stickers. Mark has 18 stickers.

㉕ How many more stickers does Jill have than Mark?

㉖ How many more stickers does Jill have than Adam? (Is there an easy way to solve this using your answer to problem 25?)

㉗ How many more stickers does Michael have than Mark?

Sara has $37. Jake has $28. Joe has $73. Heika has $54.

㉘ Who has the most money?

㉙ How much more money does Heika have than Jake?

㉚ How much money do Sara and Jake have together?

㉛ How much more money does Joe have than Jake?

㉜ How much more money does Joe have than Heika?

In your Math Journal make up three more problems based on the amounts of money Sara, Jake, Joe, and Heika have. Share them with your friends.

COOPERATIVE LEARNING

Roll and Subtract Game

Players: Two or three

Materials: Two 0–5 cubes (red), two 5–10 cubes (blue)

Object: To make the least difference (answer)

Math Focus: Subtracting two-digit numbers and place value

RULES

1. Take turns rolling all four cubes. If you roll a 10, roll that cube again.

2. Use any combination of the numbers rolled to make two two-digit numbers. Find the difference of these numbers.

3. The player with the least difference (answer) is the winner.

OTHER WAYS TO PLAY THIS GAME

1. Find the greatest difference.

2. Try to make a difference as close as possible to 40 (or 50, 60, 70, and so on).

In your Math Journal explain how you played this game. How did you make the least difference?

LESSON 17

Using Addition and Subtraction

Solve.

Martin has 75¢.

1. Can he buy popcorn and go on the ride?

2. Can he buy ice cream and go on the ride?

3. If Martin buys popcorn and ice cream, how much will he have left?

Kim has 46¢. Nancy has 38¢.

4. How much do they have all together?

5. How much more do they need to buy a pretzel?

6. How much more money does Kim have than Nancy?

7. There are 27 children in Mrs. Pinto's class. Fifteen are boys. How many girls are in Mrs. Pinto's class?

8. In Mr. Epstein's class there are 13 boys and 16 girls. How many children are in Mr. Epstein's class?

9. How many boys are in Mrs. Pinto's and Mr. Epstein's classes all together?

10. How many more girls are in Mr. Epstein's class than are in Mrs. Pinto's class?

Solve.

Jenny and her mom started at home. They drove 32 miles east. Later they turned around and drove 17 miles west.

⑪ How far are Jenny and her mom from home?

⑫ How far have they driven?

Mr. Cheng started at home. He drove 32 miles east. Then he drove 41 more miles east.

⑬ How far is Mr. Cheng from home?

⑭ How far has he driven?

Mr. Cheng and Mr. Smith started at the same location and drove in opposite directions. Mr. Cheng drove 63 miles. Mr. Smith drove 51 miles.

⑮ Who drove farther?

⑯ How much farther?

⑰ How far apart are they?

A bird known as the Arctic tern flies about 25,000 miles every year, going from the Arctic to Antarctica and back again.

In your Math Journal make up two problems like the ones on this page. Share your problems with the class.

LESSON 18

Addition and Subtraction: Applications

Solve.

1. Chloe's tomato plant is 38 inches tall. One week ago it was 25 inches tall. How much did it grow last week?

2. Mr. Batra lives 18 miles from Dallas. He drove there and back. How far did he drive?

3. Kevin had 80¢. He spent some money at the bakery. Now he has 28¢. How much did Kevin spend?

4. Marie had some CDs. She gave 12 of them to her brother. She has 19 CDs left. How many did she start with?

5. Hank can take 36 pictures with the roll of film in his camera. He has already taken nine pictures. How many does he have left?

6. Hank put a new roll of film in his camera. He took some pictures yesterday and took six pictures today. How many pictures does he have left?

Solve.

7. How much will the tennis ball and truck cost?

8. How much will the feather and paint set cost?

9. How much will the book and yo-yo cost?

10. Luis has only $1. At most, how many of the six things can he buy?

11. Which of the six things can Luis buy?

12. How much more money does he need to buy all six things?

13. Luis bought the book, the tennis ball, and the paint set. How much did he spend?

14. How much change did Luis get back?

For Sale

Book .... 26¢
Yo-yo.................... 37¢
Tennis ball......... 13¢
Paint set............ 29¢
Truck.................. 49¢
Feather...............10¢

Reviewing Addition and Subtraction

C⬤⬤PERATIVE LEARNING

Roll a Two-Digit Problem Game

Players:	**Two or more**
Materials:	**One 0–5 cube (red)**
Object:	**To get the greatest sum (or least difference)**
Math Focus:	**Place value and mathematical reasoning**

RULES

1. Use blanks to outline an addition (or subtraction) problem on your paper, like this:

$$\begin{array}{r} \_\_\ \_\_ \\ + \_\_\ \_\_ \\ \hline \end{array} \quad \textbf{or} \quad \begin{array}{r} \_\_\ \_\_ \\ - \_\_\ \_\_ \\ \hline \end{array}$$

2. The first player rolls the cube four times.

3. Each time the cube is rolled, write that number in one of the blanks in your outline.

4. When all the blanks have been filled in, find the sum (or difference) of the two numbers.

5. The player with the greatest sum (or least difference greater than or equal to 0) wins the round.

87¢   **39¢**   **46¢**   **73¢**   **50¢**

Solve.

1. How much more does the book cost than the rock?

2. How much more does the tape cost than the shell?

3. If Eduardo has $1.00, can he buy three items?

4. What is the greatest number of different items Eduardo can buy with his dollar? List each set of items Eduardo can buy. Tell how much each set would cost.

5. Look at each set of items you listed in problem 4. How much money would Eduardo have left after paying for each set?

6. How much do the colored pencils and the shell cost all together?

7. Does the book cost more or less than the colored pencils and the shell together? What is the difference in cost?

Make up some more problems based on the picture and write them in your Math Journal. Answer your problems. Let others in your class solve the problems. Do they get the same answers?

◆ **LESSON 19** Reviewing Addition and Subtraction

Solve.

8 One month ago the panda weighed 19 kilograms. Now he weighs 26 kilograms. How much weight did he gain last month?

9 Kyle had 30¢. Then he earned 65¢. How much money does Kyle have?

10 Does Kyle have enough money to buy two postcards that cost 45¢ each?

11 Kyle bought an apple for 45¢. How much money does he have left?

Josh and Maya traded sports cards.

12 Maya traded 15 baseball cards to Josh for 12 football cards and eight hockey cards. How many cards did Josh trade to Maya?

13 How many more cards does Maya have now than she had before?

14 If Josh started with 85 cards, how many does he have now?

15 If Maya started with 19 football cards, how many does she have now?

← **Old Falls 18 miles**
New Falls 28 miles →

Solve.

16 Which town is farther away?

17 How much farther?

Courtney measured her two dogs.

Buffy is 73 centimeters tall.

Flip is 78 centimeters tall.

18 Which dog is taller?

19 By how much?

Janna read 46 pages of a book on Monday. On Tuesday, she read 39 pages.

20 On which day did she read more pages?

21 How many more?

22 How many pages did she read on Monday and Tuesday all together?

23 How many more pages does she need to read to finish the book?

The Whizzo factory produced 67 doodads last year.
It produced 94 doodads this year.

24 During which year were more doodads produced?

25 How many more?

26 How many doodads were produced last year and this year all together?

THINKING STORY

Talk about the Thinking Story "Swing Low, Sweet Willy (Part 2)."

Adding and Subtracting Two-Digit Numbers

Check your math skills.

Solve these problems. Watch the signs.

1
```
   18
+  47
```

2
```
   63
+  27
```

3
```
   63
−  27
```

4
```
   85
−  35
```

5
```
   91
−  64
```

6
```
   43
−  41
```

7
```
   72
−  28
```

8
```
    8
+  74
```

9
```
   39
−  37
```

10
```
   51
−  49
```

11
```
   32
−   9
```

12
```
   17
+  87
```

13
```
   40
+  36
```

14
```
   23
+  48
```

15
```
   78
+  18
```

16
```
   43
+  18
```

17 Jan counted 23 flowers in her garden. She picked some to put in a vase. Now there are 18 flowers in her garden. How many flowers did she pick?

18 Mrs. Fattal had 93 paintings in her collection. She sold some. Now she has 48 paintings. How many paintings did Mrs. Fattal sell?

19 Toby had been waiting 12 days for her birthday present to come in the mail. She had to wait another 18 days before it came. How many days did Toby wait all together?

Number correct ▨

Solve.

Xavier has 27¢. Yolonda has 43¢. Zack has 54¢.

20 How much more money does Zack have than Yolonda?

21 How much more money does Zack have than Xavier?

22 How much more money does Yolonda have than Xavier?

23 How much money do Xavier and Yolonda have together?

24 What items can Xavier buy? Can he afford to buy more than one item?

25 If Xavier and Yolonda put their money together, can they afford to buy the rubber stamp? If so, how much money will they have left?

26 If Zack and Yolonda put their money together, can they afford to buy the marker and the rubber stamp? If so, how much money will they have left?

27 How much more does a rubber stamp cost than a pencil?

Make up five more problems based on the picture and write them in your Math Journal. Write the answers to your problems on a separate piece of paper. See if others in your class get the same answers to your problems as you did.

LESSON 21

Three-Digit Numbers: Addition and Subtraction

436 + 287 = ___?___

Use play money or other manipulatives to follow this example.

$$\begin{array}{r} 436 \\ + 287 \\ \hline \end{array}$$
Start at the right.
Add the ones.
6 + 7 = 13

$$\begin{array}{r} 1 \\ 436 \\ + 287 \\ \hline 3 \end{array}$$
13 = 1 ten and 3

$$\begin{array}{r} 1 \\ 436 \\ + 287 \\ \hline 3 \end{array}$$
Add the tens.
1 + 3 + 8 = 12
There are 12 tens.

$$\begin{array}{r} 11 \\ 436 \\ + 287 \\ \hline 23 \end{array}$$
12 tens = 1 hundred and 2 tens

$$\begin{array}{r} 11 \\ 436 \\ + 287 \\ \hline 723 \end{array}$$
Add the hundreds.
1 + 4 + 2 = 7
There are 7 hundreds.

$745 - 179 = \underline{\ ?\ }$

Use play money or other manipulatives to follow this example.

$\begin{array}{r} 745 \\ -\ 179 \\ \hline \end{array}$

Start at the right.

Subtract the ones.

Can't subtract 9 from 5.

$\begin{array}{r} \scriptstyle 3\ 15 \\ 7\cancel{4}\cancel{5} \\ -\ 179 \\ \hline \end{array}$

Regroup the 4 tens and 5.

4 tens and 5 = 3 tens and 15

$\begin{array}{r} \scriptstyle 3\ 15 \\ 7\cancel{4}\cancel{5} \\ -\ 179 \\ \hline 6 \end{array}$

Subtract the ones. $15 - 9 = 6$

Subtract the tens.

Can't subtract 7 from 3.

$\begin{array}{r} \scriptstyle 13 \\ \scriptstyle 6\ \cancel{3}\ 15 \\ \cancel{7}\cancel{4}\cancel{5} \\ -\ 179 \\ \hline 6 \end{array}$

Regroup the 7 hundreds and 3 tens.

7 hundreds and 3 tens = 6 hundreds and 13 tens

$\begin{array}{r} \scriptstyle 13 \\ \scriptstyle 6\ \cancel{3}\ 15 \\ \cancel{7}\cancel{4}\cancel{5} \\ -\ 179 \\ \hline 566 \end{array}$

Subtract the tens.

$13 - 7 = 6$

There are 6 tens.

Subtract the hundreds.

$6 - 1 = 5$

There are 5 hundreds.

◆ LESSON 21 Three-Digit Numbers: Addition and Subtraction

Solve these problems. Watch the signs.

1
```
  435
+ 256
```

2
```
  379
- 182
```

3
```
  607
+ 284
```

4
```
  200
+ 500
```

5
```
  317
- 248
```

6
```
  379
+ 256
```

7
```
  345
- 213
```

8
```
  315
+ 100
```

9
```
  594
-  57
```

10
```
  594
+  57
```

11
```
  594
- 257
```

12
```
  594
- 200
```

13
```
  314
- 107
```

14
```
  310
- 169
```

15
```
  247
+ 253
```

16
```
  247
+ 200
```

Solve.

17 It was cloudy in Binghamton 319 days last year. It was cloudy there 177 days this year. How many more days was it cloudy last year than this year?

18 Mr. and Mrs. Schwartz are building a brick path in their garden. Last week they used 167 bricks. This week they plan to use 167 more bricks. At the end of this week, how many bricks will they have used all together?

19 Dr. Johnson wrote a book. His first draft had 321 pages. By the time his book was finished, he had written 130 more pages. How many pages did Dr. Johnson write?

20 The oak tree in the Nelsons' backyard is 183 years old. The elm tree in the Kings' backyard is 137 years old. How much older is the oak tree?

Eleven of the worked-out examples have errors. See if you can find them without doing the arithmetic. Be ready to explain how you found the errors without doing the arithmetic.

㉑
$$\begin{array}{r} 436 \\ +\ 296 \\ \hline 140 \end{array}$$

㉒
$$\begin{array}{r} 821 \\ -\ 473 \\ \hline 345 \end{array}$$

㉓
$$\begin{array}{r} 607 \\ -\ 329 \\ \hline 278 \end{array}$$

㉔
$$\begin{array}{r} 399 \\ +\ 146 \\ \hline 253 \end{array}$$

㉕
$$\begin{array}{r} 345 \\ +\ 111 \\ \hline 234 \end{array}$$

㉖
$$\begin{array}{r} 108 \\ +\ 456 \\ \hline 264 \end{array}$$

㉗
$$\begin{array}{r} 889 \\ -\ 707 \\ \hline 782 \end{array}$$

㉘
$$\begin{array}{r} 473 \\ -\ 208 \\ \hline 265 \end{array}$$

㉙
$$\begin{array}{r} 892 \\ +\ 108 \\ \hline 784 \end{array}$$

㉚
$$\begin{array}{r} 743 \\ -\ 477 \\ \hline 266 \end{array}$$

㉛
$$\begin{array}{r} 109 \\ +\ 246 \\ \hline 355 \end{array}$$

㉜
$$\begin{array}{r} 572 \\ -\ 444 \\ \hline 127 \end{array}$$

㉝
$$\begin{array}{r} 234 \\ +\ 159 \\ \hline 993 \end{array}$$

㉞
$$\begin{array}{r} 987 \\ -\ 789 \\ \hline 198 \end{array}$$

㉟
$$\begin{array}{r} 369 \\ +\ 436 \\ \hline 806 \end{array}$$

㊱
$$\begin{array}{r} 852 \\ +\ 147 \\ \hline 799 \end{array}$$

㊲
$$\begin{array}{r} 158 \\ +\ 349 \\ \hline 507 \end{array}$$

㊳
$$\begin{array}{r} 987 \\ -\ 339 \\ \hline 648 \end{array}$$

㊴
$$\begin{array}{r} 451 \\ -\ 158 \\ \hline 293 \end{array}$$

㊵
$$\begin{array}{r} 315 \\ -\ 157 \\ \hline 158 \end{array}$$

Adding and Subtracting Three-Digit Numbers

506 − 148 = ___?___

```
   506
 − 148
```

Start at the right.

Subtract the ones.

Can't subtract 8 from 6.

Can't regroup 0 tens and 6.

```
 4 9 16
   5̶0̶6̶
 − 148
```

5 hundreds is the same as 50 tens.

Regroup 50 tens and 6.

50 tens and 6 = 49 tens and 16.

49 tens and 16 = 4 hundreds 9 tens and 16.

```
 4 9 16
   5̶0̶6̶
 − 148
   358
```

Subtract the ones.

Subtract the tens.

Subtract the hundreds.

Subtract.

| ❶ | 961
 − 309 | ❷ | 401
 − 266 | ❸ | 181
 − 175 | ❹ | 791
 − 432 | ❺ | 874
 − 362 |

Solve these problems. Watch the signs.

6 402
− 176

7 777
+ 222

8 654
+ 101

9 686
− 458

10 800
− 455

11 486
+ 264

12 500
− 375

13 569
+ 232

14 308
− 205

15 203
− 57

16 616
+ 215

17 492
+ 55

18 452
− 207

19 278
+ 278

20 906
+ 44

21 874
− 325

22 $6 + 9 + 1 = \blacksquare$

23 $8 - 4 + 6 = \blacksquare$

24 $3 + 9 + 4 - 7 = \blacksquare$

25 $7 + 2 - 3 + 4 = \blacksquare$

26 $5 - 5 + 5 - 5 = \blacksquare$

27 $6 + 8 + 9 + 8 = \blacksquare$

28 $8 + 3 + 7 + 2 = \blacksquare$

29 $4 + 5 + 6 + 3 = \blacksquare$

Solve.

30 Last year Cara counted 533 pennies in her bank. This year she counted 491 pennies. How many more pennies were in her bank last year?

31 There were 324 parking spaces in the parking lot. Then some trees were planted. Now there are only 255 parking spaces. How many more parking spaces were there before the trees were planted?

◆ LESSON 22 Adding and Subtracting Three-Digit Numbers

Tape/CD player $229

Television $345

Fax machine $451

VCR $209

Radio $137

Solve.

Ms. Chen has $347. Mrs. Gold has $280. Ms. Lopez has $318.

32 Is there anything above that none of the women has enough money to buy?

33 Does Ms. Chen have enough money to buy any of the items shown?

34 If Ms. Chen and Mrs. Gold combine their money, how much money will they have? Could they buy the fax machine? If so, how much money would they have left?

35 If Mrs. Gold and Ms. Lopez combine their money, how much money will they have? Could they buy the fax machine? If so, how much money would they have left?

36 Could any one person buy the radio and the VCR?

37 If Ms. Chen, Mrs. Gold, and Ms. Lopez combine their money, will they have enough to buy the radio, VCR, television, and tape/CD player?

In your Math Journal make up four more problems. Write the answers on a separate piece of paper. Exchange problems with your classmates. Do you get the same answers?

GAME

Roll a Three-Digit Problem Game

Players:	Two or more
Materials:	One 0–5 cube (red)
Object:	To get the greatest sum (or least difference)
Math Focus:	Adding three-digit numbers, inequalities, and mathematical reasoning

RULES

1. Use blanks to outline an addition (or subtraction) problem on your paper, like this:

$$+\ \underline{}\ \underline{}\ \underline{} \qquad \textbf{or} \qquad -\ \underline{}\ \underline{}\ \underline{}$$

2. The first player rolls the cube six times.

3. Each time the cube is rolled, write that number in one of the blanks in your outline.

4. When all the blanks have been filled in, find the sum (or difference) of the two numbers.

5. The player with the greatest sum (or least difference) wins the round.

Review of Addition and Subtraction

Solve these problems. Watch the signs.

1 435
   + 217

2 755
   − 694

3 804
   + 102

4 705
   − 349

5 212
   + 349

6 825
   − 312

7 212
   + 379

8 208
   − 199

9 723
   + 239

10 325
    + 184

11 359
    − 260

12 954
    − 675

13 532
    + 268

14 447
    − 186

15 284
    + 437

16 261
    + 316

17 212
    − 143

18 430
    − 194

19 658
    + 171

20 707
    − 270

Solve.

21 The library needs $705 for six new windows. Members of the community raised $337 at a bake sale. How much more money is needed for the new windows?

22 Mrs. Packs used to drive 370 miles to Boxtown. A new highway was built, and now she has to drive only 355 miles to Boxtown. How many more miles did Mrs. Packs have to drive before the new highway was built?

23 Last year about 224 inches of snow fell in Winterville. About 105 inches of snow fell in Star City. How many more inches of snow fell in Winterville?

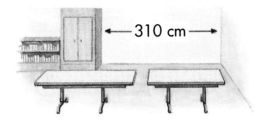

One table in the classroom is 166 centimeters long. The other table is 137 centimeters long. It is 310 centimeters from the cabinet to the wall.

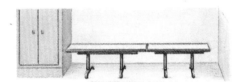

The two tables are put end-to-end next to the cabinet.

24 How many centimeters long are the two tables all together?

25 How far is it from the table on the right to the wall?

26 Could you squeeze into that space?

A table 142 centimeters long is brought in from another classroom.

27 Of the three tables in the classroom, which two will fit best between the cabinet and the wall?

28 Using the two tables from problem 27, how far is it from the table on the right to the wall?

There are two bookshelves in the classroom. One is 243 centimeters long, and the other is 182 centimeters long.

29 What is the difference in the lengths of the two bookshelves?

30 If the bookshelves were put end-to-end, how long would they be all together?

◆ LESSON 23   Review of Addition and Subtraction

The Hill School has 342 students. The Valley School has 419 students.

③ How many students are there in the two schools all together?

③ How many more students does the Valley School have?

③ Today, 58 students are absent from the Hill School. How many students are at the school?

③ Which of the two school buildings is larger?

Next year 35 students are moving from the Valley School to the Hill School.

③ Which school will have more students next year?

③ How many more students will there be in the school that has more students next year?

③ How many more students would need to move to the Hill School for both schools to have the same number of students?

③ If each school loses 20 students, how many more students will there be at the Valley School?

③ How many students will there be all together?

GAME

Play the "Checkbook" game.

Use the map to solve the problems.

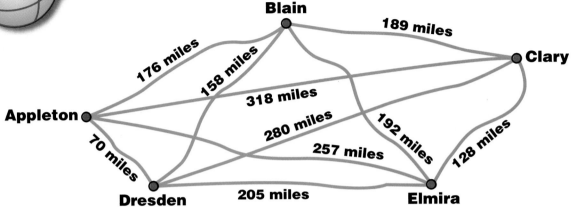

40 How far is it from Appleton to Elmira?

41 How much farther is it from Appleton to Elmira than from Appleton to Dresden?

42 If you travel from Appleton to Blain, and then from Blain to Clary, how far will you go?

43 If you travel from Appleton to Dresden to Elmira, how far will you go? How much shorter would it be to go directly from Appleton to Elmira?

44 How far is it to go from Appleton to Clary, and then back to Appleton?

45 How far is it to travel from Dresden to Blain to Elmira? How much shorter would it be to go directly from Dresden to Elmira?

Make up three more problems based on the map and write them in your Math Journal. Write your answers on a separate piece of paper. Exchange problems with your classmates. Did you get the same answers?

Adding Columns

Keith's class estimated and compared prices.
Keith made this chart to show his results.

Item	Estimate	Actual Price Good-Buy Market	Actual Price Big-Food Market
tuna fish (light, in water)	90¢	89¢	93¢
pinto beans (Veggie Time brand)	50¢	65¢	63¢
soap (bath size, Bubbler brand)	75¢	68¢	71¢
Totals	215¢	222¢	227¢

Look at the chart Keith made and answer these questions.

❶ Which store had a total price closer to Keith's estimate?

❷ Which store charged more for each of the three items?

❸ Which store had the greater total price? How much greater?

Use a computer or other means to make a chart like Keith's. Estimate and compare prices. Then use your own chart to answer these questions.

❹ Which store had a total price closer to your estimate?

❺ Which store charged more for the three items all together?

❻ Did every item cost more in the more expensive store?

Solve these problems. Watch the signs.

7 $\begin{array}{r} 300 \\ -\ 125 \\ \hline \end{array}$ **8** $\begin{array}{r} 425 \\ +\ 395 \\ \hline \end{array}$ **9** $\begin{array}{r} 136 \\ -\ 85 \\ \hline \end{array}$ **10** $\begin{array}{r} 843 \\ -\ 616 \\ \hline \end{array}$

11 $\begin{array}{r} 741 \\ -\ 681 \\ \hline \end{array}$ **12** $\begin{array}{r} 578 \\ -\ 249 \\ \hline \end{array}$ **13** $\begin{array}{r} 685 \\ +\ 293 \\ \hline \end{array}$ **14** $\begin{array}{r} 233 \\ -\ 177 \\ \hline \end{array}$

15 $\begin{array}{r} 35 \\ 32 \\ +\ 41 \\ \hline \end{array}$ **16** $\begin{array}{r} 15 \\ 39 \\ +\ 24 \\ \hline \end{array}$ **17** $\begin{array}{r} 64 \\ 27 \\ +\ 59 \\ \hline \end{array}$ **18** $\begin{array}{r} 17 \\ 98 \\ 68 \\ +\ 32 \\ \hline \end{array}$

19 $\begin{array}{r} 23 \\ 76 \\ 18 \\ +\ 34 \\ \hline \end{array}$ **20** $\begin{array}{r} 71 \\ 66 \\ 65 \\ +\ 59 \\ \hline \end{array}$ **21** $\begin{array}{r} 47 \\ 36 \\ 24 \\ +\ 13 \\ \hline \end{array}$ **22** $\begin{array}{r} 64 \\ 21 \\ +\ 48 \\ \hline \end{array}$

Solve.

There are four shelves in Maria's room. There are 27 books on the first shelf, 31 books on the second shelf, 23 books on the third shelf, and 18 books on the fourth shelf.

23 Which shelf has the most books?

24 How many more books does that shelf have than the shelf that has the fewest books?

25 How many books are on the four shelves all together?

Talk about the Thinking Story "Bargains Galore."

Practice with Numbers

Add.

❶
```
    7
    8
+   6
```

❷
```
   76
   13
+   4
```

❸
```
   38
   25
+  36
```

❹
```
   25
   25
+  25
```

❺
```
   29
   36
   21
+  14
```

❻
```
   73
   17
   19
+  25
```

❼
```
   30
   20
   10
+  60
```

❽
```
   25
   25
   25
+  25
```

❾
```
   40
  120
   30
+ 140
```

❿
```
   92
  240
  178
+ 415
```

⓫
```
   28
  109
   93
+ 177
```

⓬
```
  366
  774
+ 240
```

⓭
```
  505
  672
+ 134
```

⓮
```
  247
  383
+ 712
```

⓯
```
  451
  392
  876
+ 109
```

⓰
```
  360
  218
  543
+ 851
```

⓱
```
   77
   90
   16
+   8
```

⓲
```
   45
  789
   83
+  19
```

⓳
```
  530
  213
  138
+ 333
```

⓴
```
   25
  100
   25
+  50
```

Number correct ▩

Solve.

Jonathan brought 25 cups to the school party. Anita brought 50 cups. Shana brought 15 cups.

㉑ How many cups did they bring all together?

㉒ There will be 120 children at the school party. How many more cups are needed?

㉓ Miss Nakamura must drive from Amigo to Berry Point to Carson City to Dial Falls and back to Amigo. How far is that?

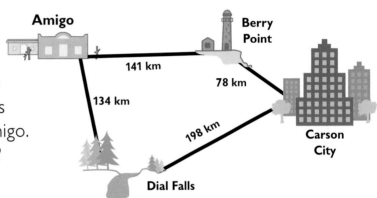

Amigo

Berry Point

141 km

78 km

134 km

198 km

Carson City

Dial Falls

㉔ Mr. Ryan drives from Amigo to Dial Falls to Carson City to Berry Point to Amigo. How far is that?

㉕ Mr. Wolf lives in Carson City. He wants to visit his brother in Amigo. What is the shortest route that Mr. Wolf can take?

㉖ The Andersons are planning a trip from their home near Dial Falls to Berry Point. What is the shortest route they can take?

㉗ How many kilometers shorter is this route than the other route the Andersons could take?

◆ **LESSON 25 Practice with Numbers**

Look at each series of numbers. Do you see a pattern?
Using your pattern, copy and complete the series. Be
ready to explain your pattern.

28 48, 52, 56, 60, ■, ■, ■, ■, ■, ■, 88

29 11, 13, 15, 17, ■, ■, ■, ■, ■, ■, 31

30 80, 83, 86, 89, ■, ■, ■, ■, ■, ■, 110

31 573, 575, 577, ■, ■, ■, ■, ■, ■, 591

32 156, 153, 150, 147, ■, ■, ■, ■, ■, ■, 126

33 600, 603, 606, 609, ■, ■, ■, ■, ■, ■, 630

34 516, 514, 512, 510, ■, ■, ■, ■, ■, ■, 496

35 230, 227, 224, 221, ■, ■, ■, ■, ■, ■, ■, ■, 194

36 652, 655, 658, ■, ■, ■, ■, ■, ■, 679

37 100, 104, 108, ■, ■, ■, ■, ■, ■, ■, ■, ■, ■, 152

38 261, 257, 253, ■, ■, ■, ■, ■, ■, ■, ■, 217

39 220, 216, 212, ■, ■, ■, ■, ■, ■, ■, ■, ■, 172

40 122, 120, 118, ■, ■, ■, ■, ■, ■, ■, ■, ■, 98

Be careful.

41 3, 6, 9, 12, 10, 13, 16, 19, 17, 20, 23, ■, ■, ■, ■, ■, ■, 34

42 2, 4, 6, 5, 7, 9, 8, 10, 12, 11, ■, ■, ■, ■, ■, ■, ■, ■, 20

43 4, 5, 7, 10, 11, 13, 16, 17, 19, 22, ■, ■, ■, ■, ■, ■, 35

44 1, 3, 2, 4, 3, 5, 4, 6, ■, ■, ■, ■, ■, ■, 8

45 7, 10, 8, 6, 9, 7, 5, 8, 6, 4, ■, ■, ■, ■, ■, ■, ■, ■, ■, ■, ■, 0

Four Rolls of Four Cubes Game

Players:	Two, three, or four
Materials:	Two 0–5 cubes (red), two 5–10 cubes (blue)
Object:	To make the greatest total score
Math Focus:	Adding columns of two-digit numbers

RULES

1. Take turns rolling all four cubes and making two two-digit numbers to add. Do this four times in each turn. (If you roll a 10, roll that cube again.)

2. Each time you roll, all the players add the two numbers you make. The player after you writes each sum for you, but all four sums count in your score.

3. After you have rolled four times, the next player rolls four times, and so on, until all players have rolled.

4. Each player adds his or her four sums to get a total score.

5. The player with the greatest total score wins the round.

SAMPLE GAME

Beth rolled:	Beth made:	For a sum of:	
7 9 2 5	95 and 72	167	
6 5 0 3	63 and 50	113	Andy wrote these down for Beth.
5 8 1 5	85 and 51	136	
9 8 2 0	92 and 80	172	

Beth's total was 558. Andy completed four turns and had a total of 550. Beth won this round.

Adding and Subtracting Four-Digit Numbers

Solve these problems. Watch the signs.

1   4083
   + 2196

2   1000
   − 750

3   4893
   − 962

4   584
   + 1208

5   4761
   − 2819

6   5000
   − 1234

7   750
   + 250

8   1750
   + 1250

9   6133
   − 2533

10   4861
   + 2222

11   7019
   − 5342

12   1971
   + 842

13   750
     250
   + 350

14   29
    35
    62
  + 47

15   315
    708
     95
  + 116

16   480
    565
    249
  + 197

17   18
   705
    63
  + 142

18   532
   621
  + 247

19   416
    76
   319
  + 386

20   291
    78
   119
  + 401

21   3085
   + 2354

22   2174
   − 1891

23   527
   222
  + 171

24   469
    79
  + 98

GAME

Roll a Four-Digit Problem Game

COOPERATIVE LEARNING

Players:	Two or more
Materials:	One 0–5 cube (red)
Object:	To get the greatest sum (or least difference)
Math Focus:	Adding four-digit numbers, inequalities, and mathematical reasoning

RULES

1. Use blanks to outline an addition (or subtraction) problem on your paper, like this:

$$\begin{array}{r} \underline{}\ \underline{}\ \underline{}\ \underline{} \\ +\ \underline{}\ \underline{}\ \underline{}\ \underline{} \\ \hline \end{array}$$ **or** $$\begin{array}{r} \underline{}\ \underline{}\ \underline{}\ \underline{} \\ -\ \underline{}\ \underline{}\ \underline{}\ \underline{} \\ \hline \end{array}$$

2. The first player rolls the cube eight times.

3. Each time the cube is rolled, write that number in one of the blanks in your outline.

4. When all the blanks have been filled in, find the sum (or difference) of the two numbers.

5. The player with the greatest sum (or least difference) wins the round.

MATH JOURNAL

In your Math Journal explain your strategy for playing this game. How did you make the greatest sum or least difference?

Four-Digit Numbers: Addition and Subtraction

Solve these problems. Watch the signs.

1 4783 + 2651   **2** 3489 − 2438   **3** 4853 − 3657

4 8074 − 2356   **5** 6173 + 3827   **6** 7004 − 4191

7 5000 + 2500   **8** 5918 − 3677   **9** 6701 + 2360

10 3417 − 2846   **11** 7172 + 609   **12** 3657 + 4407

13 6004 + 2333   **14** 9085 − 7896   **15** 1133 + 5636

16 3871 − 2566   **17** 4718 + 2719   **18** 9107 − 7281

19 8525 + 2475   **20** 6731 − 812   **21** 2336 − 2232

22 8943 − 356   **23** 3647 − 1353   **24** 3303 + 898

25 7583 − 2583   **26** 8400 + 3891   **27** 4808 − 1383

28 8000 − 2386   **29** 9876 + 1234   **30** 5455 − 3649

31 8878 + 563   **32** 4282 + 3622   **33** 9463 − 8713

Number correct

Complete the table. Show about how many years ago these famous people were born.

SOCIAL STUDIES CONNECTION

	Name	Year of Birth	Born About This Many Years Ago
34	Joan of Arc	1412	■
35	Jane Austen	1775	■
36	Geronimo	1829	■
37	Pablo Casals	1876	■
38	Lise Meitner	1878	■
39	Albert Einstein	1879	■
40	Helen Keller	1880	■
41	Tsung-Dao Lee	1926	■
42	Martin Luther King, Jr.	1929	■
43	Barbara Jordan	1936	■

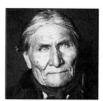
Geronimo

Helen Keller

Martin Luther King, Jr.

44 About how old was Martin Luther King, Jr. when Barbara Jordan was born?

45 About how many years apart were Jane Austen and Pablo Casals born?

46 About how many years apart were you and Albert Einstein born?

47 Lise Meitner died in 1968. About how old was Tsung-Dao Lee that year?

MATH JOURNAL

Choose three of these people and find out why they are famous. Write about them in your Math Journal.

LESSON
28

Applications: Four-Digit Addition and Subtraction

SOCIAL STUDIES CONNECTION

Complete the table. Show about how many years ago each thing was invented.

	Invention	Inventor	Year Invented	About How Many Years Ago?
1	Lightning rod	Benjamin Franklin	1752	▪
2	Telephone	Alexander Graham Bell	1876	▪
3	Radio	Guglielmo Marconi	1895	▪
4	Airplane	Orville and Wilbur Wright	1903	▪
5	Gas mask	Garrett Augustus Morgan	1912	▪
6	Television	Vladimir Zworykin	1923	▪
7	Automobile	Nicolas-Joseph Cugnot	1769	▪
8	Motion pictures	Thomas Edison	1893	▪
9	Videocassette recorder	Alexander M. Pontiatoff	1956	▪
10	CD-ROM	James T. Russell	1965	▪

11 Benjamin Franklin was born in 1706. About how old was he when he invented the lightning rod?

Solve.

Linda and David ran for school president.

Linda got 1134 votes. David got 1078 votes.

12 Who won?

13 By how many votes?

14 How many people voted?

It is 3144 miles from Portland to Boston. It is 1520 miles from Boston to Miami. Miss Ortiz drove from Portland to Boston to Miami.

15 How far did Miss Ortiz drive?

16 How far is it back to Portland if Miss Ortiz drives back the same way she came?

George Washington was born in 1732. Abraham Lincoln was born in 1809.

17 Which man was heavier?

18 How many pounds heavier?

19 About how many years apart were George Washington and Abraham Lincoln born?

Talk about the Thinking Story "How Close Is Close Enough?"

LESSON 29

Exploring Negative Numbers

Solve these problems with your calculator and without your calculator. Do you get the same answer each way?

1. $7 + 8 = $ ■
2. $70 + 80 = $ ■
3. $700 + 800 = $ ■
4. $7000 + 8000 = $ ■
5. $0 + 5 + 5 = $ ■
6. $14 - 9 = $ ■
7. $140 - 90 = $ ■
8. $1400 - 900 = $ ■
9. $14,000 - 9,000 = $ ■
10. $8 + 10 + 10 = $ ■
11. $0 + 5 + 5 + 5 + 5 + 5 = $ ■
12. $8 + 10 + 10 + 10 + 10 + 10 = $ ■

Use the number line to help solve these problems. Also solve them with your calculator. Are the answers the same?

13. $12 - 3 - 3 - 3 = $ ■
14. $10 - 3 - 3 - 3 - 3 = $ ■
15. $7 - 2 - 2 - 2 = $ ■
16. $7 - 2 - 2 - 2 - 2 = $ ■
17. $1 - 6 = $ ■
18. $-3 + 2 = $ ■
19. $-3 + 2 + 2 = $ ■
20. $0 + 5 = $ ■
21. $0 - 5 = $ ■
22. $-7 + 10 = $ ■
23. $4 - 3 + 1 - 4 = $ ■
24. $5 + 1 - 2 - 3 = $ ■

Solve.

25. The thermometer outside Mr. Harfoot's house read 8° Celsius when he went to bed. By the next morning, the temperature had dropped 11 degrees. What did the thermometer read then?

26. The top of Mount Sanford is 800 feet above sea level. The bottom of Furn Valley is 1000 feet below that. How many feet below sea level is Furn Valley?

Race from 15 to -15 and Back Game

COOPERATIVE LEARNING

GAME

Players:	**Two**
Materials:	**One 0–5 cube (red), one 5–10 cube (blue)**
Object:	**To get from 15 to –15 and back first**
Math Focus:	**Adding, subtracting, and mathematical reasoning**

RULES

1. Players take turns rolling the 0–5 cube or the 5–10 cube and add or subtract the number rolled. A player *must* roll the 0–5 cube two times before finishing.

2. Start at 15, go to or past –15, and then go back to 15.

3. The first player back to 15 who has rolled the 0–5 cube two times or more wins.

SAMPLE GAME

Wendy Rolled	Wendy Scored	Peter Rolled	Peter Scored
5 *	15 − 5 = (10)	8	15 − 8 = (7)
7	10 − 7 = (3)	8	7 − 8 = (−1)
10	3 − 10 = (−7)	8	−1 − 8 = (−9)
8	−7 − 8 = (−15)	0 *	−9 − 0 = (−9)
8	−15 + 8 = (−7)	4 *	−9 − 4 = (−13)
9	−7 + 9 = (2)	3 *	−13 − 3 = (−16)
4 *	2 + 4 = (6)	8	−16 + 8 = (−8)
9	6 + 9 = (15)	1 *	−8 + 1 = (−7)

An * marks the times the 0–5 cube was rolled. Scores are in parentheses.

Wendy won this game.

30 Race the Calculator

Solve these problems. If you use a calculator, you must push the keys for all the numbers and signs shown.

① 1 + 1 = ■

② 10 + 10 = ■

③ 100 + 100 = ■

④ 11 − 7 = ■

⑤ 110 − 70 = ■

⑥ 1100 − 700 = ■

⑦ 100 − 1 = ■

⑧ 1000 − 1 = ■

⑨ 100 − 20 = ■

⑩ 8 + 5 = ■

⑪ 80 + 50 = ■

⑫ 800 + 500 = ■

⑬ 7 + 9 = ■

⑭ 807 + 509 = ■

⑮ 500 + 500 = ■

⑯ 700 + 300 = ■

Write **C** if you would use a calculator to solve the problem. Write **N** if you would not. Then solve each problem.

⑰ ○ 1000 − 1 = ■

⑱ ○ 251 + 749 = ■

⑲ ○ 7856 + 1947 = ■

⑳ ○ 1992 − 1983 = ■

㉑ ○ 4763 − 1763 = ■

㉒ ○ 4703 − 2865 = ■

㉓ ○ 6047 − 2539 = ■

㉔ ○ 5000 − 3000 = ■

㉕ ○ 25 + 75 = ■

㉖ ○ 10 + 10 = ■

㉗ ○ 250 + 750 = ■

㉘ ○ 4567 − 3456 = ■

㉙ ○ 2633 − 888 = ■

㉚ ○ 2145 + 1884 = ■

㉛ ○ 1000 + 909 = ■

㉜ ○ 3108 − 277 = ■

㉝ ○ 500 + 600 = ■

㉞ ○ 2413 + 300 = ■

George Washington became president of the United States in 1789. He was born in 1732. What keys would you push on your calculator to find out how old he was when he became president? Would you push: 1, 7, 8, 9, −, 1, 7, 3, 2, = ? That would give you the right answer. But if Washington had not yet had his birthday that year, he would have been a year younger than the calculator shows.

John Adams was born in 1735. His son, John Quincy Adams, was born in 1767. Both men were United States presidents. John Adams became president in 1796, and John Quincy Adams became president in 1825. Neither had yet had a birthday in the year in which he became president.

For each problem, tell if you would use a calculator or not to find the answer. If you would use a calculator, say what keys you would push. If you would not use one, tell how you would get the answer. You don't need to find the answer.

35 How old was John Adams when he became president? (Did you remember to subtract 1 because he hadn't yet had his birthday that year?)

36 How old was John Quincy Adams when he became president?

37 Who was older when he became president, John Quincy Adams or John Adams? What keys would you push to find out how much older?

38 John Kennedy was born in 1917. He became president in 1961, before his birthday that year. How old was he when he became president?

Inequalities and Equalities

Fifteen of these statements have errors. Write *T* if the statement is true. Write *F* if it is false.

1. $18 > 20$
2. $7 > 5$
3. $4 = 4$

4. $107 < 54$
5. $2869 > 2895$
6. $2929 > 2900$

7. $5097 < 5196$
8. $2743 = 2743$
9. $4365 > 3$

10. $4096 = 4906$
11. $1111 < 222$
12. $910 > 466$

13. $980 < 1025$
14. $4010 = 4001$
15. $5190 > 519$

16. $78 < 54$
17. $81 < 2$
18. $867 > 867$

19. $701 > 45$
20. $6982 < 5982$
21. $27 > 26$

22. $2000 > 1999$
23. $873 = 378$
24. $4987 < 5001$

25. $3425 < 3462$
26. $6311 > 6315$
27. $326 > 236$

28. $3020 < 3008$
29. $900 = 9000$
30. $801 > 701$

31. $7794 = 7940$
32. $722 < 2300$
33. $4511 > 4115$

What is the right sign? Draw <, >, or =.

34 8 ● 11

35 612 ● 613

36 5738 ● 5738

37 483 ● 438

38 8259 ● 8260

39 1000 ● 100

40 900 ● 1000

41 8209 ● 8209

42 1764 ● 1734

43 6015 ● 6020

44 752 ● 752

45 2001 ● 2010

46 35 ● 62

47 5341 ● 2376

48 345 ● 543

49 222 ● 1110

50 345 ● 345

51 921 ● 899

52 696 ● 701

53 3121 ● 3121

54 760 ● 76

55 68 ● 86

56 192 ● 202

57 499 ● 409

Solve.

58 After nine innings of baseball, Ben's team has 12 runs and Leon's team has six runs. Whose team has more runs?

59 Skyhouse Stadium holds 12,860 people. Fulton Stadium holds 11,980 people. Which stadium holds more people?

60 Deb's vacation was 12 days long. Julie's vacation lasted 14 days. Whose vacation was longer?

Rounding to 10s, 100s, and 1000s

Often we don't need an exact number to answer a problem. We can "round" numbers to a number that is close but easier to use. For example, to know about how much 1998 + 3407 is, you might round them both to the nearest hundred: 2000 and 3400. Then add those numbers to get 5400. Rounding usually won't give the exact answer, but it should be close.

When rounding to the nearest hundred, look at the digits to the right of the hundreds place. If they make a number greater than 50, round up. If they make a number less than 50, round down. If they make exactly 50, you may round up or down, depending on the situation.

Round each number to the nearest hundred.

❶	573	❷	804	❸	96	❹	149
❺	2345	❻	2355	❼	9654	❽	5003
❾	5555	❿	451	⓫	5076	⓬	34

Round each number to the nearest ten.

⓭	573	⓮	804	⓯	96	⓰	149
⓱	2345	⓲	2355	⓳	9654	⓴	5003
㉑	5555	㉒	451	㉓	5076	㉔	34

Round each number to the nearest thousand.

㉕	2597	㉖	2463	㉗	8516	㉘	5553
㉙	3020	㉚	5173	㉛	7435	㉜	1530

If you round two numbers up or down and then add, the estimated sum may not be close. The same thing can happen if you round one number up and one number down before subtracting. In such cases you may want to correct for rounding errors.

$$752 \longrightarrow 800$$
$$\underline{+ \ 860} \longrightarrow \underline{+ \ 900}$$

For example, to estimate the sum of 752 and 860 to the nearest hundred, you might round the numbers up to 800 and 900. Then the estimated sum is 1700. However, since both numbers were rounded up a large amount, you should take your estimate down to the next closest hundred, or 1600. The precise answer is 1612.

Estimate the answers to the nearest hundred. Watch the signs.

33 1255 + 1862 = ▦   34 590 + 289 = ▦

35 848 − 649 = ▦   36 89 + 22,543 = ▦

37 34 + 1766 = ▦   38 4325 − 2281 = ▦

39 760 + 760 = ▦   40 2345 − 1955 = ▦

41 3052 − 1948 = ▦   42 3450 − 1850 = ▦

Find the precise answers to problems 33–42. Compare them with your estimates.

Write a short statement in your Math Journal about how to make good estimates.

Choosing Reasonable Answers

You can use rounding to find mistakes in answers. This can help you choose the right answers.

In each problem, one answer is correct. Decide which one is correct. You can approximate or use your knowledge of odd numbers and even numbers.

❶
$4937 + 2098 =$
- **a.** 735
- **b.** 7035
- **c.** 5035

❷
$3448 + 2648 =$
- **a.** 6096
- **b.** 5996
- **c.** 6196

❸
$4937 - 2098 =$
- **a.** 2839
- **b.** 3838
- **c.** 238

❹
$3448 - 2648 =$
- **a.** 900
- **b.** 800
- **c.** 700

❺
$5307 + 2909 =$
- **a.** 8215
- **b.** 816
- **c.** 8216

❻
$3456 + 75 =$
- **a.** 3631
- **b.** 1331
- **c.** 3531

❼
$5307 - 2909 =$
- **a.** 2403
- **b.** 248
- **c.** 2398

❽
$3456 - 75 =$
- **a.** 3581
- **b.** 3481
- **c.** 3381

❾
$1094 - 937 =$
- **a.** 216
- **b.** 157
- **c.** 2018

❿
$9028 - 6154 =$
- **a.** 2873
- **b.** 2874
- **c.** 2875

SOCIAL STUDIES CONNECTION

For each problem, give an approximate answer that is within 50 of the exact answer. Try to get the answer by rounding and approximating.

11 Joan of Arc was born in 1412. George Washington was born in 1732. About how many years earlier was Joan of Arc born?

12 The artist Michelangelo was born in 1475. The artist Pablo Picasso was born in 1881. Who was born first? About how many years were there between their births?

13 Queen Elizabeth I was born in 1533. Queen Elizabeth II was born in 1926. About how many years apart were they born?

14 Explorer Marco Polo was born in about 1254. Christopher Columbus was born in 1451. About how many years apart were they born?

15 Mount Whitney in California is 14,494 feet high. Woodall Mountain in Mississippi is 806 feet high. How much difference is there in the heights of the two mountains?

16 The highest point of Guadalupe Peak is 8749 feet. The highest point on Black Mesa is 4973 feet. About how much difference is there in the heights of the two points?

17 The area of Jefferson County is 1095 square miles. The area of Jerome County is 600 square miles. About how much difference is there in the area of the two counties?

LESSON 34

Approximating Sums and Differences

What is the correct sign? Draw <, >, or =.
Compare methods of solving. Which do you think are
the easiest?

1 246 + 40 ● 546 + 140

2 3 + 82 ● 2 + 83

3 3000 + 2000 ● 3001 + 2001

4 12 − 3 ● 14 − 1

5 102 + 86 ● 586 + 240

6 8 + 43 ● 43 + 8

7 100 − 7 ● 200 − 7

8 21 − 8 ● 28 − 1

9 43 − 0 ● 53 − 10

10 157 + 861 ● 57 + 61

11 7 + 43 ● 43 + 72

12 1000 − 3 ● 1000 − 43

13 18 − 9 ● 19 − 10

14 156 − 56 ● 166 − 66

15 126 − 100 ● 126 − 10

16 34 + 27 ● 27 + 34

17 4259 + 675 ● 4259 + 575

18 720 − 39 ● 720 − 49

19 1085 − 200 ● 1085 + 200

20 116 + 49 ● 47 + 116

21 3128 + 99 ● 1743 + 83

22 211 − 20 ● 111 − 20

23 1134 + 1113 ● 1471 + 2717

24 320 − 20 ● 270 + 30

25 4000 − 400 ● 44 + 1000

26 718 + 67 ● 520 + 67

Solve.

27 There were two football games Friday night. In the first game the final score was 28 to 10. The score of the second game was 38 to 14. Which game had the greatest difference in scores?

Solve.

Tony had 89¢. His
mother gave him 68¢.

28 Can Tony buy a book?

29 Can he buy a car?

30 Can he buy two cars?

31 Which costs more, two books or two cars?

32 How wide is the doorway?

33 How wide is the piano from front to back?

34 Will the piano fit through the doorway?

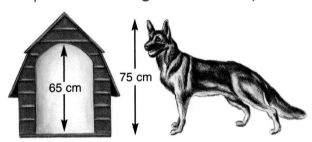

35 How tall is Corky?

36 How tall is the doorway to the doghouse?

37 Will Corky fit through the doorway?

◆ **LESSON 34** **Approximating Sums and Differences**

Inequality Game

GAME

Players:	**Two**
Materials:	**Two 0–5 cubes (red), two 5–10 cubes (blue)**
Object:	**To fill in an inequality statement correctly**
Math Focus:	**Adding two-digit numbers, identifying inequalities, and mathematical reasoning**

RULES

1. Make one of these game forms on a sheet of paper:

   ___ ___ < ___ ___ **or** ___ ___ > ___ ___

2. The first player rolls all four cubes, makes two two-digit numbers, and writes their sum on either side of the inequality sign. If the player rolls a 10, he or she rolls that cube again.

3. The second player rolls all four cubes, makes two two-digit numbers, and writes their sum in the remaining space.

4. If the inequality statement is true, the second player wins. If the inequality statement is false, the first player wins.

5. Take turns being first.

In your **Math Journal** explain your strategy for playing this game. What tips would you give someone playing this game for the first time?

Savannah, Terry, Andy, Maggie, Bryce, Susan, Angela, and Minae wanted to find out who could run the farthest in 15 minutes. They ran on a track that was 1000 meters around. Each meter was marked on the track so they could tell how far they had run.

Savannah ran around the track four times plus another 535 meters. How far was that? The students made a table to show how far each ran.

Savannah	Terry	Andy	Maggie	Bryce	Susan	Angela	Minae
4535							

Use a computer or other means to copy the table. Fill it in using the following information.

Terry ran around the track three times and another 987 meters. Andy ran around the track five times and another 48 meters. Maggie ran around the track four times and another 535 meters. Bryce ran around the track four times and another 378 meters. Susan ran around the track four times and another 355 meters. Angela ran around the track four times exactly. Minae ran around the track four times and another 378 meters.

38 Who ran the longest distance?

39 Who ran the shortest distance?

40 Did any runners run the same distance? If so, who?

LESSON 35 Add to Find the Perimeter

Solve these problems. Watch the signs.

① 5 + 7 = ■   ② 10 + 4 = ■   ③ 16 + 5 = ■

④ 8 + 9 = ■   ⑤ 12 + 6 = ■   ⑥ 3 + 9 = ■

⑦ 16 − 9 = ■   ⑧ 10 − 7 = ■   ⑨ 6 − 2 = ■

⑩ 15 − 9 = ■   ⑪ 11 − 6 = ■   ⑫ 15 − 11 = ■

⑬
```
   23
+  54
```
⑭
```
   47
+  26
```
⑮
```
   48
−   7
```
⑯
```
   48
−  26
```

⑰
```
   82
−  39
```
⑱
```
    7
+  28
```
⑲
```
  100
−   25
```
⑳
```
   27
   92
+  46
```

㉑
```
    36
    23
+  154
```
㉒
```
    95
   105
   216
+  150
```
㉓
```
   8756
−  3849
```
㉔
```
   2046
+  3598
```

Solve.

㉕ The Andersons' living room is 11 feet by 10 feet. What is the perimeter of the room?

㉖ Mrs. Pae's living room is 13 feet by 8 feet. Whose room has the greater perimeter, the Andersons' or Mrs. Pae's?

Find the perimeter.

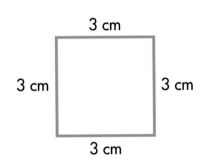

③ Square

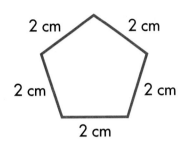

③ Regular Pentagon

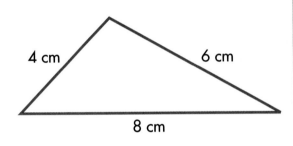

③ Triangle

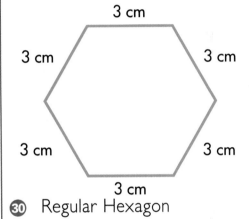

③ Regular Hexagon

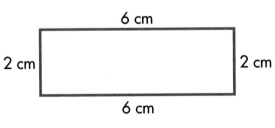

③ Rectangle

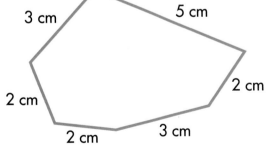

③ Hexagon

Make up two problems about perimeter. Write them in your Math Journal.

◆ **LESSON 35** Add to Find the Perimeter

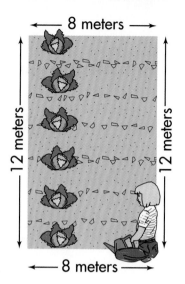

8 meters

12 meters   12 meters

8 meters

Solve.

33 How long a fence does Abby need to go around her garden?

34 Mr. Wing gave Abby 25 meters of fence. How many more meters of fence does she need?

35 What is the shape of Abby's garden?

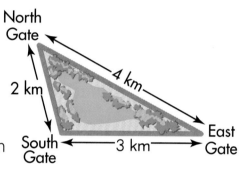

North Gate

4 km

2 km

South Gate   3 km   East Gate

36 Lorena jogged around the park one time. How far did she jog?

37 What is the shape of the park?

38 On another day, Lorena jogged from the East Gate to the North Gate to the South Gate, and then walked back to the East Gate. How far did she jog?

39 How far did she walk?

40 Mr. Zalesky built a house. He lived in it for six years. Then Dr. Ortega lived in it for 12 years. Then she sold it to Mr. Howe. Mr. Howe has lived in it for 11 years. How old is the house?

Trees are the largest living things on Earth. Some are even bigger than whales. The heaviest tree is the giant sequoia, which can weigh up to 2 million pounds.

Let's look at geometric shapes.

The base of a parallelogram is 5 centimeters long.

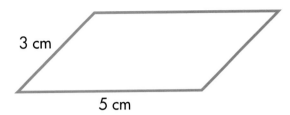

A side is 3 centimeters long. You can use this information to find the perimeter of the parallelogram. That is because opposite sides of a parallelogram are equal.

41 Suppose you know the perimeter of a parallelogram. Could you figure out how long a side plus the base is? How?

42 Draw a parallelogram that has a perimeter of 26 cm.

43 Draw a rectangle that has a perimeter of 26 cm.

44 Try to draw a triangle that has a perimeter of about 15 cm. Is this harder than drawing a rectangle with a given perimeter? Why?

45 Try to draw a hexagon (six-sided figure) with a perimeter of about 18 cm.

46 Try to draw a pentagon (five-sided figure) with a perimeter of 25 cm.

47 Draw a square with a perimeter of 20 cm.

Practice with Approximating Sums and Differences

In each problem, two of the answers are clearly wrong and one is correct. Choose the correct answer. Explain why your answers make sense.

①
48 + 27 =
- **a.** 45
- **b.** 25
- **c.** 75

②
371 + 629 =
- **a.** 500
- **b.** 1000
- **c.** 10,000

③
276 + 28 =
- **a.** 304
- **b.** 84
- **c.** 204

④
912 + 162 =
- **a.** 74
- **b.** 174
- **c.** 1074

⑤
206 + 209 =
- **a.** 215
- **b.** 415
- **c.** 615

⑥
5763 + 2194 =
- **a.** 5757
- **b.** 757
- **c.** 7957

⑦
329 + 329 =
- **a.** 258
- **b.** 358
- **c.** 658

⑧
4328 + 3672 =
- **a.** 4000
- **b.** 500
- **c.** 8000

⑨
612 + 398 =
- **a.** 110
- **b.** 1010
- **c.** 9010

⑩
1009 + 3986 =
- **a.** 4995
- **b.** 995
- **c.** 9995

In each problem, two of the answers are clearly wrong and one is correct. Choose the correct answer. Explain why your answers make sense.

11 $3705 - 1698 =$
a. 107
b. 5007
c. 2007

12 $5000 - 2500 =$
a. 250
b. 2500
c. 9500

13 $750 + 750 =$
a. 150
b. 750
c. 1500

14 $8003 - 2986 =$
a. 5017
b. 8017
c. 9017

15 $2250 + 2250 =$
a. 500
b. 4500
c. 8500

16 $17 + 8983 =$
a. 2000
b. 9000
c. 4000

17 $5000 - 250 =$
a. 250
b. 2500
c. 4750

18 $864 - 468 =$
a. 396
b. 5396
c. 96

19 $2401 + 2401 =$
a. 0
b. 2402
c. 4802

20 $3068 + 932 =$
a. 2000
b. 3000
c. 4000

Pick one of the problems. In your Math Journal explain the strategy you used to find the reasonable answer.

◆ LESSON 36 Practice with Approximating Sums and Differences

This table shows the length and depth of each of the Great Lakes.

Lake	Length (in miles)	Deepest Part (in feet)
Superior	383	1333
Huron	247	750
Michigan	321	923
Erie	241	210
Ontario	193	778

For each problem, three possible answers are given. Two are clearly wrong. The other is correct. Choose the correct answer.

㉑ The difference in depth between the deepest and shallowest Great Lake is:

a. 223 feet **b.** 823 feet **c.** 1123 feet

㉒ The difference in length between the longest and shortest Great Lake is:

a. 90 miles **b.** 190 miles **c.** 290 miles

㉓ Lake Superior is how much longer than the next longest Great Lake?

a. 704 miles **b.** 162 miles **c.** 62 miles

㉔ Lake Superior is how much deeper than the next deepest Great Lake?

a. 410 feet **b.** 610 feet **c.** 810 feet

GAME

Make 1000 Game

Players:	Two
Materials:	Two 0–5 cubes (red), two 5–10 cubes (blue)
Object:	To make the greater sum not over 1000
Math Focus:	Multidigit addition, place value, and mathematical reasoning

RULES

1. Each player chooses a different starting number between 250 and 750.

2. One player rolls all four cubes. If a 10 is rolled, roll that cube again.

3. Each player makes a 1-, 2-, or 3-digit number and adds it to his or her starting number. If a player's sum is over 1000, that player loses the round. If both players go over 1000, they choose new starting numbers and begin again.

4. The player with the greater sum not over 1000 wins the round.

SAMPLE GAME

Charles chose 472 as his number. Nora chose 285.

Nora rolled 7, 6, 2, and 4 and made the number 672. She added 285 + 672 = 957.

Charles made the number 476 and added 472 + 476 = 948.

Nora won this round.

MATH JOURNAL

Would you choose a starting number closer to 250 or to 750? Explain why in your Math Journal.

Telling Time

What time is it? How many minutes after the hour?
The first problem has been done for you.

1

8:05

5 minutes after 8

2

■ minutes after ■

3

■ minutes after ■

4

■ minutes after ■

5

■ minutes after ■

6

■ minutes after ■

7

■ minutes after ■

8

■ minutes after ■

What time is it? How many minutes before the next hour? The first problem has been done for you.

⑨

2:55

5 minutes to 3

⑩

■ minutes to ■

⑪

■ minutes to ■

⑫

■ minutes to ■

⑬

■ minutes to ■

⑭

■ minutes to ■

There are 86,400 seconds in one day and 31,536,000 seconds in one 365-day year.

GAME

Play the "Minutes" game.

LESSON
38

Practice Telling Time

Tell which clocks show the same time.

1

a.  4:15

2

b. 7:08

3

c. 6:00

4

d. 3:19

5

e. 12:30

Tell the time in three ways. The first one has been done for you.

6  2:45

45 minutes after **2**
15 minutes to **3**

7

▦ minutes after ▦
▦ minutes to ▦

8

▦ minutes after ▦
▦ minutes to ▦

9

▦ minutes after ▦
▦ minutes to ▦

10

▦ minutes after ▦
▦ minutes to ▦

11

▦ minutes after ▦
▦ minutes to ▦

12

▦ minutes after ▦
▦ minutes to ▦

13

▦ minutes after ▦
▦ minute to ▦

LESSON 39

Unit 1 Review

MATH JOURNAL

Study the chart.

① Make up three problems based on the chart and solve them. Write them in your Math Journal.

GEOGRAPHY CONNECTION

Lessons 26–28

How Deep Are Some Bodies of Water?

Body of Water	Greatest Depth (in meters)
Pacific Ocean	10,924
Atlantic Ocean	8,605
Indian Ocean	7,125
Caribbean Sea	8,605
Arctic Ocean	5,450
Mediterranean Sea	5,150
Gulf of Mexico	3,504
South China Sea	7,258
Sea of Japan	3,053
Red Sea	2,266

ALGEBRA READINESS

Solve these problems. Watch the signs.

② $\blacksquare - 3 = 7$ ③ $\blacksquare + 8 = 16$ ④ $4 + \blacksquare = 12$

Lesson 7

⑤ $\blacksquare + 7 = 13$ ⑥ $10 - \blacksquare = 3$ ⑦ $8 + \blacksquare = 13$

What is the right sign? Draw <, >, or =.

Lessons
31, 34

8 350 + 20 ● 375 + 25   **9** 638 − 138 ● 138 + 138

10 63 + 20 ● 64 + 2   **11** 187 + 69 ● 109 + 70

12 35 + 35 ● 39 + 40   **13** 38 + 58 ● 48 + 48

14 87 + 26 ● 26 + 87   **15** 1002 ● 500 + 500

Add or subtract. Watch the signs.

Lesson 25

16
```
   37
   62
+  48
```

17
```
   370
   545
   698
+   85
```

18
```
   546
−  209
```

19
```
   52
   74
+  98
```

20
```
   719
−   34
```

21
```
   2743
+  3981
```

22
```
   1998
−  1299
```

23
```
   3783
−  2941
```

Answer these questions.

Lesson 35

24 What is the perimeter?

25 What is the shape?

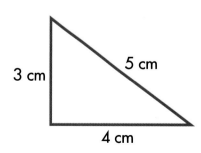

3 cm

5 cm

4 cm

Unit Test

Count up or down. Fill in the missing numbers.

1 | 7 | 8 | ■ | ■ | ■ | ■ | 13 | 14 |

2 | 363 | 362 | ■ | ■ | ■ | 358 | ■ | 356 |

3 | 1096 | 1097 | ■ | ■ | ■ | 1101 | ■ | 1103 |

4 | 3905 | 3906 | ■ | ■ | ■ | ■ | ■ | 3912 |

Write each number as a numeral.

5 six hundred eighteen

6 eight hundred three

7 two hundred nine

8 three thousand one hundred twelve

9 seventy-three

10 one hundred forty-one

11 five thousand four hundred

12 two thousand nine hundred ninety

Solve these problems. Watch the signs.

13 $5 + 5 = $ ■

14 $8 + 7 = $ ■

15 $19 - 12 = $ ■

16 $16 - 10 = $ ■

17 $12 - 5 = $ ■

18 $5 + 16 = $ ■

19 $4 + 4 = $ ■

20 $9 + 7 = $ ■

21 $18 - 4 = $ ■

22 $15 - 5 = $ ■

23 $14 - 8 = $ ■

24 $7 + 9 = $ ■

25 $7 + 7 = $ ■

26 $13 - 4 = $ ■

27 $11 + 11 = $ ■

Solve these problems. Watch the signs.

28. 58
    − 37

29. 58
    + 37

30. 83
    − 46

31. 249
    + 138

32. 493
    + 576

33. 1247
    − 1058

34. 37
     58
    + 43

35. 256
     709
     432
    + 88

36. 321
     713
    + 186

37. 800
    − 300

38. 5000
     200
      80
    +   5

39. 465
     280
     122
    + 123

40. $5 + \blacksquare = 11$

41. $\blacksquare + 7 = 12$

42. $6 + \blacksquare = 15$

43. $\blacksquare − 7 = 8$

44. $20 − \blacksquare = 12$

45. $19 − \blacksquare = 10$

46. $18 − \blacksquare = 7$

47. $8 + \blacksquare = 13$

48. $\blacksquare + 3 = 11$

49. $\blacksquare + 19 = 20$

50. $5 − \blacksquare = 1$

51. $4 + \blacksquare = 19$

Round to the nearest ten.

52. 71

53. 158

54. 25

55. 58

56. 14

57. 91

58. 415

59. 8

60. 67

61. 83

62. 353

63. 692

Solve.

64. In January, 24 inches of snow fell in Shelbyville. By the end of February, a total of 41 inches of snow had fallen during the year. How many inches of snow fell in February?

65. A jigsaw puzzle has 500 pieces. Jody has only 148 pieces left. How many pieces have been put together already?

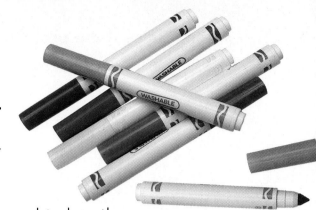

◆ Unit 1 Test

Solve.

66 Miss Annino had 17 markers. She gave out some. She has nine markers left. How many did she give out?

67 How much money does Erin need to buy the three masks?

$2   **$3**   **$5**

68 Juan was born in 1984. Mr. Cerda was born in 1940. How many centimeters taller than Juan is Mr. Cerda?

69 Emiko wants to buy a taco for 69¢. She has 30¢. How much more money does she need?

70

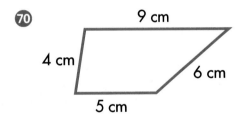

9 cm
4 cm
6 cm
5 cm

The perimeter is ■ centimeters.

71

6 ft
4 ft   4 ft
6 ft

The perimeter is ■ feet.

72

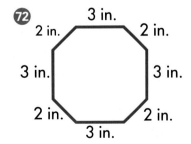

3 in.
2 in.   2 in.
3 in.   3 in.
2 in.   2 in.
3 in.

The perimeter is ■ inches.

73

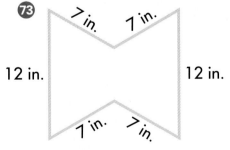

7 in.   7 in.
12 in.   12 in.
7 in.   7 in.

The perimeter is ■ inches.

What is the correct sign? Draw <, >, or =.

74 43 ● 34

75 174 + 50 ● 40 + 170

76 1011 ● 1011

77 25 − 9 ● 35 − 19

78 83 + 2746 ● 88 + 2747

79 44 ● 440

80 86 − 43 ● 87 − 44

81 88 + 1000 ● 8800

82 300 + 70 ● 400 − 30

83 115 ● 511

84 2882 ● 280 + 82

85 71 + 78 ● 75 + 70

Tell the time in two ways.

86 ▮

87 ▮ minutes after ▮

88 ▮

89 ▮ minutes to ▮

Solve.

90 Isaac woke up at 8:00 this morning. He took a shower for 15 minutes. Then he spent 25 minutes getting dressed. Then he ate breakfast, which took 35 minutes. At about what time did Isaac finish eating breakfast?

Extend Your Thinking

Add or subtract. Then use this code chart to solve the riddle.

A	B	C	D	E	F	G	H	I	J	K	L	M
1	2	3	4	5	6	7	8	9	10	11	12	13
N	O	P	Q	R	S	T	U	V	W	X	Y	Z
14	15	16	17	18	19	20	21	22	23	24	25	26

1 Where should you leave your dog when you go shopping?

```
  22      7        1820
– 13    + 7       – 1819
 ☐       ☐          ☐
```

```
  80    92      9     50      3      1      556
– 78  – 91    + 9   – 39    + 6   + 13    – 549
 ☐     ☐      ☐     ☐       ☐      ☐       ☐
```

```
  67      7      886
– 55    + 8    – 866
 ☐       ☐       ☐
```

Add or subtract. Then use this code to solve the riddles.

A	B	C	D	E	F	G	H	I	J	K	L	M
1	2	3	4	5	6	7	8	9	10	11	12	13
N	O	P	Q	R	S	T	U	V	W	X	Y	Z
14	15	16	17	18	19	20	21	22	23	24	25	26

2 Which presidents of the United States are not buried in the United States?

```
  22      4     28     15    987          11    672     50
-  2   +  4   - 13   +  4   - 982       + 12   - 664   - 35
  ☐      ☐     ☐      ☐     ☐            ☐      ☐       ☐
```

```
   0     50     73          10     11    886     6     24
+  1   - 32   - 68        +  9   +  9   - 877   + 6   - 12
  ☐      ☐     ☐            ☐      ☐      ☐      ☐      ☐
```

```
 1820     13     18    556     22
- 1819   -  1   -  9   - 534   - 17
  ☐       ☐      ☐      ☐       ☐
```

Make up your own riddles and write them in your
Math Journal. Then ask a friend to solve them.

LOOKING FOR PATTERNS

+	0	1	2	3	4	5	6	7	8	9	10
0	0	1	2	3	4	5	6	7	8	9	10
1	1	2	3	4	5	6	7	8	9	10	11
2	2	3	4	5	6	7	8	9	10	11	12
3	3	4	5	6	7	8	9	10	11	12	13
4	4	5	6	7	8	9	10	11	12	13	14
5	5	6	7	8	9	10	11	12	13	14	15
6	6	7	8	9	10	11	12	13	14	15	16
7	7	8	9	10	11	12	13	14	15	16	17
8	8	9	10	11	12	13	14	15	16	17	18
9	9	10	11	12	13	14	15	16	17	18	19
10	10	11	12	13	14	15	16	17	18	19	20

MATH JOURNAL

Work with one or more friends. Use the addition table. Look for interesting patterns in it. Write about them in your Math Journal.

Here's one pattern. Look at a two by two square anywhere in the table, like the blue square below.

5	6	7	8
6	7	8	9
7	8	9	10
8	9	10	11

The numbers 7 and 9 are on one diagonal of the square. The numbers 8 and 8 are on the other diagonal of the square. What is the sum of 7 and 9? What is the sum of 8 and 8? Does this work for every two by two square in the table?

Try this with three by three squares on the table. Does it work for all three by three squares?

In a three by three square, do any rows or columns have the same sum as the diagonals? Which rows and columns? Does this work for all three by three squares?

UNIT 2

Multiplication and Division

UNDERSTANDING INVERSE OPERATIONS

- **area**

- **number patterns**

- **missing factors**

- **remainders**

- **algebra readiness**

SCHOOL TO WORK CONNECTION

Artists use math . . .

A quilter is an artist who designs a pattern with fabric. Quilters choose shapes that tessellate, or fit together. The artist must figure out how many times the pattern could repeat. Careful calculations are needed to make sure the pattern isn't too large for the quilt.

LESSON
41

Approximating the Area

Solve.

Tim is going to paint both walls.

❶ On which wall do you think he will use more paint?

❷ Which wall is longer?

❸ Which wall has a larger area?

Flossie the cow is hungry.

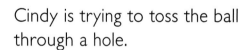

❹ Which patch of grass has more grass for Flossie to eat?

❺ Which patch of grass is longer?

❻ Which patch of grass has a larger area?

Cindy is trying to toss the ball through a hole.

❼ Which hole is the easiest to get the ball through?

❽ Which hole is the hardest to get the ball through?

❾ Which hole has the largest area?

❿ Which hole has the smallest area?

⓫ Noah has a sheet of paper. He wants more room to write. So he cuts his sheet into two pieces. Now does he have more room to write?

Solve.

Every day Rose jogs once around the outside of Cedar Park. She jogs 6 kilometers north, 1 kilometer east, 6 kilometers south, and then 1 kilometer west.

12 Draw an outline of Cedar Park.

13 How far does Rose jog each day?

Every day Lee jogs once around the outside of Plum Park. She jogs 3 kilometers north, 3 kilometers west, 3 kilometers south, and then 3 kilometers east.

14 Draw an outline of Plum Park.

15 How far does Lee jog each day?

16 Who jogs farther each day, Rose or Lee?

17 Which park has a larger area, Cedar Park or Plum Park?

18 Could the smaller park fit inside the larger park?

Every day Pete jogs once around the outside of Klima Park. He jogs 5 kilometers north, 2 kilometers east, 5 kilometers south, and then 2 kilometers west.

19 Draw an outline of Klima Park.

20 How far does Pete jog each day?

21 Who jogs the farthest each day, Rose, Lee, or Pete?

22 Which park has the largest area, Cedar Park, Plum Park, or Klima Park?

Talk about the Thinking Story "The Case of the Fading Violets."

Finding the Area

Area is the number of square units (such as square cm) inside a figure.

What is the area? The first one has been done for you.

1   1 cm

1 cm

1 square centimeter

2

☐ square centimeters

3

☐ square centimeters

4

☐ square centimeters

5

☐ square centimeters

6

☐ square centimeters

7

☐ square centimeters

8

☐ square centimeters

What is the area? The first one has been done for you.

9

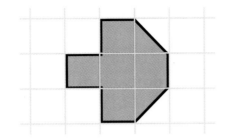

6 square centimeters

10

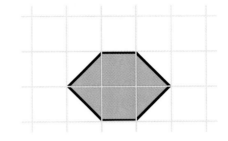

■ square centimeters

11

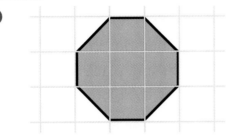

■ square centimeters

12

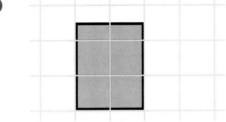

■ square centimeters

13

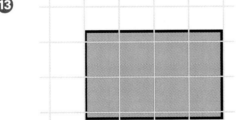

About ■ square centimeters

14

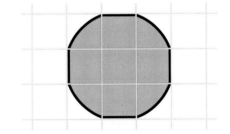

About ■ square centimeters

15

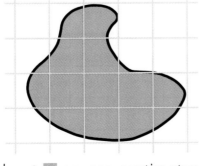

About ■ square centimeters

16

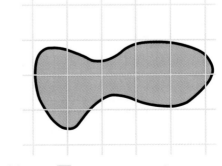

About ■ square centimeters

Number Patterns: Skip Counting

Use a computer or other means to draw three copies of the grid below. Then do each of the following exercises on a separate grid.

1 On the first grid, color the boxes you reach when counting by 2s and circle the number in the boxes you reach when counting by 5s. Place an **X** in the boxes you reach when counting by 10s.

2 On the second grid, circle the number in the boxes you reach when counting by 9s and place an **X** in the boxes you reach when counting by 11s.

3 On the third grid, circle the number in the boxes you reach when counting by 8s and color the boxes you reach when counting by 12s.

0	1	2	3	4	5	6	7	8	9
10	11	12	13	14	15	16	17	18	19
20	21	22	23	24	25	26	27	28	29
30	31	32	33	34	35	36	37	38	39
40	41	42	43	44	45	46	47	48	49
50	51	52	53	54	55	56	57	58	59
60	61	62	63	64	65	66	67	68	69
70	71	72	73	74	75	76	77	78	79
80	81	82	83	84	85	86	87	88	89
90	91	92	93	94	95	96	97	98	99

◆ Look at the grid at the bottom of the page. How is it different from the grid on page 132?

Use a computer or other means to draw three copies of the grid below. Then do each of the following exercises on a separate grid.

4 On the first grid, color the boxes you reach when counting by 2s and circle the number in the boxes you reach when counting by 5s.

5 On the second grid, circle the number in the boxes you reach when counting by 9s and place an **X** in the boxes you reach when counting by 7s.

6 On the third grid, circle the number in the boxes you reach when counting by 4s and color the boxes you reach when counting by 10s. Place an **X** in the boxes you reach when counting by 8s.

0	1	2	3	4	5	6	7
8	9	10	11	12	13	14	15
16	17	18	19	20	21	22	23
24	25	26	27	28	29	30	31
32	33	34	35	36	37	38	39
40	41	42	43	44	45	46	47
48	49	50	51	52	53	54	55
56	57	58	59	60	61	62	63

In your Math Journal write about a number pattern you see in one of the grids.

Understanding Multiplication

Solve these problems.

2 + 2 + 2 + 2 + 2

1 There are two marbles in each bag.
How many marbles are there? 5 × 2 = ▦

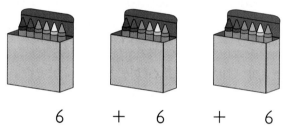

6 + 6 + 6

2 There are six crayons in each box.
How many crayons are there? 3 × 6 = ▦

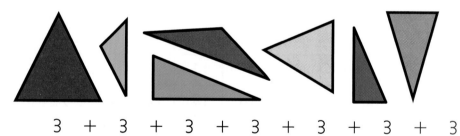

3 + 3 + 3 + 3 + 3 + 3 + 3

3 Each triangle has three sides.
How many sides are there all together? 7 × 3 = ▦

4 + 4 + 4 + 4 + 4

4 There are four cans in each box.
How many cans are there? 5 × 4 = ▦

134 • Multiplication and Division

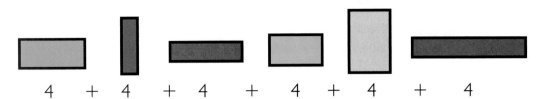

4 + 4 + 4 + 4 + 4 + 4

5 Each rectangle has four sides. How many sides are there all together?　　　　6 × 4 = ■

5 + 5 + 5 + 5

6 Each star has five points. How many points are there all together?　　　　4 × 5 = ■

3 + 3 + 3 + 3

7 There are three people seated in each row. There are four rows. How many people are seated?　　　　4 × 3 = ■

3 + 3 + 3

8 Each pile has three dollars. How many dollars are there all together?　　　　3 × 3 = ■

Using Information in Displays

Some airplanes have six seats in each row. Answer the questions for this kind of airplane.

1 How many seats are there in two rows?

2 How many seats are there in seven rows? Did you count? Did you add 6 + 6 + 6 + 6 + 6 + 6 + 6? Did you do something else?

3 How many seats are there in three rows?

4 How many seats are there in four rows?

5 How many seats are there in six rows?

6 How many seats are there in ten rows? Is this the same as six 10s?

7 How many seats are there in nine rows? Is this six less than your answer to question 6?

8 How many seats are there in eight rows?

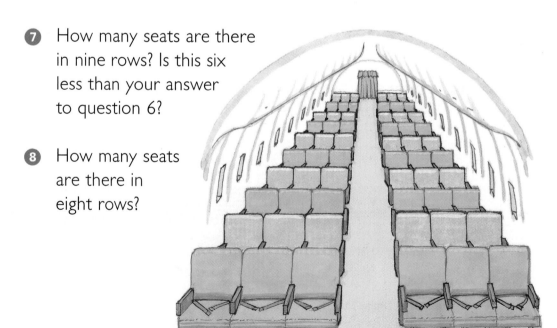

Some airplanes have only four seats in each row.
Answer the questions for this kind of airplane.

9 How many seats are there
in two rows?

10 How many seats are there
in three rows?

11 How many seats are there
in four rows?

12 How many seats are there
in ten rows?

13 How many seats are there
in nine rows?

14 How many seats are there
in five rows?

15 How many seats are there
in eight rows?

16 How many seats are there
in seven rows?

17 How many seats are there
in one row?

18 How many seats are there
in six rows?

Applying Multiplication: Area

Estimate the area of the orange part of each rectangle.

1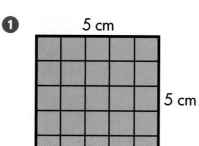
5 cm
5 cm

2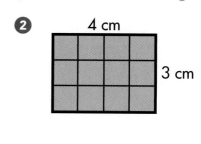
4 cm
3 cm

3
6 cm
2 cm

4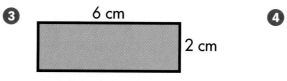
6 cm
3 cm

5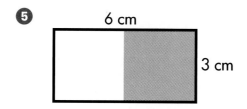
6 cm
3 cm

6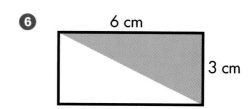
6 cm
3 cm

7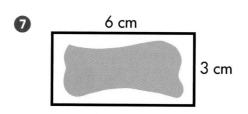
6 cm
3 cm

8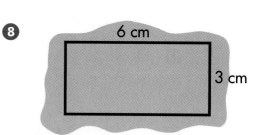
6 cm
3 cm

Mr. Eng told Portia about the Speedway Racetrack. "If you drive around it one time, you will go exactly 4 miles," he said. "But most races are more than one time around."

"If a race is two times around, how many miles is that?" Portia wondered. She also wondered about longer races.

Help Portia by copying and completing this chart. You can use a computer or other means.

	Number of Times Around the Track	Number of Miles
9	1	4
10	2	▪
11	3	▪
12	4	▪
13	5	▪
14	6	▪
15	7	▪
16	8	▪
17	9	▪
18	10	▪

In your Math Journal explain how multiplication can sometimes help make adding easier.

Estimating Products

Solve.

Each bag has five, six, or seven peanuts. Aaron bought three bags.

1 What is the fewest number of peanuts Aaron might have?

2 What is the greatest number of peanuts Aaron might have?

3 How many peanuts would you estimate Aaron has?

4 If Aaron bought four bags, how many peanuts would you estimate he has?

Gina caught four fish. Every fish weighed between 2 and 3 pounds.

5 Can Gina have 14 pounds of fish all together?

6 Can she have 3 pounds?

7 Can she have 10 pounds?

8 Can she have 9 pounds?

9 How many pounds of fish would you estimate Gina has?

Solve.

Most airlines have different kinds of airplanes. Some airplanes have six seats in a row. Some have five seats in a row. Some have four seats in a row. Some small planes have only three seats in a row.

⑩ Suppose you are sitting in the third row. What is the greatest number of people who might be in front of you? (Don't count people in your row. Only people in rows 1 and 2 are in front of you.) Remember, there are different kinds of planes.

⑪ Suppose all seats are full. What is the fewest number of people who might be in front of you if you sit in the third row?

⑫ Suppose you are sitting in the 11th row. What is the greatest number of people who might be in front of you?

⑬ Suppose all seats are full. What are the possible numbers of people who might be in front of you if you sit in the 11th row?

⑭ Suppose you are sitting in the sixth row. What is the greatest number of people who might be in front of you?

⑮ Suppose all seats are full. What is the fewest number of people who might be in front of you if you sit in the sixth row?

⑯ If all seats are full, what are the possible numbers of people who might be in front of you if you sit in the ninth row?

⑰ If all seats are full, what are the possible numbers of people who might be in front of you if you sit in the fifth row?

◆ **LESSON 47** Estimating Products

CO⊘PERATIVE LEARNING

Mul-Tack-Toe Game

Players:	**Two**
Materials:	**Two Mul-Tack-Toe cards (like those below), two 0–5 cubes (red), eight counters or coins for each player**
Object:	**To cover three boxes in a line**
Math Focus:	**Multiplication facts**

RULES

1. Each player chooses one of the two Mul-Tack-Toe cards.

2. Players take turns rolling the two 0–5 cubes.

3. Both players calculate the product of the two numbers rolled. If the product is on a player's card, he or she puts a counter on that box.

4. The first player to cover three boxes in a line (horizontally, diagonally, or vertically) wins the round.

15	16	6
25	4	5
10	0	2

Card 1

12	1	10
0	4	20
8	9	15

Card 2

Multiply.

18 $2 \times 1 =$ ▇ **19** $4 \times 1 =$ ▇ **20** $5 \times 7 =$ ▇

21 $2 \times 2 =$ ▇ **22** $5 \times 2 =$ ▇ **23** $6 \times 4 =$ ▇

24 $3 \times 2 =$ ▇ **25** $6 \times 5 =$ ▇ **26** $1 \times 2 =$ ▇

27 $5 \times 4 =$ ▇ **28** $1 \times 5 =$ ▇ **29** $7 \times 7 =$ ▇

30 $4 \times 4 =$ ▇ **31** $5 \times 5 =$ ▇ **32** $3 \times 6 =$ ▇

33 $3 \times 3 =$ ▇ **34** $2 \times 7 =$ ▇ **35** $4 \times 5 =$ ▇

36 $4 \times 3 =$ ▇ **37** $6 \times 6 =$ ▇ **38** $2 \times 4 =$ ▇

39 $5 \times 3 =$ ▇ **40** $7 \times 5 =$ ▇ **41** $5 \times 1 =$ ▇

42 $6 \times 3 =$ ▇ **43** $6 \times 2 =$ ▇ **44** $3 \times 4 =$ ▇

45 $7 \times 3 =$ ▇ **46** $7 \times 1 =$ ▇ **47** $5 \times 1 =$ ▇

48 $4 \times 2 =$ ▇ **49** $4 \times 6 =$ ▇ **50** $2 \times 3 =$ ▇

51 $6 \times 1 =$ ▇ **52** $1 \times 3 =$ ▇ **53** $7 \times 4 =$ ▇

Multiplication and Money

Roger wanted to buy different-shaped dog biscuits for his dog Puggy. He made a chart to help him choose what to buy.

Use a computer or other means to copy and fill in the chart.

Dog Biscuits

Amount	Bones 10¢	Steaks 7¢	Cats 5¢	Doughnuts 8¢	Nuts 2¢
1					
2					
3					
4					
5					
6					

Solve.

1. How much would five dog doughnuts cost?

2. How much would six dog bones cost?

3. How much would five steaks cost?

4. How much would six of each item cost all together?

5. Write that amount in dollars and cents.

6. Roger does not want to spend more than $2.00. Does he have enough money to buy six of each item? Does he have enough money to buy two of each item?

Multiply. Solve for *n*.

⑦ $6 \times 5 = n$　　⑧ $8 \times 6 = n$　　⑨ $4 \times 7 = n$

⑩ $3 \times 2 = n$　　⑪ $7 \times 3 = n$　　⑫ $6 \times 6 = n$

⑬ $4 \times 10 = n$　　⑭ $3 \times 7 = n$　　⑮ $2 \times 5 = n$

⑯ $7 \times 5 = n$　　⑰ $2 \times 6 = n$　　⑱ $4 \times 4 = n$

Solve.

Carolyn has seven nickels. She wants to buy a fan that costs 95¢.

⑲ How much money does Carolyn have in cents?

⑳ How much more does she need to buy the fan?

Solve these problems. Use shortcuts when you can. Watch the signs.

㉑　　324
　　+ 479

㉒　　821
　　− 731

㉓　　601
　　+ 399

㉔　　900
　　− 500

㉕　　456
　　− 251

㉖　　273
　　+ 438

㉗　　564
　　+ 286

㉘　　700
　　− 299

Using the Multiplication Table

Solve.

1 Gloria wants to buy 15 lemons. Each bag has 3 lemons. How many bags must she buy?

2 One marble costs 4¢. Jared has 28¢. How many marbles can he buy?

3 Each box has five pencils. Marty needs 20 pencils. How many boxes must he buy?

Think about each problem. Then write which number sentence tells you the answer.

4 One pen costs 9¢. How much will eight pens cost?

    a. 8 + 9 = 17   **b.** 8 × 9 = 72

5 Marcia is nine years old. How old will she be in four years?

    a. 9 × 4 = 36   **b.** 9 + 4 = 13

6 One pack of gum has seven pieces. How many pieces are there in four packs?

    a. 4 + 7 = 11   **b.** 4 × 7 = 28

GAME

Play the "Multiplication Table" game.

Multiplication Table

X	0	1	2	3	4	5	6	7	8	9	10
0	0	0	0	0	0	0	0	0	0	0	0
1	0	1	2	3	4	5	6	7	8	9	10
2	0	2	4	6	8	10	12	14	16	18	20
3	0	3	6	9	12	15	18	21	24	27	30
4	0	4	8	12	16	20	24	28	32	36	40
5	0	5	10	15	20	25	30	35	40	45	50
6	0	6	12	18	24	30	36	42	48	54	60
7	0	7	14	21	28	35	42	49	56	63	70
8	0	8	16	24	32	40	48	56	64	72	80
9	0	9	18	27	36	45	54	63	72	81	90
10	0	10	20	30	40	50	60	70	80	90	100

Find the answers in the multiplication table.

7. $7 \times \blacksquare = 49$

8. $\blacksquare \times 9 = 81$

9. $3 \times \blacksquare = 27$

10. $5 \times \blacksquare = 30$

11. $\blacksquare \times 3 = 21$

12. $5 \times \blacksquare = 50$

13. $4 \times \blacksquare = 36$

14. $\blacksquare \times 9 = 63$

15. $3 \times 3 = \blacksquare$

16. $7 \times 8 = \blacksquare$

17. $4 \times 8 = \blacksquare$

18. $8 \times \blacksquare = 16$

19. $6 \times 7 = \blacksquare$

20. $8 \times 8 = \blacksquare$

21. $6 \times \blacksquare = 36$

LESSON
50

The Order Property of Multiplication

Multiply.

① $7 \times 5 = $ ■ 　② $8 \times 7 = $ ■ 　③ $5 \times 3 = $ ■

④ $4 \times 9 = $ ■ 　⑤ $3 \times 8 = $ ■ 　⑥ $4 \times 6 = $ ■

⑦ $10 \times 6 = $ ■ 　⑧ $6 \times 7 = $ ■ 　⑨ $7 \times 2 = $ ■

⑩ $5 \times 7 = $ ■ 　⑪ $7 \times 8 = $ ■ 　⑫ $3 \times 5 = $ ■

⑬ $9 \times 4 = $ ■ 　⑭ $8 \times 3 = $ ■ 　⑮ $6 \times 4 = $ ■

⑯ $6 \times 10 = $ ■ 　⑰ $7 \times 6 = $ ■ 　⑱ $2 \times 7 = $ ■

⑲ $\begin{array}{r} 9 \\ \times\ 9 \\ \hline \end{array}$ 　⑳ $\begin{array}{r} 8 \\ \times\ 8 \\ \hline \end{array}$ 　㉑ $\begin{array}{r} 9 \\ \times\ 8 \\ \hline \end{array}$ 　㉒ $\begin{array}{r} 8 \\ \times\ 9 \\ \hline \end{array}$

㉓ $\begin{array}{r} 7 \\ \times\ 7 \\ \hline \end{array}$ 　㉔ $\begin{array}{r} 7 \\ \times\ 9 \\ \hline \end{array}$ 　㉕ $\begin{array}{r} 9 \\ \times\ 7 \\ \hline \end{array}$ 　㉖ $\begin{array}{r} 5 \\ \times\ 8 \\ \hline \end{array}$

㉗ $\begin{array}{r} 8 \\ \times\ 5 \\ \hline \end{array}$ 　㉘ $\begin{array}{r} 5 \\ \times\ 5 \\ \hline \end{array}$ 　㉙ $\begin{array}{r} 9 \\ \times\ 3 \\ \hline \end{array}$ 　㉚ $\begin{array}{r} 3 \\ \times\ 9 \\ \hline \end{array}$

MATH JOURNAL

In your Math Journal write two sets of multiplication facts showing that order does not affect the product of two factors.

What is the area?

31 5 cm

3 cm

32 3 cm

5 cm

33 4 cm

2 cm

34 2 cm

4 cm

Solve.

35 Nadia has ten nickels. How much money does she have in cents?

36 Brent has five dimes. How much money does he have in cents?

37 Rachel has three $5 bills. How much money does she have in dollars?

38 Bart has four $10 bills. How much money does he have in dollars?

Talk about the Thinking Story "Lemonade Incorporated (Part 1)."

Multiplication Functions

Manolita dreamed about a powerful number machine. When she put something into the machine, five times as many came out.

The chart shows what Manolita dreamed she put into the machine.

Complete the chart. The first one has been done for you.

	In		Out
❶	3 turtles	3 × 5	**15 turtles**
❷	6 bananas	6 × 5	
❸	9 dollars	9 × 5	
❹	7 roses	7 × 5	
❺	8 books	8 × 5	
❻	9 keys	9 × 5	
❼	4 pillows	4 × 5	
❽	5 pizzas	5 × 5	

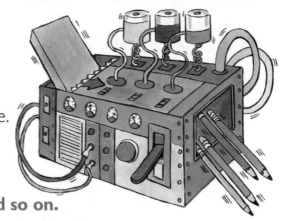

Manolita dreamed about a machine that makes pencils. The machine could make four pencils every minute.

Fill in the chart. Show how many pencils the machine could make in two minutes, in three minutes, and so on.

	Number of Minutes	Number of Pencils
9	1	4
10	2	▪
11	3	▪
12	4	▪
13	5	▪
14	6	▪
15	7	▪
16	8	▪
17	9	▪
18	10	▪

Solve.

19 Sylvia wants to hang five posters. Each poster needs four tacks. How many tacks does she need?

20 Each crate holds eight containers of milk. There are six empty crates. How many containers can they hold?

21 Bananas come in bunches of seven. There are six bunches left on the shelf. How many bananas are there?

22 There are four quarters in one dollar. Jill has nine dollars' worth of quarters. How many quarters does she have?

GAME

Play the "Shopping" game.

52 Multiplying by 10

Multiply.

① 5 × 10 = ■

② 7 × 10 = ■

③ 30 × 10 = ■

④ 4 × 10 = ■

⑤ 9 × 10 = ■

⑥ 10 × 16 = ■

⑦ 10 × 10 = ■

⑧ 11 × 10 = ■

⑨ 67 × 10 = ■

⑩ 12 × 10 = ■

⑪ 10 × 15 = ■

⑫ 10 × 13 = ■

⑬ 19 × 10 = ■

⑭ 20 × 10 = ■

⑮ 22 × 10 = ■

⑯ 10 × 21 = ■

⑰ 10 × 48 = ■

⑱ 10 × 8 = ■

⑲ 50 × 10 = ■

⑳ 80 × 10 = ■

㉑ 10 × 61 = ■

㉒ 81 × 10 = ■

㉓ 10 × 78 = ■

㉔ 52 × 10 = ■

㉕ 10 × 35 = ■

㉖ 78 × 10 = ■

㉗ 17 × 10 = ■

㉘ 10 × 45 = ■

㉙ 18 × 10 = ■

㉚ 10 × 59 = ■

Multiply.

31 $90 \times 10 = \blacksquare$ **32** $10 \times 100 = \blacksquare$ **33** $296 \times 10 = \blacksquare$

34 $91 \times 10 = \blacksquare$ **35** $10 \times 101 = \blacksquare$ **36** $301 \times 10 = \blacksquare$

37 $92 \times 10 = \blacksquare$ **38** $102 \times 10 = \blacksquare$ **39** $10 \times 296 = \blacksquare$

40 $99 \times 10 = \blacksquare$ **41** $110 \times 10 = \blacksquare$ **42** $10 \times 300 = \blacksquare$

43 $100 \times 10 = \blacksquare$ **44** $273 \times 10 = \blacksquare$ **45** $400 \times 10 = \blacksquare$

Solve these problems. Watch the signs.

46
$$\begin{array}{r} 37 \\ + 43 \\ \hline \end{array}$$

47
$$\begin{array}{r} 872 \\ + 365 \\ \hline \end{array}$$

48
$$\begin{array}{r} 379 \\ - 287 \\ \hline \end{array}$$

49
$$\begin{array}{r} 600 \\ - 450 \\ \hline \end{array}$$

50
$$\begin{array}{r} 750 \\ - 750 \\ \hline \end{array}$$

51
$$\begin{array}{r} 897 \\ - 225 \\ \hline \end{array}$$

52
$$\begin{array}{r} 6242 \\ + 3758 \\ \hline \end{array}$$

53
$$\begin{array}{r} 310 \\ 430 \\ + 180 \\ \hline \end{array}$$

54
$$\begin{array}{r} 337 \\ + 389 \\ \hline \end{array}$$

55
$$\begin{array}{r} 827 \\ - 295 \\ \hline \end{array}$$

56
$$\begin{array}{r} 562 \\ + 248 \\ \hline \end{array}$$

57
$$\begin{array}{r} 75 \\ 38 \\ + 65 \\ \hline \end{array}$$

Multiplying by 100 and 1000

Multiply.

1 $7 \times 100 = $ ▪

2 $8 \times 1000 = $ ▪

3 $10 \times 100 = $ ▪

4 $14 \times 100 = $ ▪

5 $20 \times 100 = $ ▪

6 $100 \times 57 = $ ▪

7 $100 \times 90 = $ ▪

8 $99 \times 100 = $ ▪

9 $3 \times 1000 = $ ▪

10 $8 \times 1000 = $ ▪

11 $10 \times 1000 = $ ▪

12 $50 \times 10 = $ ▪

13 $10 \times 73 = $ ▪

14 $10 \times 300 = $ ▪

15 $80 \times 10 = $ ▪

16 $83 \times 10 = $ ▪

17 $40 \times 10 = $ ▪

18 $83 \times 100 = $ ▪

19 $10 \times 10 = $ ▪

20 $1000 \times 83 = $ ▪

21 $100 \times 10 = $ ▪

22 $6 \times 100 = $ ▪

23 $1000 \times 10 = $ ▪

24 $60 \times 10 = $ ▪

In your Math Journal explain the strategy you use to multiply by 100. How else could you find the product (answer)?

Solve.

25 Sharla has 13 $10 bills. Does she have enough money to buy the skates?

Skates $109.00

26 Mr. Baccari, the park ranger, has 3500 yards of fencing. The park has four sides. Each side is 1000 yards long. Does Mr. Baccari have enough fencing to surround the park?

27 There are seven boxes of balloons. Each box has 100 balloons. There are 629 children. Can each child have a balloon?

28 There are 65 trays of cookies. Each tray has ten cookies on it. Can each child in problem 27 have a cookie?

Solve these problems. Watch the signs.

29 $7 + 3 + 2 + 8 - 10 = \blacksquare$ **30** $3 + 6 + 5 - 2 + 1 - 7 = \blacksquare$

31 $6 + 6 + 6 + 6 + 6 = \blacksquare$ **32** $10 - 6 + 7 - 6 + 5 = \blacksquare$

33 $4 + 3 + 5 + 2 - 7 = \blacksquare$ **34** $7 + 6 + 4 - 3 + 5 = \blacksquare$

35 $3 + 4 - 2 + 1 + 7 - 6 = \blacksquare$ **36** $5 + 4 + 5 - 6 + 1 - 9 = \blacksquare$

37 $5 + 3 + 2 - 8 + 3 - 5 = \blacksquare$ **38** $2 + 3 + 5 - 8 + 3 + 3 = \blacksquare$

LESSON 54

Using Mental Math to Multiply

Lynne bought some things for her birthday party. The chart shows what she bought.

Write the missing amounts.

	Item	How Many	Unit Price	Total Price
1	Whistle	3	7¢	▪
2	Party Hat	10	9¢	▪
3	Noisemaker	3	10¢	▪
4	Balloon	4	6¢	▪

Solve.

5 How many people do you think Lynne expected to come to the party?

6 Which costs more, a whistle or a balloon?

7 How much money did Lynne spend?

8 Write that amount in dollars and cents.

9 Each invitation cost $1. How much did Lynne spend on invitations?

10 Which costs more, ten balloons or five noisemakers?

11 Did Lynne spend more on whistles and noisemakers than party hats?

Multiply.

12 $8 \times 1 = \blacksquare$ 13 $8 \times 7 = \blacksquare$ 14 $8 \times 9 = \blacksquare$

15 $10 \times 3 = \blacksquare$ 16 $5 \times 0 = \blacksquare$ 17 $3 \times 5 = \blacksquare$

18 $2 \times 6 = \blacksquare$ 19 $9 \times 1 = \blacksquare$ 20 $9 \times 5 = \blacksquare$

21 $2 \times 10 = \blacksquare$ 22 $6 \times 2 = \blacksquare$ 23 $1 \times 9 = \blacksquare$

24 $2 \times 9 = \blacksquare$ 25 $7 \times 2 = \blacksquare$ 26 $8 \times 3 = \blacksquare$

27 $0 \times 8 = \blacksquare$ 28 $10 \times 7 = \blacksquare$ 29 $2 \times 7 = \blacksquare$

30 $\begin{array}{r} 9 \\ \times\ 2 \\ \hline \end{array}$ 31 $\begin{array}{r} 2 \\ \times\ 6 \\ \hline \end{array}$ 32 $\begin{array}{r} 10 \\ \times\ 2 \\ \hline \end{array}$ 33 $\begin{array}{r} 4 \\ \times\ 2 \\ \hline \end{array}$

34 $\begin{array}{r} 2 \\ \times\ 5 \\ \hline \end{array}$ 35 $\begin{array}{r} 7 \\ \times\ 8 \\ \hline \end{array}$ 36 $\begin{array}{r} 10 \\ \times\ 3 \\ \hline \end{array}$ 37 $\begin{array}{r} 2 \\ \times\ 7 \\ \hline \end{array}$

38 $\begin{array}{r} 4 \\ \times\ 10 \\ \hline \end{array}$ 39 $\begin{array}{r} 8 \\ \times\ 2 \\ \hline \end{array}$ 40 $\begin{array}{r} 7 \\ \times\ 7 \\ \hline \end{array}$ 41 $\begin{array}{r} 3 \\ \times\ 4 \\ \hline \end{array}$

LESSON 55

Multiplying by 3 and 5

Multiply.

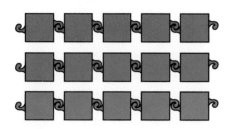

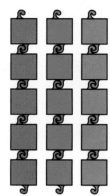

1 $3 \times 5 = $ ■

2 $5 \times 3 = $ ■

 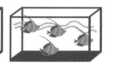

3 $4 \times 3 = $ ■

4 $3 \times 4 = $ ■

5 $3 \times 7 = $ ■

6 $7 \times 3 = $ ■

7 $6 \times 3 = $ ■

8 $3 \times 6 = $ ■

Multiply.

9 $3 \times 5 = $ ■

10 $5 \times 3 = $ ■

11 $7 \times 3 = $ ■

12 $10 \times 7 = $ ■

13 $5 \times 2 = $ ■

14 $4 \times 3 = $ ■

15 $5 \times 7 = $ ■

16 $0 \times 10 = $ ■

17 $5 \times 10 = $ ■

18 $2 \times 8 = $ ■

19 $6 \times 5 = $ ■

20 $4 \times 7 = $ ■

21 $4 \times 5 = $ ■

22 $9 \times 5 = $ ■

23 $3 \times 8 = $ ■

24 $5 \times 1 = $ ■

25 $5 \times 4 = $ ■

26 $2 \times 9 = $ ■

27
$$\begin{array}{r} 8 \\ \times\ 7 \\ \hline \end{array}$$

28
$$\begin{array}{r} 10 \\ \times\ \ 9 \\ \hline \end{array}$$

29
$$\begin{array}{r} 8 \\ \times\ 3 \\ \hline \end{array}$$

30
$$\begin{array}{r} 3 \\ \times\ 9 \\ \hline \end{array}$$

31
$$\begin{array}{r} 5 \\ \times\ 4 \\ \hline \end{array}$$

32
$$\begin{array}{r} 7 \\ \times\ 1 \\ \hline \end{array}$$

33
$$\begin{array}{r} 9 \\ \times\ 3 \\ \hline \end{array}$$

34
$$\begin{array}{r} 5 \\ \times\ 5 \\ \hline \end{array}$$

35
$$\begin{array}{r} 8 \\ \times\ 5 \\ \hline \end{array}$$

36
$$\begin{array}{r} 3 \\ \times\ 7 \\ \hline \end{array}$$

37
$$\begin{array}{r} 9 \\ \times\ 6 \\ \hline \end{array}$$

38
$$\begin{array}{r} 4 \\ \times\ 7 \\ \hline \end{array}$$

39
$$\begin{array}{r} 10 \\ \times\ \ 5 \\ \hline \end{array}$$

40
$$\begin{array}{r} 8 \\ \times\ 8 \\ \hline \end{array}$$

41
$$\begin{array}{r} 7 \\ \times\ 8 \\ \hline \end{array}$$

42
$$\begin{array}{r} 3 \\ \times\ 3 \\ \hline \end{array}$$

LESSON 56

Multiplying by 9

Multiply.

1. $9 \times 1 = $ ■
2. $4 \times 9 = $ ■
3. $9 \times 5 = $ ■
4. $9 \times 2 = $ ■
5. $9 \times 6 = $ ■
6. $9 \times 4 = $ ■
7. $9 \times 3 = $ ■
8. $9 \times 9 = $ ■
9. $9 \times 7 = $ ■
10. $9 \times 8 = $ ■
11. $5 \times 9 = $ ■
12. $8 \times 9 = $ ■
13. $7 \times 9 = $ ■
14. $9 \times 10 = $ ■
15. $10 \times 9 = $ ■

Add.

16. $9 + 9 = $ ■
17. $8 + 8 = $ ■
18. $7 + 7 = $ ■
19. $6 + 6 = $ ■
20. $5 + 5 = $ ■
21. $4 + 4 = $ ■
22. $3 + 3 = $ ■
23. $5 + 6 = $ ■
24. $4 + 5 = $ ■
25. $6 + 7 = $ ■
26. $8 + 7 = $ ■
27. $4 + 3 = $ ■
28. $9 + 8 = $ ■
29. $8 + 6 = $ ■
30. $7 + 9 = $ ■

Solve.

31. Every month Julie receives nine dollars for her allowance. How much money will she have in nine months if she saves it all?

32. There are eight baseball teams in the tournament. Each team has nine players. How many players are in the tournament?

33. Jan, Reggie, and Marta each borrowed nine books from the library. How many books do they have all together?

34. Each page of Hanna's book has nine pictures. There are ten pages in her book. How many pictures are in her book?

Multiply.

③⑤ $\begin{array}{r} 9 \\ \times\ 3 \\ \hline \end{array}$ ③⑥ $\begin{array}{r} 5 \\ \times\ 9 \\ \hline \end{array}$ ③⑦ $\begin{array}{r} 8 \\ \times\ 1 \\ \hline \end{array}$ ③⑧ $\begin{array}{r} 5 \\ \times\ 4 \\ \hline \end{array}$

③⑨ $\begin{array}{r} 7 \\ \times\ 3 \\ \hline \end{array}$ ④⓪ $\begin{array}{r} 9 \\ \times\ 8 \\ \hline \end{array}$ ④① $\begin{array}{r} 3 \\ \times\ 3 \\ \hline \end{array}$ ④② $\begin{array}{r} 2 \\ \times\ 9 \\ \hline \end{array}$

④③ $\begin{array}{r} 8 \\ \times\ 2 \\ \hline \end{array}$ ④④ $\begin{array}{r} 9 \\ \times\ 9 \\ \hline \end{array}$ ④⑤ $\begin{array}{r} 9 \\ \times\ 4 \\ \hline \end{array}$ ④⑥ $\begin{array}{r} 9 \\ \times\ 6 \\ \hline \end{array}$

④⑦ $8 \times 5 = \blacksquare$ ④⑧ $6 \times 1 = \blacksquare$ ④⑨ $6 \times 9 = \blacksquare$

⑤⓪ $7 \times 9 = \blacksquare$ ⑤① $7 \times 8 = \blacksquare$ ⑤② $2 \times 7 = \blacksquare$

⑤③ $4 \times 9 = \blacksquare$ ⑤④ $6 \times 5 = \blacksquare$ ⑤⑤ $3 \times 8 = \blacksquare$

⑤⑥ $10 \times 6 = \blacksquare$ ⑤⑦ $5 \times 7 = \blacksquare$ ⑤⑧ $0 \times 9 = \blacksquare$

FANTASTIC FACT

Something or someone who makes a short-lived sensation is known as a *nine-day wonder.*

◆ LESSON 56   Multiplying by 9

A baseball team has nine players on the field at one time. Answer the questions about those players.

59 In a baseball game between the Cubs and the Astros, how many players are there?

60 In a tournament with six teams, how many players are there?

61 In a league with five teams, how many players are there?

62 In a league with eight teams, how many players are there?

63 Suppose each player on a team came to bat four times during a game. How many "at bats" were there?

64 How many shoes are needed for the players on one team?

65 How many shoes are needed for all the players in a game?

66 How many gloves are needed for all the players in a game?

A regular baseball game has nine innings.

67 The Cubs played four regular baseball games this week. How many innings did they play?

68 The Cubs played three of the games at their home stadium. How many innings did they play there?

Add the Products Game

Players:	Two, three, or four
Materials:	Two 0–5 cubes (red)
Object:	To score a total of 50 or more
Math Focus:	Multiplication facts and addition

RULES

1. Take turns rolling both cubes.
2. On each turn, find the product of the two numbers you roll.
3. Add the product to your last score.
4. The first player whose score totals 50 or more is the winner.

If your score was:	And you rolled:	Your new score would be:
12	**3** **2**	18
36	**4** **0**	36
25	**5** **1**	30

OTHER WAYS TO PLAY THIS GAME

1. Use one 0–5 cube and one 5–10 cube. Try to score a total of 150 or more.
2. Use two 5–10 cubes. Try to score a total of 450 or more.

Multiplying by 4 and 8

Use a computer or other means to copy and complete the chart.

How Many Legs?

Number of Each			
1	2	4	8
❶ 2			
❷ 3			
❸ 4			
❹ 5			
❺ 6			
❻ 7			
❼ 8			
❽ 9			
❾ 10			

Solve.

❿ How many horseshoes are needed to shoe seven horses?

⓫ How many sneakers are there on five basketball players?

⓬ How many legs do eight spiders have?

Multiply. Solve for _n_.

⑬ $8 \times 8 = n$ ⑭ $6 \times 2 = n$ ⑮ $6 \times 7 = n$

⑯ $7 \times 2 = n$ ⑰ $6 \times 3 = n$ ⑱ $5 \times 8 = n$

⑲ $4 \times 8 = n$ ⑳ $6 \times 4 = n$ ㉑ $4 \times 3 = n$

㉒ $5 \times 9 = n$ ㉓ $6 \times 5 = n$ ㉔ $6 \times 6 = n$

㉕ $10 \times 10 = n$ ㉖ $6 \times 8 = n$ ㉗ $9 \times 3 = n$

㉘ $9 \times 4 = n$ ㉙ $6 \times 9 = n$ ㉚ $2 \times 7 = n$

㉛ $8 \times 7 = n$ ㉜ $7 \times 4 = n$ ㉝ $4 \times 5 = n$

㉞ $4 \times 4 = n$ ㉟ $9 \times 8 = n$ ㊱ $7 \times 8 = n$

Solve these problems. Watch the signs.

㊲
```
    8376
  − 3475
```

㊳
```
    2258
  + 3769
```

㊴
```
    8475
  − 3376
```

㊵
```
    6210
  + 3256
```

㊶
```
    7000
  − 6000
```

㊷
```
    1888
  +  999
```

LESSON 58

Multiplication Practice

Multiply.

1. $2 \times 7 = $ ■

2. $5 \times 2 = $ ■

3. $2 \times 2 = $ ■

4. $4 \times 7 = $ ■

5. $5 \times 4 = $ ■

6. $2 \times 4 = $ ■

7. $8 \times 7 = $ ■

8. $5 \times 8 = $ ■

9. $2 \times 8 = $ ■

10. $2 \times 6 = $ ■

11. $2 \times 8 = $ ■

12. $6 \times 2 = $ ■

13. $4 \times 6 = $ ■

14. $4 \times 8 = $ ■

15. $6 \times 4 = $ ■

16. $8 \times 6 = $ ■

17. $8 \times 8 = $ ■

18. $6 \times 8 = $ ■

19. $9 \times 2 = $ ■

20. $2 \times 4 = $ ■

21. $2 \times 5 = $ ■

22. $9 \times 4 = $ ■

23. $4 \times 4 = $ ■

24. $4 \times 5 = $ ■

25. $9 \times 8 = $ ■

26. $8 \times 4 = $ ■

27. $8 \times 5 = $ ■

28. $6 \times 2 = $ ■

29. $2 \times 3 = $ ■

30. $2 \times 9 = $ ■

31. $6 \times 4 = $ ■

32. $4 \times 3 = $ ■

33. $4 \times 9 = $ ■

34. $6 \times 8 = $ ■

35. $8 \times 3 = $ ■

36. $8 \times 9 = $ ■

Multiply.

37. 9 × 7

38. 9 × 6

39. 9 × 9

40. 8 × 9

41. 5 × 9

42. 5 × 6

43. 5 × 10

44. 0 × 8

45. 7 × 2

46. 9 × 3

47. 6 × 3

48. 1 × 7

49. 5 × 3

50. 3 × 7

51. 7 × 7

52. 8 × 8

53. 5 × 5

54. 7 × 8

55. 8 × 4

56. 0 × 6

57. 5 × 7

58. 4 × 4

59. 6 × 8

60. 1 × 9

61. 3 × 3

62. 9 × 3

63. 6 × 6

64. 2 × 9

65. 10 × 3

66. 5 × 8

Talk about the Thinking Story "Lemonade Incorporated (Part 2)."

Multiplying by 6

Solve.

Jason lives in East City. Every day he drives
3 miles to Centerville and then back home.

1 How many miles does he drive in one day?

2 How many miles does he drive in five days?

3 Jason stops at a gas station 2 miles from
home. How far is the gas station from
Centerville?

4 How many people live in East City?

At the corner store in Centerville there are six eggs
in each carton.

5 On Monday the store sold five cartons. How many
eggs were sold on Monday?

6 On Tuesday the store sold three cartons. How many
eggs were sold on Tuesday?

7 On Friday the store sold twice as many cartons as were
sold on Tuesday. How many eggs were sold on Friday?

At the shoe store in Centerville, every pair of shoes
costs $60.

8 Liang bought a pair of sneakers and a pair of loafers.
How much did she spend?

9 If Liang has $400, can she buy seven pairs of shoes?

10 How much do ten pairs of shoes cost?

Multiply.

⑪ $\begin{array}{r} 6 \\ \times\ 3 \\ \hline \end{array}$ ⑫ $\begin{array}{r} 8 \\ \times\ 7 \\ \hline \end{array}$ ⑬ $\begin{array}{r} 9 \\ \times\ 6 \\ \hline \end{array}$ ⑭ $\begin{array}{r} 6 \\ \times\ 8 \\ \hline \end{array}$ ⑮ $\begin{array}{r} 7 \\ \times\ 9 \\ \hline \end{array}$

⑯ $\begin{array}{r} 7 \\ \times\ 4 \\ \hline \end{array}$ ⑰ $\begin{array}{r} 6 \\ \times\ 2 \\ \hline \end{array}$ ⑱ $\begin{array}{r} 5 \\ \times\ 3 \\ \hline \end{array}$ ⑲ $\begin{array}{r} 3 \\ \times\ 5 \\ \hline \end{array}$ ⑳ $\begin{array}{r} 6 \\ \times\ 7 \\ \hline \end{array}$

㉑ $6 \times 5 = \blacksquare$ ㉒ $4 \times 4 = \blacksquare$ ㉓ $4 \times 1 = \blacksquare$

㉔ $4 \times 8 = \blacksquare$ ㉕ $5 \times 5 = \blacksquare$ ㉖ $4 \times 3 = \blacksquare$

㉗ $8 \times 6 = \blacksquare$ ㉘ $6 \times 6 = \blacksquare$ ㉙ $3 \times 6 = \blacksquare$

㉚ $6 \times 4 = \blacksquare$ ㉛ $8 \times 8 = \blacksquare$ ㉜ $1 \times 6 = \blacksquare$

㉝ $2 \times 2 = \blacksquare$ ㉞ $9 \times 9 = \blacksquare$ ㉟ $5 \times 6 = \blacksquare$

㊱ $3 \times 3 = \blacksquare$ ㊲ $10 \times 10 = \blacksquare$ ㊳ $2 \times 4 = \blacksquare$

㊴ $5 \times 7 = \blacksquare$ ㊵ $7 \times 7 = \blacksquare$ ㊶ $6 \times 10 = \blacksquare$

㊷ $6 \times 9 = \blacksquare$ ㊸ $4 \times 9 = \blacksquare$ ㊹ $8 \times 5 = \blacksquare$

◆ **LESSON 59** Multiplying by 6

Mul-Tack-Toe Game

COOPERATIVE LEARNING

GAME

Players:	**Two**
Materials:	**Two Mul-Tack-Toe cards (like those below), two 0–5 cubes (red), two 5–10 cubes (blue), eight counters or coins for each player**
Object:	**To cover three boxes in a line**
Math Focus:	**Multiplication facts and mathematical reasoning**

RULES

1. Each player chooses one of the two Mul-Tack-Toe cards.

2. Players take turns rolling any two cubes.

3. Both players calculate the product of the two numbers rolled. If the product is on a player's card, he or she puts a counter on that box.

4. The first player to cover three boxes in a line (horizontally, diagonally, or vertically) wins the round.

36	6	16
28	0	72
12	100	40

Card 1

18	1	20
56	0	63
30	8	24

Card 2

Suppose that your card looks like this:

In your Math Journal tell what cubes you would roll next and why.

●	●	16
28	0	72
●	100	40

Solve.

Every window in the Morales's h[...]
six panes.

45 There are eight windows in [...]
many windowpanes are the[...]

46 The Morales's dining room [...]
many windowpanes are the[...]
dining room together?

47 The playroom has three w[...]
panes are there in the playroom[...]

48 The kitchen has four windows. How many
windowpanes are there in the kitchen?

49 There are four bedrooms. Each has two windows.
How many windowpanes are in the four bedrooms
all together?

50 There are eight rooms with windows in the Morales's
house. Can you figure out how many windowpanes
they have all together? If so, write the answer. If not,
explain why.

LESSON 60

Squares of 1 to 10

What is the area? Write the number of square centimeters.

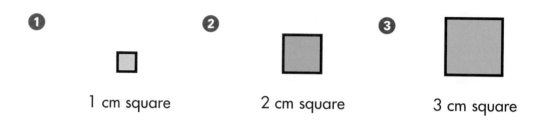

1

1 cm square

2

2 cm square

3

3 cm square

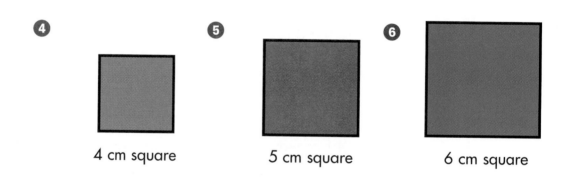

4

4 cm square

5

5 cm square

6

6 cm square

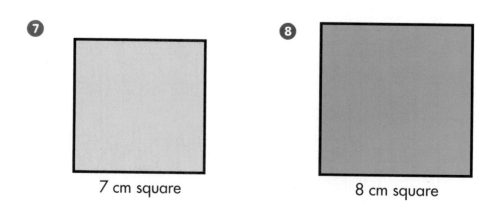

7

7 cm square

8

8 cm square

Solve.

9 The Bears scored four touchdowns and no field goals.
Each touchdown is worth six points. How many points did the Bears score?

10 The Lions scored eight field goals and no touchdowns.
Each field goal is worth three points.
How many points did the Lions score?

11 Who won?

12 By how much?

13 How many field goals does it take to equal the points scored in three touchdowns?

Solve these problems. Watch the signs.

14 $9 - 2 = $ ■

15 $8 + 7 = $ ■

16 $7 + 5 = $ ■

17 $14 - 7 = $ ■

18 $6 + 9 = $ ■

19 $5 + 13 = $ ■

20 $19 - 5 = $ ■

21 $10 + 5 = $ ■

22 $17 - 7 = $ ■

23 $20 - 10 = $ ■

24 $8 + 8 = $ ■

25 $9 + 9 = $ ■

26 $16 - 9 = $ ■

27 $7 + 0 = $ ■

28 $11 - 4 = $ ■

Multiplying by 7

Multiply.

1 7 × 8 = ▪

2 7 × 0 = ▪

3 3 × 7 = ▪

4 1 × 7 = ▪

5 7 × 5 = ▪

6 8 × 7 = ▪

7 7 × 10 = ▪

8 7 × 9 = ▪

9 7 × 6 = ▪

10 5 × 7 = ▪

11 7 × 7 = ▪

12 7 × 4 = ▪

13 4 × 7 = ▪

14 7 × 100 = ▪

15 6 × 7 = ▪

16 7 × 2 = ▪

17 2 × 7 = ▪

18 9 × 7 = ▪

19
$$\begin{array}{r} 9 \\ \times\ 7 \\ \hline \end{array}$$

20
$$\begin{array}{r} 7 \\ \times\ 3 \\ \hline \end{array}$$

21
$$\begin{array}{r} 7 \\ \times\ 1 \\ \hline \end{array}$$

22
$$\begin{array}{r} 10 \\ \times\ 7 \\ \hline \end{array}$$

PROBLEM SOLVING

Solve these problems.

23 Debbie reads 100 pages every day. How many pages does she read in one week?

24 The grocery store is having a sale. If you buy one six-pack of soda, you get one can free. If Debbie buys eight six-packs, how many cans of soda will she have?

Multiply. Check your math skills.

25 $6 \times 9 = $ ■   **26** $7 \times 5 = $ ■   **27** $6 \times 8 = $ ■

28 $5 \times 4 = $ ■   **29** $4 \times 7 = $ ■   **30** $5 \times 5 = $ ■

31 $8 \times 8 = $ ■   **32** $8 \times 6 = $ ■   **33** $5 \times 6 = $ ■

34 $6 \times 7 = $ ■   **35** $8 \times 3 = $ ■   **36** $5 \times 7 = $ ■

37 $9 \times 8 = $ ■   **38** $9 \times 9 = $ ■   **39** $2 \times 6 = $ ■

40 $3 \times 10 = $ ■   **41** $0 \times 7 = $ ■   **42** $9 \times 2 = $ ■

43 $8 \times 7 = $ ■   **44** $10 \times 5 = $ ■   **45** $9 \times 4 = $ ■

46 $4 \times 8 = $ ■   **47** $8 \times 1 = $ ■   **48** $9 \times 6 = $ ■

49 $3 \times 9 = $ ■   **50** $7 \times 7 = $ ■   **51** $10 \times 3 = $ ■

52 $5 \times 8 = $ ■   **53** $6 \times 6 = $ ■   **54** $3 \times 7 = $ ■

55 $7 \times 3 = $ ■   **56** $3 \times 8 = $ ■   **57** $9 \times 7 = $ ■

Number correct ■

Multiplication

Multiply.

1 $2 \times 0 = \blacksquare$ **2** $2 \times 3 = \blacksquare$ **3** $10 \times 0 = \blacksquare$

4 $5 \times 2 = \blacksquare$ **5** $9 \times 0 = \blacksquare$ **6** $2 \times 2 = \blacksquare$

7 $3 \times 5 = \blacksquare$ **8** $1 \times 8 = \blacksquare$ **9** $4 \times 4 = \blacksquare$

10 $8 \times 2 = \blacksquare$ **11** $5 \times 10 = \blacksquare$ **12** $6 \times 4 = \blacksquare$

13 $8 \times 10 = \blacksquare$ **14** $6 \times 6 = \blacksquare$ **15** $3 \times 3 = \blacksquare$

16 $9 \times 4 = \blacksquare$ **17** $7 \times 2 = \blacksquare$ **18** $8 \times 1 = \blacksquare$

19 $6 \times 8 = \blacksquare$ **20** $2 \times 6 = \blacksquare$ **21** $7 \times 8 = \blacksquare$

22 $9 \times 7 = \blacksquare$ **23** $3 \times 9 = \blacksquare$ **24** $2 \times 9 = \blacksquare$

25 $\begin{array}{r} 8 \\ \times\ 5 \\ \hline \end{array}$ **26** $\begin{array}{r} 10 \\ \times\ 8 \\ \hline \end{array}$ **27** $\begin{array}{r} 3 \\ \times\ 1 \\ \hline \end{array}$ **28** $\begin{array}{r} 9 \\ \times\ 9 \\ \hline \end{array}$

29 $\begin{array}{r} 4 \\ \times\ 5 \\ \hline \end{array}$ **30** $\begin{array}{r} 6 \\ \times\ 3 \\ \hline \end{array}$ **31** $\begin{array}{r} 1 \\ \times\ 4 \\ \hline \end{array}$ **32** $\begin{array}{r} 4 \\ \times\ 8 \\ \hline \end{array}$

33 $\begin{array}{r} 5 \\ \times\ 5 \\ \hline \end{array}$ **34** $\begin{array}{r} 4 \\ \times\ 3 \\ \hline \end{array}$ **35** $\begin{array}{r} 5 \\ \times\ 0 \\ \hline \end{array}$ **36** $\begin{array}{r} 7 \\ \times\ 4 \\ \hline \end{array}$

Multiply. Check your math skills.

37. $8 \times 6 = \blacksquare$
38. $8 \times 8 = \blacksquare$
39. $0 \times 0 = \blacksquare$
40. $6 \times 9 = \blacksquare$
41. $6 \times 5 = \blacksquare$
42. $1 \times 6 = \blacksquare$
43. $8 \times 7 = \blacksquare$
44. $7 \times 7 = \blacksquare$
45. $2 \times 5 = \blacksquare$
46. $2 \times 7 = \blacksquare$
47. $9 \times 2 = \blacksquare$
48. $3 \times 6 = \blacksquare$
49. $10 \times 6 = \blacksquare$
50. $4 \times 4 = \blacksquare$

(51) $7 \times 9 = \blacksquare$

(52) $6 \times 0 = \blacksquare$

(53) $4 \times 2 = \blacksquare$

(54) $4 \times 10 = \blacksquare$

(55) $4 \times 6 = \blacksquare$

(56) $3 \times 3 = \blacksquare$

(57) $3 \times 4 = \blacksquare$

(58) $3 \times 7 = \blacksquare$

(59) $6 \times 7 = \blacksquare$

(60) $2 \times 4 = \blacksquare$

(61) $\begin{array}{r} 8 \\ \times\ 3 \\ \hline \end{array}$

(62) $\begin{array}{r} 7 \\ \times\ 4 \\ \hline \end{array}$

(63) $\begin{array}{r} 1 \\ \times\ 1 \\ \hline \end{array}$

(64) $\begin{array}{r} 5 \\ \times\ 9 \\ \hline \end{array}$

(65) $\begin{array}{r} 9 \\ \times\ 5 \\ \hline \end{array}$

(66) $\begin{array}{r} 2 \\ \times\ 2 \\ \hline \end{array}$

(67) $\begin{array}{r} 8 \\ \times\ 9 \\ \hline \end{array}$

(68) $\begin{array}{r} 10 \\ \times\ 10 \\ \hline \end{array}$

(69) $\begin{array}{r} 5 \\ \times\ 7 \\ \hline \end{array}$

(70) $\begin{array}{r} 2 \\ \times\ 8 \\ \hline \end{array}$

Number correct $\blacksquare$

LESSON 63

Using Multiplication

John, Maya, Josh, and Laura went shopping for school supplies. Markers cost 9¢, scissors cost 39¢, pencil sharpeners cost 19¢, and pencils cost 7¢.

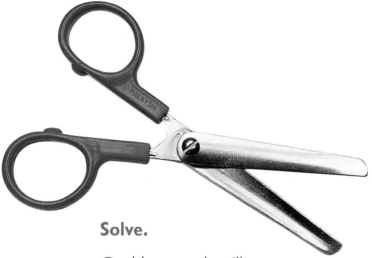

Solve.

1. How much will five pencils cost?

2. How much will two pencil sharpeners cost?

3. How much more will five markers cost than one pair of scissors?

4. John has seven nickels. How much money is that in cents?

5. Maya has six dimes. Can she buy two pairs of scissors?

6. Josh has 25¢. How much will he have left if he buys two markers?

7. Laura has 30¢. How many pencils can she buy?

8. How much more money would she need to buy seven pencils?

Solve.

9 Each person has $8. How much do they have all together?

10 Each woman weighs 55 kilograms. How much do the two women weigh together?

11 Each man is 2 meters tall. If they lie end to end, how long a line will the three men make?

12 Each man can jump a stream that is 2 meters wide. How wide a stream can the three men jump?

13 Each woman has one brother and two sisters. How many brothers and sisters do the two women have all together?

14 Each person drives 20 miles to work. How far do they drive all together?

15 Each man has three children. How many children do the three men have all together?

16 Each woman jogs 12 miles every week. How many miles do the two women together jog each week?

THINKING STORY

Talk about the Thinking Story "The Race Is Not to the Swift (Part 1)."

Mid-Unit Review

Every day Kevin jogs once around the outside of Elm Park. He jogs 5 kilometers north, 2 kilometers east, 5 kilometers south, and then 2 kilometers west.

Every day Pat jogs once around the outside of Oak Park. She jogs 4 kilometers north, 4 kilometers east, 4 kilometers south, and then 4 kilometers west.

Solve.

1 Draw an outline of Elm Park.

2 Draw an outline of Oak Park.

3 Who jogs farther each day, Kevin or Pat?

4 How many kilometers will Kevin and Pat each jog in one day?

What is the area?

5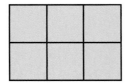

■ square centimeters

6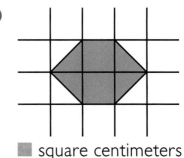

■ square centimeters

Fill in the missing numbers.

7 3, 6, 9, ■, ■, ■

8 77, 70, 63, ■, ■, ■

9 20, 22, 24, ■, ■, ■

10 210, 220, 230, ■, ■, ■

Solve.

⑪ Each star has five points. There are three stars. How many points are there all together?

$3 \times 5 = \blacksquare$

⑫ Each lamb has four legs. There are four lambs. How many legs are there all together?

$4 \times 4 = \blacksquare$

Some airplanes have six seats in a row.

⑬ For this kind of airplane, how many seats are there in two rows?

⑭ How many seats are there in five rows?

⑮ How many seats are there in seven rows?

Six cars enter the park. Each car has two, three, or four people in it.

⑯ What is the least number of people that might be in the cars?

⑰ What is the greatest number of people that might be in the cars?

Multiply.

⑱ $3 \times 4 = \blacksquare$ ⑲ $1 \times 6 = \blacksquare$ ⑳ $8 \times 5 = \blacksquare$

㉑ $5 \times 6 = \blacksquare$ ㉒ $2 \times 3 = \blacksquare$ ㉓ $6 \times 7 = \blacksquare$

㉔ $4 \times 2 = \blacksquare$ ㉕ $3 \times 5 = \blacksquare$ ㉖ $9 \times 9 = \blacksquare$

㉗ $1 \times 5 = \blacksquare$ ㉘ $6 \times 6 = \blacksquare$ ㉙ $7 \times 8 = \blacksquare$

㉚ $7 \times 3 = \blacksquare$ ㉛ $3 \times 7 = \blacksquare$ ㉜ $8 \times 4 = \blacksquare$

㉝ $4 \times 5 = \blacksquare$ ㉞ $1 \times 9 = \blacksquare$ ㉟ $5 \times 5 = \blacksquare$

LESSON 64

Understanding Division

Use manipulatives to act out these problems.

1 There are 24 shells and three children. How many shells are there for each child?

24 ÷ 3 = ▪

2 There are 12 coins in three rows. How many coins are in each row?

12 ÷ 3 = ▪

3 There are 35 cabbage plants. There are five rows. How many plants are there in each row?

35 ÷ 5 = ▪

④ Three new pencils weigh 18 grams all together. How many grams does each pencil weigh?

18 ÷ 3 = ■

⑤ There are ten fish in two tanks. Each tank has the same number of fish. How many fish are in each tank?

10 ÷ 2 = ■

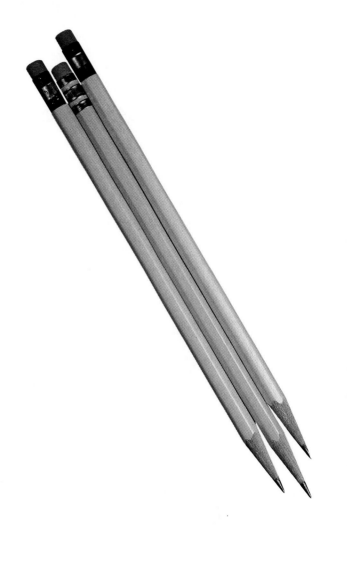

⑥ There are 20 baseball cards on the table. Four children take turns picking cards until they each have the same number. How many cards does each child have?

⑦ Micah has 10¢. He has only nickels. How many nickels does Micah have?

10 ÷ 5 = ■

⑧ Alyssa, Heidi, and Grant found 24¢. They want to share it equally. How many cents should each child get?

24 ÷ 3 = ■

◆ **LESSON 64** **Understanding Division**

Solve these problems. Watch the signs.

⑨   345
   + 722

⑩   609
   − 345

⑪   812
   − 799

⑫   400
   + 500

⑬   325
   + 549

⑭   179
   − 88

⑮   503
   + 333

⑯   956
   − 469

Multiply.

⑰   4
   × 5

⑱   6
   × 4

⑲   8
   × 7

⑳   3
   × 6

㉑   10
   × 10

㉒   7
   × 6

㉓   9
   × 1

㉔   4
   × 8

㉕   7
   × 2

㉖   5
   × 9

㉗   5
   × 8

㉘   4
   × 4

㉙   10
   × 6

㉚   9
   × 2

㉛   6
   × 8

㉜   6
   × 7

㉝   7
   × 7

㉞   3
   × 8

㉟   10
   × 8

㊱   9
   × 7

㊲   5
   × 5

㊳   7
   × 3

㊴   3
   × 4

㊵   5
   × 6

◆ Jeff and Laura are playing the "Missing Factor" game. Laura sees a 5 on Jeff's back. The class tells them the product is 35. What number should Laura say is on her back?

◆ In the next game, Sam and Lee go to the front of the room. Sam sees a 4 on Lee's back. The class says the product is 16. What number should Sam say is on his back?

Copy and complete the table.

Missing Factor Game

	Student 1	Student 2	Product
41	Jeff: 5	Laura:	35
42	Lee: 4	Sam: ▨	16
43	Suki: 7	Henry: ▨	35
44	Leah: ▨	Alan: 6	30

Your class can play this game. Two students go to the front of the room. Without letting them see, attach a numbered sheet of paper to each student's back.

The two students look at each other's number (but not their own). Then the students ask the class, "What is the product of the two numbers?"

The class gives the product, and each student must figure out what number is on his or her back.

Repeat the game with different pairs of students, using different numbers.

LESSON 65

Missing Factors and Division

ALGEBRA READINESS

Solve these problems.

1 $7 \times \blacksquare = 56$

2 $56 \div 7 = \blacksquare$

3 $7\overline{)56}$

4 $\blacksquare \times 9 = 36$

5 $36 \div 9 = \blacksquare$

6 $9\overline{)36}$

7 $\blacksquare \times 8 = 48$

8 $48 \div 8 = \blacksquare$

9 $8\overline{)48}$

PROBLEM SOLVING

10 Martina wants to buy 18 tennis balls. They come in cans of three. How many cans should she buy?

$\blacksquare \times 3 = 18$

$18 \div 3 = \blacksquare$

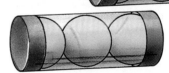

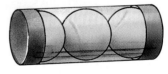

11 Zachary needs $35. He can earn $7 a week mowing lawns. In how many weeks can Zachary earn the money he needs?

$\blacksquare \times 7 = 35$ $\qquad$ $35 \div 7 = \blacksquare$

12 Five friends want to share a bag of oranges equally. The bag contains 30 oranges. How many oranges should each person get?

$\blacksquare \times 5 = 30$ $\qquad$ $30 \div 5 = \blacksquare$

Divide.

⑬ 32 ÷ 8 = ▨   ⑭ 21 ÷ 3 = ▨   ⑮ 7 ÷ 1 = ▨

⑯ 56 ÷ 7 = ▨   ⑰ 49 ÷ 7 = ▨   ⑱ 30 ÷ 10 = ▨

⑲ 72 ÷ 8 = ▨   ⑳ 64 ÷ 8 = ▨   ㉑ 12 ÷ 4 = ▨

㉒ 21 ÷ 7 = ▨   ㉓ 18 ÷ 2 = ▨   ㉔ 45 ÷ 9 = ▨

㉕ 4)‾16‾   ㉖ 9)‾36‾   ㉗ 6)‾24‾

㉘ 7)‾42‾   ㉙ 7)‾63‾   ㉚ 6)‾36‾

㉛ 4)‾36‾   ㉜ 3)‾27‾   ㉝ 9)‾81‾

㉞ 2)‾8‾   ㉟ 8)‾56‾   ㊱ 5)‾35‾

Solve.

㊲ The Brandts bought 21 tomato plants. They have room in their garden for three rows of plants. How many plants should they put in each row?

㊳ Arthur has a piece of rope that is 12 feet long. He needs to cut it into three equal lengths. How long should each piece be?

㊴ Three paper-cup dispensers need to be refilled. There are 90 cups in the refill pack. How many cups should go in each dispenser to fill them equally?

㊵ Two campers decided to take turns staying up through the night to keep their fire going. If there are ten hours of nighttime, how long will each camper's shift be?

Related Multiplication and Division Facts

Solve these problems. Watch the signs.

1. $4 \times 5 = \blacksquare$

2. $20 \div 4 = \blacksquare$

3. $10 \times 7 = \blacksquare$

4. $7 \times 6 = \blacksquare$

5. $42 \div 6 = \blacksquare$

6. $35 \div 5 = \blacksquare$

7. $8 \times 8 = \blacksquare$

8. $70 \div 10 = \blacksquare$

9. $5 \times 8 = \blacksquare$

10. $40 \div 5 = \blacksquare$

11. $8 \times 7 = \blacksquare$

12. $7 \times 7 = \blacksquare$

13. $54 \div 6 = \blacksquare$

14. $18 \div 2 = \blacksquare$

15. $3 \times 6 = \blacksquare$

16. $9 \times 6 = \blacksquare$

17. $2 \times 9 = \blacksquare$

18. $3 \times 7 = \blacksquare$

19. $56 \div 8 = \blacksquare$

20. $49 \div 7 = \blacksquare$

21. $18 \div 3 = \blacksquare$

22. $5 \times 7 = \blacksquare$

23. $4 \times 7 = \blacksquare$

24. $8 \times 4 = \blacksquare$

25. $64 \div 8 = \blacksquare$

26. $28 \div 7 = \blacksquare$

27. $32 \div 8 = \blacksquare$

28. $21 \div 3 = \blacksquare$

29. $10 \times 4 = \blacksquare$

30. $5 \times 9 = \blacksquare$

31. $6 \times 5 = \blacksquare$

32. $9 \times 9 = \blacksquare$

33. $40 \div 10 = \blacksquare$

34. $45 \div 5 = \blacksquare$

35. $30 \div 5 = \blacksquare$

36. $81 \div 9 = \blacksquare$

Solve.

37 From 1912 to 1959, there were 48 states in the United States. The flag had 48 stars, one for each state. The stars were in the shape of a rectangle with six rows. How many stars were in each row?

38 Between January and August of 1959, there were 49 states in the United States. The flag had 49 stars. The stars were in the shape of a rectangle. How many rows do you think there were? How many stars were in each row? What kind of rectangle was that?

39 Now the United States has 50 states. If the stars on the flag were in the shape of a rectangle with five rows, how many stars would be in each row? Draw how the flag would look. Do you like how it looks?

40 What other rectangular shapes are possible with 50 stars? Do you like how any of them look?

Look at a United States flag. Write in your Math Journal about the design of the stars. Can you think of other ways to arrange them? Suppose we have 51 states someday. How would you arrange that many stars?

Practice with Missing Factors and Division

Solve these problems.

① $3 \times \blacksquare = 12$

② $8 \times \blacksquare = 64$

③ $5 \times \blacksquare = 20$

④ $4 \times \blacksquare = 32$

⑤ $5 \times \blacksquare = 40$

⑥ $4 \times \blacksquare = 24$

⑦ $7 \times \blacksquare = 49$

⑧ $7 \times \blacksquare = 35$

⑨ $8 \times \blacksquare = 32$

⑩ $8 \times \blacksquare = 16$

⑪ $8 \times \blacksquare = 24$

⑫ $6 \times \blacksquare = 36$

⑬ $3 \times \blacksquare = 15$

⑭ $9 \times \blacksquare = 9$

⑮ $\blacksquare \times 3 = 12$

⑯ $5 \times \blacksquare = 40$

⑰ $5 \times \blacksquare = 30$

⑱ $9 \times \blacksquare = 54$

⑲ $5 \times \blacksquare = 50$

⑳ $6 \times \blacksquare = 42$

Solve.

㉑ There are 16 computers. Four computers will fit on a table. How many tables are needed?

㉒ Mr. Biggs will have 54 students taking a test in his classroom. He has space for six rows of desks. How many desks will he put in each row?

㉓ The waiters at Leon's Restaurant share their tips equally. Last night they made $80 all together. How much did each waiter earn?

GAME

Play the "Multigo" game.

Solve these problems. Watch the signs.

24 $3 \times 2 = \blacksquare$ **25** $4 \times 2 = \blacksquare$ **26** $18 \div 2 = \blacksquare$

27 $5 \times 2 = \blacksquare$ **28** $6 \times 2 = \blacksquare$ **29** $6 \times 5 = \blacksquare$

30 $7 \times 2 = \blacksquare$ **31** $8 \times 2 = \blacksquare$ **32** $3 \times 5 = \blacksquare$

33 $9 \times 2 = \blacksquare$ **34** $10 \times 2 = \blacksquare$ **35** $32 \div 4 = \blacksquare$

36 $12 \div 2 = \blacksquare$ **37** $6 \div 2 = \blacksquare$ **38** $16 \div 4 = \blacksquare$

39 $10 \div 2 = \blacksquare$ **40** $8 \div 2 = \blacksquare$ **41** $30 \div 6 = \blacksquare$

42 $3 \times 4 = \blacksquare$ **43** $12 \div 3 = \blacksquare$ **44** $7 \times 7 = \blacksquare$

45 $5 \times 4 = \blacksquare$ **46** $20 \div 5 = \blacksquare$ **47** $15 \div 5 = \blacksquare$

48 $8 \times 7 = \blacksquare$ **49** $56 \div 8 = \blacksquare$ **50** $36 \div 9 = \blacksquare$

51 $24 \div 6 = \blacksquare$ **52** $9 \times 3 = \blacksquare$ **53** $10 \div 2 = \blacksquare$

54 $48 \div 6 = \blacksquare$ **55** $9 \times 4 = \blacksquare$ **56** $9 \times 6 = \blacksquare$

57 $24 \div 3 = \blacksquare$ **58** $9 \times 5 = \blacksquare$ **59** $3 \times 1 = \blacksquare$

Using Division

Divide.

1 3)24   **2** 4)24   **3** 6)24   **4** 8)24

5 3)27   **6** 9)81   **7** 8)72   **8** 7)42

9 8)16   **10** 5)25   **11** 8)64   **12** 7)35

13 4)28   **14** 7)49   **15** 5)10   **16** 8)56

17 2)18   **18** 3)18   **19** 6)18   **20** 9)18

21 6)48   **22** 9)54   **23** 5)40   **24** 8)32

25 4)24   **26** 6)54   **27** 2)6   **28** 9)45

Solve.

29 Jean, Val, and Todd wanted some ice cubes. They used two trays that made 12 ice cubes each. If they shared the ice cubes equally, how many did each person get?

30 Mr. Marshall wants to take his four nieces to the movies. If he brings $50, how much money can he spend equally on each niece and himself?

Missing Divisor Game

Players: Two

Materials: About seven counters, one 0–5 cube (red),
one 5–10 cube (blue), the seven problems below

Object: To cover more problems

Math Focus: Solving missing divisor problems, relating
multiplication and division, and mathematical
reasoning

RULES

ALGEBRA READINESS

1. Copy the problems below.

2. Take turns rolling either cube.

3. If the number you roll is the missing divisor in a
   problem not yet covered, place a counter on that
   problem. Then write the entire problem on your
   paper.

4. The game ends when all seven problems are covered.

5. The player who has covered more problems is the
   winner.

$$28 \div \blacksquare = 7 \qquad 10 \div \blacksquare = 5$$

$$24 \div \blacksquare = 3 \qquad 54 \div \blacksquare = 9$$

$$\blacksquare \overline{)63} \quad {}^{7} \qquad \blacksquare \overline{)15} \quad {}^{5} \qquad \blacksquare \overline{)30} \quad {}^{6}$$

◆ **LESSON 68 Using Division**

Divide.

31 5)25 ▢

32 6)48 ▢

33 8)64 ▢

34 5)35 ▢

35 ▢)42 7

36 ▢)49 7

37 ▢)16 2

38 ▢)18 6

39 2)▢ 6

40 7)▢ 9

41 8)▢ 4

42 6)30 ▢

Solve these problems.

43 Faith needs $15 to buy a paint set. Her allowance is $5 a week. How long will it take her to save up for the paint set?

44 Evan uses three eggs to make a batch of pancakes. How many batches of pancakes can he make with nine eggs?

45 There are 56 balloons to blow up. All the balloons have been passed out, and each student got seven of them. How many students are there?

46 Dani collects stamps. She has 36 stamps for her album. Each page holds nine stamps. How many pages can she fill?

47 Lori is packing apples in plastic bags. She can fit nine apples in each bag. How many bags does she need for 54 apples?

Solve.

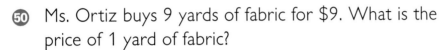

48 Sara is handing out paintbrushes.
If she has 12 paintbrushes,
how many should she leave
at each of six tables?

49 Mark is packing T-shirts.
He has 72 T-shirts that he
must pack eight to a box.
How many boxes will he need?

50 Ms. Ortiz buys 9 yards of fabric for $9. What is the
price of 1 yard of fabric?

51 Kenji collects footballs after the team practices. Each bag
holds only six footballs. How many bags does he need
for 36 footballs if he fills every bag?

52 Julia has 24 sports cards that she wants to save in a
special album. Complete the chart to show how many
pages she will need. The first two rows are already
done for you.

Sports Card Album

If she puts this many on one page:	She'll need this many pages:
1	24
2	12
3	▪
4	▪
5	▪
6	▪
7	▪
8	▪

Division with Remainders

Use sticks or other manipulatives to divide. The first one has been done for you.

    1 R3

1 4)7   **2** 3)8   **3** 5)20   **4** 6)20

5 5)24   **6** 8)30   **7** 9)54   **8** 9)56

9 7)50   **10** 4)10   **11** 3)8   **12** 6)24

Solve.

JoAnne and her two friends want to share 20 baseball cards equally.

13 How many baseball cards should each of the three children get?

14 How many baseball cards will be left over?

Mrs. Sarton has 11 balloons to divide equally among four children.

15 How many balloons should each child get?

16 How many balloons will be left over?

Solve.

Arnaldo has 40 shells to divide equally among five friends.

17 How manyshells should each child get?

18 How many shells will be left over?

Mr. Bailey, a zookeeper, has 40 bananas for Koko the ape. Koko eats five bananas each day.

19 How many days will the bananas last?

20 How much does Koko weigh?

At the flower shop, Mr. Kane is making bouquets of 5 flowers each.

21 How many bouquets can he make?

22 How many roses will be left over?

Mrs. McIntosh needs 65 party hats for a party. The hats come in packages of eight.

23 How many packages should Mrs. McIntosh buy?

24 Will she have any extra party hats?

25 How many extra?

In your Math Journal explain why eight packages of party hats is not enough for Mrs. McIntosh's party.

Practicing Basic Operations

Solve these problems. Watch the signs.

1 8
   + 6

2 8
   − 6

3 8
   × 6

4 9
   × 7

5 9
   − 7

6 4)32

7 6)36

8 9)36

9 7)56

10 243
    + 378

11 594
    − 368

12 803
    − 246

13 185
    + 68

14 $8 + 7 = \blacksquare$

15 $5 + 9 = \blacksquare$

16 $8 - 7 = \blacksquare$

17 $15 - 7 = \blacksquare$

18 $17 - 9 = \blacksquare$

19 $24 \div 8 = \blacksquare$

20 $18 \div 9 = \blacksquare$

21 $24 \div 6 = \blacksquare$

22 $3 \times 9 = \blacksquare$

23 $63 \div 7 = \blacksquare$

24 $6 \times 7 = \blacksquare$

25 $14 \div 2 = \blacksquare$

Solve.

26 Arnie earned $6.25 for mowing the lawn. The shirt he wants to buy costs $10. After his father paid him for washing the car, Arnie had exactly enough money to buy the shirt. How much did Arnie earn for washing the car?

27 Janna has four stacks of pennies. There are eight pennies in each stack. How many pennies does Janna have?

Solve these problems. Work each problem from left to right. Watch the signs.

(28) $3 + 5 - 8 \times 4 \times 7 + 2 = \blacksquare$

(29) $5 + 2 \times 8 - 6 \div 10 + 4 = \blacksquare$

(30) $4 - 3 \times 7 \times 8 + 4 \div 6 = \blacksquare$

(31) $10 - 4 \times 5 + 6 \div 9 + 6 = \blacksquare$

(32) $43 - 3 \div 8 \times 5 - 1 \div 4 = \blacksquare$

(33) $7 + 6 - 4 \times 9 + 9 \times 0 = \blacksquare$

(34) $8 \div 4 \times 4 \div 4 \times 4 \div 4 \times 4 = \blacksquare$

(35) $17 - 3 + 3 - 3 + 3 - 3 + 3 = \blacksquare$

(36) $6 \times 5 - 10 \div 5 + 2 \times 2 = \blacksquare$

(37) $11 + 9 \div 2 \times 10 - 50 + 1 = \blacksquare$

(38) $4 + 4 \times 4 + 4 \div 4 - 4 = \blacksquare$

(39) $7 \times 2 - 2 + 8 \times 2 \div 5 = \blacksquare$

(40) $35 + 6 - 1 \div 5 + 8 \div 2 + 1 \times 5 = \blacksquare$

(41) $2 \times 3 \times 4 - 4 + 10 - 3 \div 3 = \blacksquare$

(42) $16 - 3 + 1 \div 7 \times 10 - 8 \div 6 = \blacksquare$

THINKING STORY

Talk about the Thinking Story "The Race Is Not to the Swift (Part 2)."

LESSON
71

Choosing the Correct Operation

Tell whether you would add, subtract, multiply, or divide to solve each problem. You do not have to find the answers.

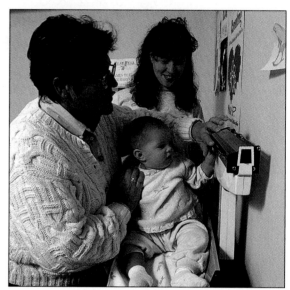

1 Three months ago Chris weighed 19 pounds. Now he weighs 22 pounds. How many pounds did he gain in the last three months?

2 Chelsea had 24 balloons. Some of them burst. Now she has four balloons. How many burst?

3 Mallory, Lindsay, Vikas, and Pete want to share 60 cookies equally. How many cookies should each child get?

4 Mrs. James bought 13 packages of candles. Each package holds six candles. How many candles did she buy?

5 Magnets cost 49¢ each. How much will two magnets cost?

6 Stickers cost 11¢ each. Lana has 45¢. How many stickers can she buy?

7 Pencils cost 8¢ each. How much will 64 pencils cost?

8. Tad saves 5¢ each day. How much money will he save in seven days?

9. Jorge, Phillip, and Cody had a race. Each child finished the race in about 20 seconds. About how long did the race take?

10. Mrs. Tyler drove from her home to the airport and back. She drove a total of 118 miles. About how far is it from her home to the airport?

11. Maria bought nine packages of paper cups. Each package has 25 cups. How many paper cups did Maria buy?

Look at the picture, then answer the question.

12. What's wrong here?

Welcome to Cuckoo Corners

Founded	1831
Population	7049
Altitude	1100 meters
Total	9980

LESSON 72

Multiplication and Division Practice

ALGEBRA READINESS

Solve for *n*. Watch the signs.

1 $50 \div 10 = n$

2 $40 \div 4 = n$

3 $49 \div 7 = n$

4 $60 \div 6 = n$

5 $60 \div 10 = n$

6 $5 \times 5 = n$

7 $5 \times 10 = n$

8 $4 \times 10 = n$

9 $48 \div 8 = n$

10 $6 \times 10 = n$

11 $40 \div 5 = n$

12 $10 \times 7 = n$

13 $40 \div 8 = n$

14 $5 \times 8 = n$

15 $9 \times 5 = n$

16 $7 \times 7 = n$

17 $6 \times 8 = n$

18 $18 \div 3 = n$

19 $6 \times 5 = n$

20 $9 \times 3 = n$

21 $3 \times 1 = n$

22 $8 \times 7 = n$

23 $42 \div 7 = n$

24 $9 \times 9 = n$

25 $25 \div 5 = n$

26 $3 \times 9 = n$

27 $27 \div 3 = n$

28 $2 \times 7 = n$

29 $64 \div 8 = n$

30 $90 \div 9 = n$

31 $9 \times 10 = n$

32 $3 \times 10 = n$

33 $2 \times 9 = n$

34 $70 \div 10 = n$

35 $6 \times 7 = n$

36 $3 \times 6 = n$

37 $1 \times 1 = n$

38 $30 \div 3 = n$

39 $45 \div 5 = n$

Solve these problems. Watch the signs.

㊵ 256 − 134	㊶ 372 + 216	㊷ 429 + 236	㊸ 700 − 250
㊹ 873 − 225	㊺ 184 + 632	㊻ 927 − 356	㊼ 313 + 97
㊽ 244 + 378	㊾ 417 − 278	㊿ 803 − 597	(51) 575 + 325
(52) 932 − 252	(53) 606 + 187	(54) 369 − 248	(55) 299 + 299
(56) 63 54 88 + 25	(57) 471 386 + 198	(58) 249 249 251 + 251	(59) 107 104 102 + 105

PROBLEM SOLVING

Solve.

(60) There were 472 movie tickets sold on Monday and 381 movie tickets sold on Tuesday. How many more movie tickets were sold on Monday than on Tuesday?

(61) Earl scored 25 points and Jamie scored 32 points in last night's basketball game. Craig scored 12 more points than Earl. How many points did they score all together?

◆ LESSON 72 Multiplication and Division Practice

REAL-WORLD CONNECTION

Most monthly calendars are in the shape of a rectangle. The days of the week, starting with Sunday, are across the top.

Solve these problems. Draw a calendar to help you.

62 How many days are in a week? So how many boxes are needed in each row?

63 If there are 30 days in a month and the first day of the month is on Sunday, how many rows will you need?

64 If there are 30 days in a month and the first day of the month is on Thursday, how many rows will you need?

65 If there are 30 days in a month and the first day of the month is on Friday, how many rows will you need?

66 If there are 30 days in a month and the first day of the month is on Saturday, how many rows will you need?

67 How many unused boxes will there be for each of the calendars in problems 63–66?

68 Repeat questions 63–67 for a 28-day month. Discuss the differences. What month has 28 days?

Guess the Cube Game

Players: Four or five
Materials: Two 0–5 cubes (red), two 5–10 cubes (blue)
Object: To guess the other player's number
Math Focus: Solving missing factor problems

GAME

RULES

ALGEBRA READINESS

1. Divide into two groups. Two students are players, and the rest are multipliers.

2. Each player chooses a cube and shows a number on it to the multipliers. The players do not show each other their numbers.

3. The multipliers tell the product of the two numbers.

4. Each player tries to guess the other player's number.

For example, you are a multiplier and the players show you a 9 and a 7. What do you say?

$$9 \times 7 = \blacksquare$$

Later you become a player. You choose the number 3.
The multiplier tells you the product is 12.
What do you say?

$$3 \times \blacksquare = 12$$

MATH JOURNAL

**Which position did you prefer—player or multiplier?
Explain why in your Math Journal.**

Functions

The function rule for this function machine is ×4.

Answer the questions and complete the function charts.

1 Suppose 3 is put into this function machine. What number will come out?

2 Suppose 7 is put into this function machine. What number will come out?

The function rule for this function machine is −7.

3 If 16 is put in, what number will come out?

4 If 7 is put in, what number will come out?

Sam made a chart. He wrote each number that he put into this function machine. He also wrote each number that came out. Then he found the function rule.

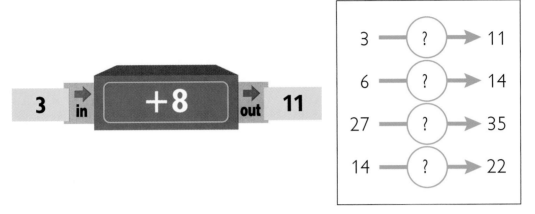

The function rule is **+8**.

Find the function rule for each set of numbers.

5

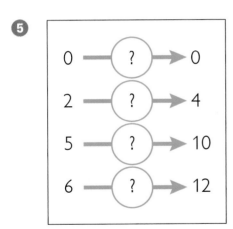

The function rule is ▇.

6

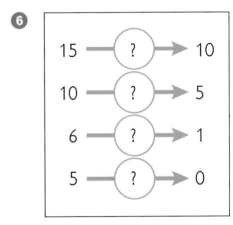

The function rule is ▇.

7

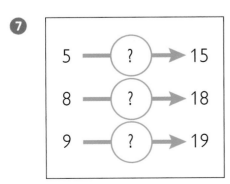

The function rule is ▇.

8

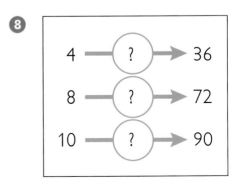

The function rule is ▇.

LESSON
74

Solving Equations with Variables

Find the value of *n*.

ALGEBRA
READINESS

1

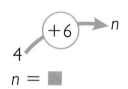

4 $\xrightarrow{+6}$ n

$n = \blacksquare$

2

n $\xleftarrow{\times 2}$ 5

$n = \blacksquare$

3 6 $\xrightarrow{-5}$ n

$n = \blacksquare$

4

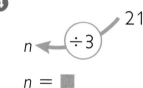

n $\xleftarrow{\div 3}$ 21

$n = \blacksquare$

Find the value of *n*. Then find the value of *m*.

5 4 $\xrightarrow{+2}$ n $\xrightarrow{\times 3}$ m $n = \blacksquare$ $m = \blacksquare$

6 5 $\xrightarrow{+2}$ n $\xrightarrow{\times 3}$ m $n = \blacksquare$ $m = \blacksquare$

7 m $\xleftarrow{\times 0}$ n $\xleftarrow{+83}$ 2 $n = \blacksquare$ $m = \blacksquare$

8 m $\xleftarrow{\times 2}$ n $\xleftarrow{\div 3}$ 12 $n = \blacksquare$ $m = \blacksquare$

208 • Multiplication and Division

Find the values of *n*, *x*, and *y*.

9

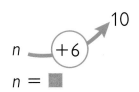

n —(+6)→ 10

$n =$ ■

10

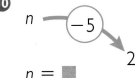

n —(−5)→ 2

$n =$ ■

11

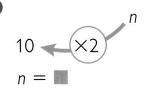

10 ←(×2)— n

$n =$ ■

12

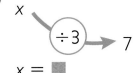

x —(÷3)→ 7

$x =$ ■

13

y ←(×3)— 7

$y =$ ■

14

21 —(÷3)→ n

$n =$ ■

15

8 ←(+8)— x

$x =$ ■

16

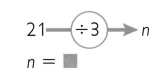

y —(×8)→ 56

$y =$ ■

17

16 —(÷4)→ x

$x =$ ■

18

x —(−7)→ 5

$x =$ ■

19

y —(÷9)→ 6

$y =$ ■

20

y —(×3)→ 24

$y =$ ■

Inverse Relationships

Write the inverse arrow operation. The first one has been done for you.

1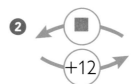

2

3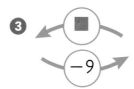

4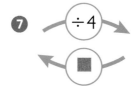

5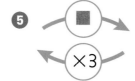

6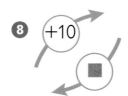

7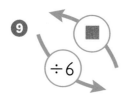

8

9

10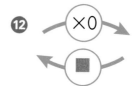

11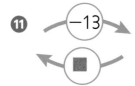

12

Use inverse arrow operations to find the value of *n*.

13
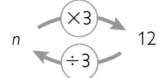 n 12 $n = \blacksquare$

14
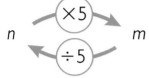 n m 38 $n = \blacksquare$

---

15 n  14 $n = \blacksquare$

---

16   13 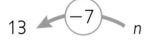 n $n = \blacksquare$

---

17 n  m 1 $n = \blacksquare$

---

18   10 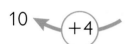 m n $n = \blacksquare$

---

19 n  m  1 $n = \blacksquare$

---

20   81  m 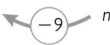 n $n = \blacksquare$

Use inverse arrow operations to find the value of _n_.

13 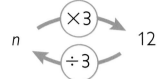 12   _n_ = ■

14 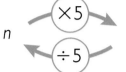 _m_ 38   _n_ = ■

15 _n_  14   _n_ = ■

16 13  _n_   _n_ = ■

17 _n_  _m_ ──6── 1   _n_ = ■

18 10  _m_ ──×3── _n_   _n_ = ■

19 _n_  _m_ ──÷2── 1   _n_ = ■

20 81  _m_ ──−9── _n_   _n_ = ■

LESSON
76

Inverse Relationships with Variables

ALGEBRA READINESS

Solve these problems. Work down the page.

$x \xrightarrow{+3} y$

1. If $x = 3$, what is y? ■
2. If $y = 3$, what is x? ■
3. If $x = 6$, what is y? ■
4. If $y = 6$, what is x? ■

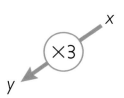
$x \xrightarrow{\times 3} y$

11. If $x = 6$, what is y? ■
12. If $y = 6$, what is x? ■
13. If $x = 9$, what is y? ■
14. If $y = 9$, what is x? ■

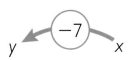
$y \xleftarrow{-7} x$

5. If $x = 56$, what is y? ■
6. If $x = 42$, what is y? ■
7. If $y = 63$, what is x? ■
8. If $y = 35$, what is x? ■

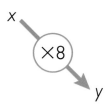
$x \xrightarrow{\times 8} y$

15. If x is 6, what is y? ■
16. If x is 9, what is y? ■
17. If y is 32, what is x? ■
18. If y is 64, what is x? ■

$x \xrightarrow{+7} y$

9. If $x = 21$, what is y? ■
10. If $y = 21$, what is x? ■

$y \xleftarrow{\times 4} x$

19. If $x = 9$, what is y? ■
20. If $y = 36$, what is x? ■

Copy and complete the function charts. You
may use a computer to draw the charts.

㉑ x —(×4)→ y

x	y
5	■
■	16
9	■
4	■
■	32

㉒ x —(−7)→ y

x	y
8	1
12	■
■	0
■	4
13	■

㉓ x —(■)→ y

x	y
4	2
10	5
16	8
6	■
■	6
■	0

㉔ x —(■)→ y

x	y
1	0
7	0
4	■
■	0
173	0

Solve these problems. Watch the signs.

㉕
$$\begin{array}{r} 9 \\ \times\ 7 \\ \hline \end{array}$$

㉖
$$\begin{array}{r} 6 \\ \times\ 6 \\ \hline \end{array}$$

㉗
$$\begin{array}{r} 3 \\ \times\ 5 \\ \hline \end{array}$$

㉘ 6)̅3̅6̅

㉙ 3)̅2̅4̅

Unit 2 Review

Solve these problems. Watch the signs.

Lesson 70

1 $3 \times 6 = \blacksquare$ **2** $12 - 7 = \blacksquare$

3 $8 \times 4 = \blacksquare$ **4** $8 - 4 = \blacksquare$

5 $4 + 8 = \blacksquare$ **6** $20 \div 5 = \blacksquare$

7 $8 \div 4 = \blacksquare$ **8** $8 + 4 = \blacksquare$

9
```
   122
+   64
```

10
```
  1734
+  580
```

11
```
   122
-   64
```

12
```
   875
   875
   225
+  145
```

13
```
   4826
-  1270
```

14
```
    548
+  1349
```

15
```
   7205
-  6347
```

16 $25 \div 5 = \blacksquare$

Divide.

Lesson 69

17 $5\overline{)25}$ **18** $6\overline{)32}$ **19** $7\overline{)42}$ **20** $2\overline{)9}$

Multiply.

Lesson 53 ㉑ 10 × 9 = ■

㉒ 16 × 10 = ■

㉓ 7 × 100 = ■

㉔ 28 × 100 = ■

㉕ 10 × 72 = ■

㉖ 100 × 10 = ■

㉗ 25 × 1000 = ■

㉘ 100 × 100 = ■

Find the function rule.

ALGEBRA READINESS

㉙

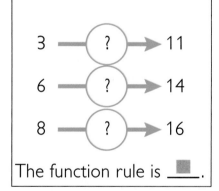

3 — ? → 11
6 — ? → 14
8 — ? → 16

The function rule is ___.

㉚

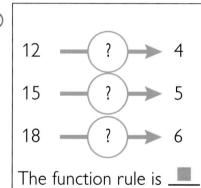

12 — ? → 4
15 — ? → 5
18 — ? → 6

The function rule is ___.

Lesson 73

Find the values of x and y.

Lesson 74 ㉛

6 —(×7)→ y   y = ■

㉜ x —(÷4)→ 8   x = ■

㉝ 6 —(−1)→ y   y = ■

㉞ x —(×2)→ n —(+4)→ 12   x = ■

◆ **LESSON 77 Unit 2 Review**

Solve.

35 There are eight cans in each box. How many cans are there in six boxes?

Lesson 58

36 How many cans are there in three boxes?

37 Kara has 90¢. Pears cost 48¢ per pound. Can she buy 2 pounds of pears?

Mr. Kimoto's garden is a square. Each side is 5 feet long.

Lesson 46

38 What is the area of Mr. Kimoto's garden?

39 How long is the border that goes around the garden?

40 A machine can cap one bottle every three seconds. How long will it take to cap eight bottles?

41 Miss Lin lives 20 miles from work. Ms. Johnson lives 15 miles from work. Which woman is older?

The table shows the approximate lengths of some long rivers in the world.

GEOGRAPHY CONNECTION

River	Length (in miles)
Nile (Africa)	4160
Amazon (South America)	4000
Mississippi (North America)	2340
Chang Jiang (Asia)	3964
Huang (Asia)	3395

Solve.

Lesson 70

42 What is the difference in length between the longest and the next-longest river?

43 How much longer is the Nile than the shortest river in the table?

44 What is the difference in length between the two Asian rivers?

45 Use this table to make up three problems. Write your answers on a separate piece of paper. Have friends solve your problems. See if you get the same answers. Did you and your friends make up some problems that were the same? Why do you think that is?

Find out the lengths and locations of two or three other rivers. In your Math Journal make a chart like the one above and write about the difference in length of the rivers.

Unit Test

Solve these problems. Watch the signs.

1 $6 + 4 = \blacksquare$ **2** $7 - 2 = \blacksquare$ **3** $5 + 3 = \blacksquare$

4 $8 + 7 = \blacksquare$ **5** $9 + 6 = \blacksquare$ **6** $13 - 4 = \blacksquare$

7 $14 - 7 = \blacksquare$ **8** $16 - 8 = \blacksquare$ **9** $15 + 5 = \blacksquare$

10
$$\begin{array}{r} 43 \\ + 18 \\ \hline \end{array}$$

11
$$\begin{array}{r} 25 \\ - 17 \\ \hline \end{array}$$

12
$$\begin{array}{r} 428 \\ + 397 \\ \hline \end{array}$$

13
$$\begin{array}{r} 382 \\ - 176 \\ \hline \end{array}$$

14
$$\begin{array}{r} 2150 \\ - 741 \\ \hline \end{array}$$

15
$$\begin{array}{r} 8674 \\ + 9182 \\ \hline \end{array}$$

16
$$\begin{array}{r} 9182 \\ - 8674 \\ \hline \end{array}$$

17
$$\begin{array}{r} 137 \\ 69 \\ + 55 \\ \hline \end{array}$$

Multiply.

18 $10 \times 7 = \blacksquare$ **19** $100 \times 5 = \blacksquare$

20 $7 \times 1000 = \blacksquare$ **21** $10 \times 100 = \blacksquare$

22 $100 \times 18 = \blacksquare$ **23** $26 \times 1000 = \blacksquare$

Multiply.

24   6   **25**   7   **26**   8   **27**   9   **28**   8
   $\times$ 4 $\times$ 3 $\times$ 5 $\times$ 6 $\times$ 7

29 $7 \times 0 = \blacksquare$ **30** $9 \times 1 = \blacksquare$ **31** $2 \times 5 = \blacksquare$

32 $8 \times 2 = \blacksquare$ **33** $7 \times 9 = \blacksquare$ **34** $6 \times 6 = \blacksquare$

35 $6 \times 8 = \blacksquare$ **36** $3 \times 9 = \blacksquare$ **37** $7 \times 4 = \blacksquare$

38 $7 \times 6 = \blacksquare$ **39** $3 \times 8 = \blacksquare$ **40** $5 \times 3 = \blacksquare$

Divide.

41 $3\overline{)24}$ **42** $6\overline{)25}$ **43** $8\overline{)16}$ **44** $2\overline{)11}$ **45** $5\overline{)34}$

46 $48 \div 8 = \blacksquare$ **47** $21 \div 7 = \blacksquare$ **48** $49 \div 7 = \blacksquare$

49 $20 \div 5 = \blacksquare$ **50** $56 \div 8 = \blacksquare$ **51** $18 \div 8 = \blacksquare$

52 $36 \div 6 = \blacksquare$ **53** $16 \div 2 = \blacksquare$ **54** $30 \div 6 = \blacksquare$

55 $24 \div 6 = \blacksquare$ **56** $60 \div 10 = \blacksquare$ **57** $32 \div 4 = \blacksquare$

◆ **Unit 2 Test**

Find the function rule.

58

7	?	15
12	?	20
30	?	38

59

4	?	20
5	?	25
6	?	30

The function rule is ■.　　The function rule is ■.

Find the value of x.

60
$$x \longrightarrow \boxed{\div 3} \longrightarrow 7 \qquad x = ■$$

61
$$x \searrow \boxed{+4} \nearrow 14 \qquad x = ■$$

62
$$6 \longleftarrow \boxed{-7} \longleftarrow x \qquad x = ■$$

63
$$x \longrightarrow \boxed{\times 5} \longrightarrow 30 \qquad x = ■$$

64
$$x \searrow \boxed{\times 2} \nearrow n \searrow \boxed{+5} \nearrow 25 \qquad x = ■$$

65
$$10 \nwarrow \boxed{-11} \searrow n \qquad \boxed{\times 3} \nwarrow x \qquad x = ■$$

66
$$x \longrightarrow \boxed{\times 3} \longrightarrow 24 \qquad x = ■$$

67
$$13 \longleftarrow \boxed{-6} \longleftarrow n \longleftarrow \boxed{+1} \longleftarrow x \quad x = ■$$

Solve these problems.

68 Marco has 55¢. How much more does he need to buy a ruler that costs 79¢?

69 Brenna has nine nickels. How much is that in cents?

70 Tacks cost 8¢ each. How much will three tacks cost?

71 There are 12 crayons. The three students want to share them equally. How many crayons should each student get?

72 Another student joins the group. Now how many crayons should each student get? Will there be any left over?

73 Another student joins the group. Now how many crayons should each student get? Will there be any left over?

Miller Park has the shape of a rectangle. It is 7 kilometers long and 3 kilometers wide.

74 What is the area of Miller Park?

75 How far is it to walk once around the park?

Extend Your Thinking

Use this code to solve the puzzle.

A	B	C	D	E	F	G	H	I	J	K	L	M
1	2	3	4	5	6	7	8	9	10	11	12	13

N	O	P	Q	R	S	T	U	V	W	X	Y	Z
14	15	16	17	18	19	20	21	22	23	24	25	26

What is a rectangle?

$18 - 17$ 2×7 $9 \div 9$ $37 - 23$ $56 \div 8$ 3×4 $35 \div 7$

4×5 4×2 $4 \div 4$ 2×10 $64 \div 8$ $8 \div 8$ $38 - 19$

$18 \div 9$ $40 \div 8$ $30 \div 6$ 7×2

3×3 $9 + 5$ $7 \div 7$ $8 + 6$

$6 \div 6$ $24 \div 8$ $18 \div 6$ 9×1 2×2 $20 \div 4$ $7 + 7$ 10×2

Use this code to solve the puzzle.

A	B	C	D	E	F	G	H	I	J	K	L	M
1	2	3	4	5	6	7	8	9	10	11	12	13
N	O	P	Q	R	S	T	U	V	W	X	Y	Z
14	15	16	17	18	19	20	21	22	23	24	25	26

What is a polygon?

$10 \div 10$ 4×4 $4 \div 4$ 6×3 9×2 3×5 4×5

5×4 $64 \div 8$ 1×1 10×2 $32 \div 4$ $6 - 5$ $27 - 8$

6×2 $35 \div 7$ $42 \div 7$ $42 - 22$

$48 \div 6$ $21 - 6$ $7 + 6$ $45 \div 9$

Make up your own puzzles and write them in your Math Journal. Ask a friend to solve them.

NUMBER TRICKS

Put your hands in front of you. Stretch out your fingers. Think of your fingers as being numbers from 1 through 10, as shown. Now, bend down finger number 3. You have two fingers up on the left and seven fingers up on the right. What is 9×3? Do you see any connection?

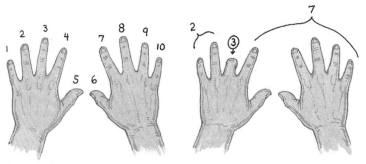

Bend down finger number 4. Do you see a connection between your fingers and 4×9? What happens when you bend down finger number 8?

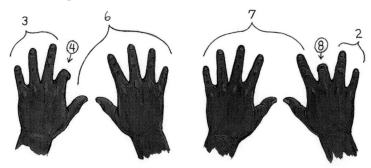

Does this work for 10×9? How about for 0×9?

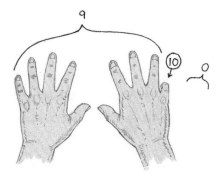

Why does this work? If you multiply 7 by 10, you get seven tens. So put up seven fingers. Now, if you subtract 7, you have one fewer ten (so put down finger number 7). But you need three more ones (because 10 − 7 = 3), so put up three fingers.

In your Math Journal write about how this trick can help you remember the multiples of 9.

Try this number trick on your friends. Start with a two-digit number that has two different digits. Reverse the digits. Subtract the lesser number from the greater number.

Then, reverse the digits of this last number and add. The sum will be 99.

For example, if you start with 48, the reversed number is 84.

$$84 - 48 = 36$$

Reverse the digits, and add: 36 + 63 = 99.

If you started with a three-digit number, what would the final number be?

UNIT 3

Fractions and Decimals

UNDERSTANDING PARTS

- **graphing**

- **measurement**

- **money**

- **adding and subtracting decimals**

Sales clerks use math . . .

Every time sales clerks ring up a sale, make change, count money, or compute sales tax they use decimals. When there is a sale, the clerk may use percents to figure out the discount price. Even if the sales clerk has a register that computes change and sale discounts, the clerk must know if the totals are reasonable.

Reading Pictographs

Every ten years the United States government takes a census, or count, of the population. The chart below is called a **pictograph**. A pictograph displays information using pictures. This pictograph shows the number of people who lived in each of seven states in 1990. Each figure stands for 1,000,000 people.

Alabama	
Alaska	
California	
Idaho	
North Carolina	
South Carolina	
Texas	

Population of states from 1990 census. Each stands for 1,000,000 people.

Use the pictograph to answer these questions.

1 Which state had fewer than 1,000,000 people?

2 Which state had the most people? About how many people did it have? Only part of the last figure is shown. What do you think that means?

3 The 1990 census showed that 29,760,021 people lived in California. Do you think that was exactly right? Explain.

4 Which state on the graph had the second greatest number of people? About how many people did it have?

5 About how many people lived in Alabama?

6 About how many people lived in Alaska?

7 About how many people lived in Idaho?

8 About how many people lived in North Carolina?

9 About how many people lived in South Carolina?

10 Compare your population estimates with actual 1990 census figures. You can find census information in an almanac or an encyclopedia.

In your Math Journal explain how pictographs are different from other kinds of charts you have used.

Reading Bar Graphs

The chart below is a **bar graph**. A bar graph uses rectangles to display information. This bar graph shows the approximate populations of some cities. These population figures came from the 1990 census.

1990 Populations of Some Cities in the United States

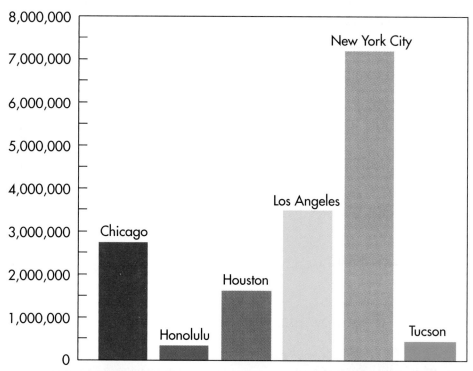

Answer the questions about the bar graph.

1. Which city had the greatest population? About how many people lived there?

2. Which city had the fewest people?

3. About how many people lived in Los Angeles?

4. Compare the population of Los Angeles with the population of New York City. Was it half as much, twice as much, or about two thirds as much?

5. About how many people lived in Chicago?

6. What was the approximate population of Honolulu?

7. What was the approximate population of Houston?

8. What was the approximate population of Tucson?

9. Here are the 1990 census figures for some more cities. Make a bar graph showing these populations. Choose your scale carefully.

City	Population
Norfolk	261,229
Philadelphia	1,585,577
Phoenix	983,403
Seattle	516,259
Washington, D.C.	606,900

In your Math Journal write a comparison of pictographs and bar graphs. How are they alike? How are they different?

Reading Line Graphs

The chart below is a **line graph**. A line graph uses points connected by a line to display information. This line graph shows the change in Todd's height through the years.

Todd's Height

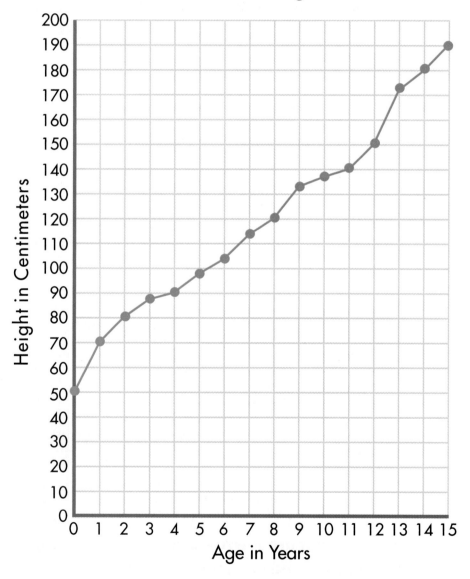

HEALTH CONNECTION

Use the graph to answer these questions.

About how tall was Todd on his

1 first birthday?

2 fifth birthday?

3 eighth birthday?

4 fourteenth birthday?

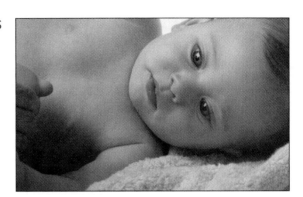

How old was Todd when he was

5 90 centimeters tall?

6 115 centimeters tall?

7 140 centimeters tall?

8 180 centimeters tall?

About how many centimeters did Todd grow between his

9 first and fifth birthdays?

10 fifth and eighth birthdays?

11 eighth and fourteenth birthdays?

12 first and fourteenth birthdays?

13 If Todd continues to grow at the same rate as he grew between his thirteenth and fifteenth birthdays, how tall do you think he will be on his sixteenth birthday?

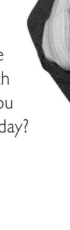

THINKING STORY

Talk about the Thinking Story "Clever Consuela."

Line Graphs

Read the graph.

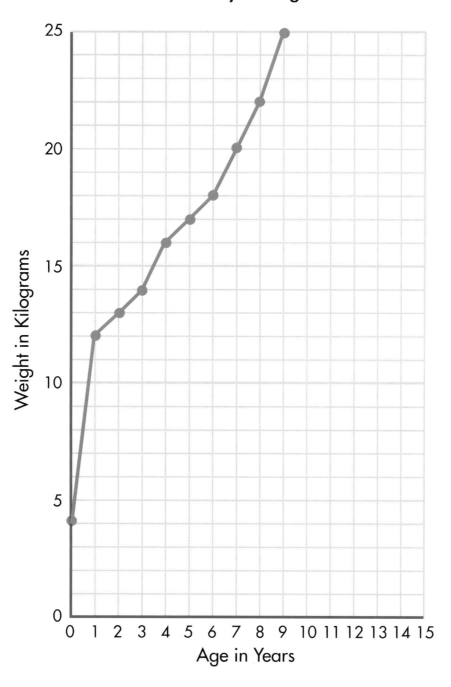

Wendy's Weight

Use the line graph to answer these questions.

About how much did
Wendy weigh on her

1 first birthday?

2 third birthday?

3 seventh birthday?

4 ninth birthday?

5 About how much do you think Wendy weighed when she was $7\frac{1}{2}$ years old?

6 About how old do you think Wendy was when she weighed 24 kilograms?

Solve these problems. Watch the signs.

7
$$\begin{array}{r} 3 \\ \times\ 4 \\ \hline \end{array}$$

8
$$\begin{array}{r} 6 \\ \times\ 5 \\ \hline \end{array}$$

9
$$\begin{array}{r} 7 \\ +\ 3 \\ \hline \end{array}$$

10
$$\begin{array}{r} 5 \\ -\ 3 \\ \hline \end{array}$$

11
$$\begin{array}{r} 8 \\ -\ 5 \\ \hline \end{array}$$

12
$$\begin{array}{r} 8 \\ +\ 7 \\ \hline \end{array}$$

13
$$\begin{array}{r} 479 \\ +\ 635 \\ \hline \end{array}$$

14
$$\begin{array}{r} 576 \\ -\ 337 \\ \hline \end{array}$$

15
$$\begin{array}{r} 856 \\ +\ 342 \\ \hline \end{array}$$

16
$$\begin{array}{r} 503 \\ -\ 327 \\ \hline \end{array}$$

17
$$\begin{array}{r} 654 \\ 327 \\ +\ \ 98 \\ \hline \end{array}$$

18
$$\begin{array}{r} 249 \\ +\ 502 \\ \hline \end{array}$$

LESSON
83

Reading a Thermometer

Temperature is measured with thermometers. Most of the world's people measure temperature in degrees Celsius (sometimes called centigrade). In the United States and a few other countries, temperature is usually measured in degrees Fahrenheit. Water freezes at 32° Fahrenheit. Water boils at 212° Fahrenheit.

Many thermometers do not show every degree. If you look carefully at a thermometer, you can decide what the markings mean.

Use the thermometer shown to answer the questions. Talk about your answers with others.

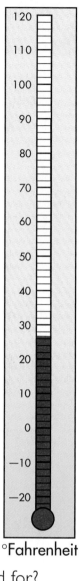

°Fahrenheit

❶ How many marks are there between 40 and 50 on this thermometer?

❷ What does the first mark above the 40 stand for?

❸ What does the third mark above the 20 stand for?

❹ What does the fourth mark above the 20 stand for?

❺ Does the temperature appear to be between 26 and 28 degrees?

❻ What temperature does this thermometer show?

❼ At that temperature would you be comfortable in your bathing suit?

❽ If the top of the red line was two marks below the 0, what would the temperature be? Would this be warm or cold?

Write the temperature shown on each Fahrenheit thermometer. Tell whether you think the temperature is *hot, comfortable,* or *cold.*

9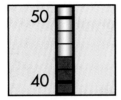

10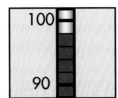

11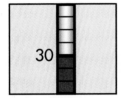

12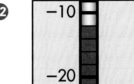

13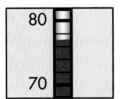

14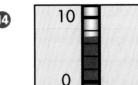

15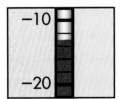

16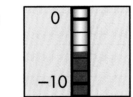

17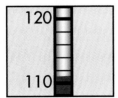

18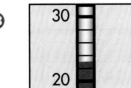

LESSON 84

Making Line Graphs

For a science project, Brad wanted to find out about how hot water cools. He left a glass of hot water in the room. Every 15 minutes he measured the temperature of the water. He made this chart. Make a line graph to show how the water cooled.

Number of Minutes After Start	Temperature
0	176°F
15	131°F
30	108°F
45	95°F
60	88°F
75	81°F
90	77°F
105	73°F
120	72°F
135	70°F
150	70°F
165	68°F
180	68°F
195	68°F
210	68°F
225	68°F
240	68°F

◆ About what temperature do you think the room was?

■ °F

Solve for _n_. Use shortcuts when you can.

1. $5 \times 6 = n$ 2. $6 \div 2 = n$ 3. $81 \div 9 = n$

4. $7 \times 8 = n$ 5. $27 \div 9 = n$ 6. $3 \times 8 = n$

7. $9 \times 9 = n$ 8. $36 \div 9 = n$ 9. $4 \times 3 = n$

10. $3 \times 2 = n$ 11. $48 \div 6 = n$ 12. $24 \div 4 = n$

13. $7 \times 0 = n$ 14. $36 \div 4 = n$ 15. $5 \times 4 = n$

Solve these problems. Watch the signs.

16.
```
  756
+ 389
```
17.
```
  937
- 638
```
18.
```
  729
+ 389
```
19.
```
  600
- 599
```

20.
```
  859
- 365
```
21.
```
  233
+ 299
```
22.
```
  992
- 793
```
23.
```
  312
+ 529
```

Divide. Watch for remainders.

24. $6\overline{)30}$ 25. $7\overline{)49}$ 26. $2\overline{)12}$ 27. $2\overline{)13}$

28. $5\overline{)35}$ 29. $4\overline{)30}$ 30. $9\overline{)81}$ 31. $9\overline{)85}$

FANTASTIC FACT

At 68°F, one gallon of water weighs about $8\frac{1}{2}$ pounds.

Metric Measurements of Length and Weight

The **meter, centimeter,** and **kilometer** are units of length.

There are 100 centimeters in 1 meter.

100 cm = 1 m

Ten soccer fields end-to-end would be about 1 kilometer long. There are 1000 meters in 1 kilometer.

1000 m = 1 km

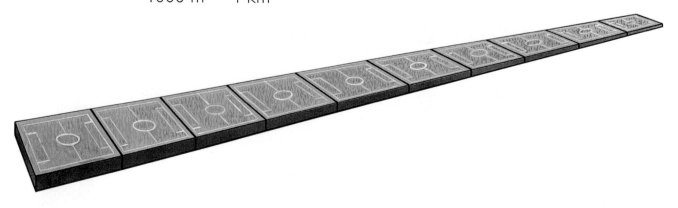

The **gram** and the **kilogram** are units of weight.

There are 1000 grams in 1 kilogram.

1000 g = 1 kg

Write the equivalent measures.

① 1 m = ▧ cm

② 1 kg = ▧ g

③ 2 m = ▧ cm

④ 4 kg = ▧ g

⑤ 7 m = ▧ cm

⑥ 6 kg = ▧ g

⑦ 1 km = ▧ m

⑧ ▧ cm = 3 m

⑨ 3 km = ▧ m

⑩ ▧ m = 5 km

⑪ 10 km = ▧ m

⑫ ▧ g = 5 kg

◆ **LESSON 85 Metric Measurements of Length and Weight**

Write the name of the unit that makes sense. Write
kilometers, meters, centimeters, kilograms,
or *grams*. Work down the page.

⓭ About 2 ▪ tall

⓮ Weighs about 75 ▪

⓳ About 130 ▪ tall

⓴ Weighs about 27 ▪

⓯ About 2 ▪ across

⓰ Weighs about 3 ▪

㉑ About 30 ▪ long

㉒ Weighs about 500 ▪

⓱ About 18 ▪ long

⓲ Weighs about 6 ▪

㉓ About 2 ▪ long

㉔ Weighs about 8 ▪

Play the "Find the Distance" game.

Choose the number that seems most reasonable.

25  weighs about ___ grams.

a. 10   **b.** 100   **c.** 1000

26 is about ___ centimeters tall.

a. 13   **b.** 130   **c.** 1300

27 is about ___ centimeters tall.

a. 30   **b.** 300   **c.** 3000

28  is about ___ meters tall.

a. 2   **b.** 20   **c.** 200

29  weighs about ___ kilograms.

a. 7   **b.** 70   **c.** 700

30  is about ___ meters tall.

a. 35   **b.** 350   **c.** 3500

31  is about ___ centimeters wide.

a. 120   **b.** 1200   **c.** 12,000

32  weighs about ___ kilograms.

a. 10   **b.** 100   **c.** 1000

LESSON
86

Estimate and Measure Metric Lengths

Estimate and then measure each length with your centimeter ruler.

1

2

3

4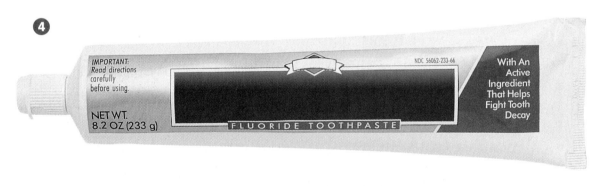

NET WT.
8.2 OZ (233 g)

NDC 56062-233-66

IMPORTANT:
Read directions
carefully
before using.

With An
Active
Ingredient
That Helps
Fight Tooth
Decay

FLUORIDE TOOTHPASTE

5

Solve these problems.

6 The poles are 12 meters apart. About how long is the rope?

7 In order to eat healthfully, Jake should not eat more than 50 grams of fat a day. On Monday his breakfast had 13 grams of fat, his lunch had 14 grams of fat, and his dinner had 21 grams of fat. Did Jake eat healthfully?

8 Marilyn is 129 centimeters tall. Jeb is 133 centimeters tall. How much taller is Jeb than Marilyn?

9 Briana lives 2 kilometers from school. If she rides her bicycle to school and back every Monday through Friday, how far does she ride each week?

10 Cesar weighs 29 kilograms. When he holds his dog Chompers, the scale shows 34 kilograms. How much does Chompers weigh?

 **Do the "Measuring" activity.**

Customary Measurements of Length and Weight

The **inch, foot, yard,** and **mile** are units of length.

There are 12 inches in 1 foot.

12 in. = 1 ft

There are 3 feet in 1 yard.

There are 36 inches in 1 yard.

It takes about 15 or 20 minutes to walk 1 mile.

There are 5280 feet in 1 mile.

246 • Fractions and Decimals

The **pound** and **ounce** are units of weight.

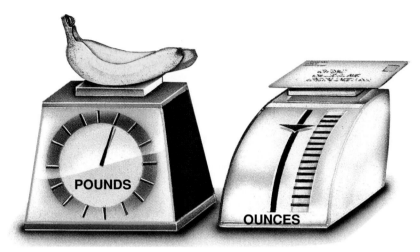

There are 16 ounces in 1 pound.

Write the equivalent measures.

❶ 1 foot = ◼ inches

❷ 4 yards = ◼ inches

❸ 2 feet = ◼ inches

❹ 1 mile = ◼ feet

❺ 1 yard = ◼ feet

❻ 2 miles = ◼ feet

❼ 10 yards = ◼ feet

❽ 1 pound = ◼ ounces

❾ 1 yard = ◼ inches

❿ 2 pounds = ◼ ounces

⓫ 2 yards = ◼ inches

⓬ 10 pounds = ◼ ounces

⓭ 4 feet = ◼ inches

⓮ 32 ounces = ◼ pounds

GAME

Play the "Customary Unit" game.

◆ LESSON 87 Customary Measurements of Length and Weight

Write the name of the unit that makes sense. Write
inches, feet, yards, miles, ounces, or *pounds.* Watch your
numbering.

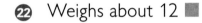

15 About 18 ▪ long

16 Weighs about 3500 ▪

21 About 1 ▪ long

22 Weighs about 12 ▪

17 About 6 ▪ tall

18 Weighs about 180 ▪

23 About 1 ▪ long

24 About 2 ▪ thick

19 About 100 ▪ long

20 About 50 ▪ wide

25 About 7 ▪ long

26 Weighs about 4 ▪

In your Math Journal make up three more problems
like this and share them with the class.

Choose the number that seems most reasonable.

27  weighs about ____ ounces.

a. 2   **b.** 20   **c.** 200

28 is about ____ inches tall.

a. 50   **b.** 500   **c.** 5000

29 is about ____ feet tall.

a. 1   **b.** 10   **c.** 100

30  is about ____ inches tall.

a. 8   **b.** 80   **c.** 800

31  weighs about ____ ounces.

a. 24   **b.** 240   **c.** 2400

32  is about ____ feet tall.

a. 1   **b.** 10   **c.** 100

33  is about ____ feet wide.

a. 4   **b.** 40   **c.** 400

34  weighs about ____ pounds.

a. 20   **b.** 200   **c.** 2000

LESSON 88

Estimate and Measure Customary Lengths and Weights

Estimate and then measure each length with an inch ruler.

1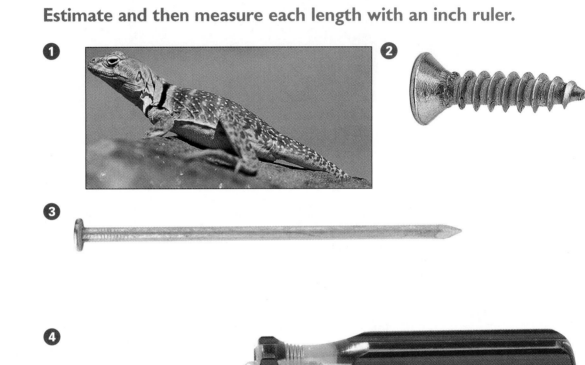

2

3

4

5

Solve these problems.

Sasha can reach up to a height of 6 feet.

6 If she stands on the stool, can she reach the top shelf?

The board is 2 feet long. Mr. Wright needs pieces that are 5 inches long.

7 How many 5-inch pieces can he get from the board?

8 How long will the leftover piece be?

9 Bill jogs 2 miles every day of the week. How far does he jog each week?

10 Mr. Hakim needs 1 pound of cream cheese for a cake. Each package is 8 ounces. How many packages should he buy?

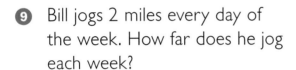

11 Meredith jumped 2 yards. Mumtaz jumped 5 feet. Who jumped farther?

12 A stick of butter weighs 4 ounces. Mrs. Demetry needs 1 pound of butter. How many sticks of butter does she need?

13 Tonya's baseball glove weighs 14 ounces. How much less than 1 pound is that?

 **Do the "Measuring" activity.**

Graphing Multiples of 5

Copy and complete this line graph of the multiples of 5.

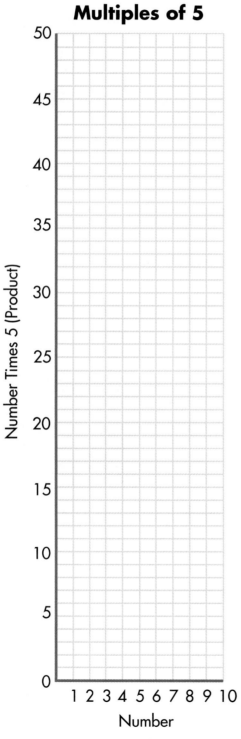

Multiples of 5

Number Times 5 (Product)

Number

1 $0 \times 5 = $ ■

2 $1 \times 5 = $ ■

3 $2 \times 5 = $ ■

4 $3 \times 5 = $ ■

5 $4 \times 5 = $ ■

6 $5 \times 5 = $ ■

7 $6 \times 5 = $ ■

8 $7 \times 5 = $ ■

9 $8 \times 5 = $ ■

10 $9 \times 5 = $ ■

11 $10 \times 5 = $ ■

Solve for *n*. Watch the signs.

⑫ $6 \times 3 = n$ ⑬ $7 \times 2 = n$ ⑭ $6 \div 2 = n$

⑮ $8 \div 2 = n$ ⑯ $4 \times 7 = n$ ⑰ $6 \times 2 = n$

⑱ $27 \div 3 = n$ ⑲ $16 \div 4 = n$ ⑳ $7 \times 4 = n$

㉑ $5 \times 5 = n$ ㉒ $6 \times 6 = n$ ㉓ $40 \div 5 = n$

㉔ $7 \times 7 = n$ ㉕ $14 \div 2 = n$ ㉖ $2 \times 9 = n$

Solve. Watch the signs.

㉗ $\begin{array}{r} 235 \\ + \ 765 \\ \hline \end{array}$ ㉘ $\begin{array}{r} 2350 \\ + \ 7650 \\ \hline \end{array}$ ㉙ $\begin{array}{r} 800 \\ - \ 401 \\ \hline \end{array}$ ㉚ $\begin{array}{r} 279 \\ - \ 186 \\ \hline \end{array}$

㉛ $\begin{array}{r} 269 \\ + \ \ 35 \\ \hline \end{array}$ ㉜ $\begin{array}{r} 2136 \\ + \ 725 \\ \hline \end{array}$ ㉝ $\begin{array}{r} 9712 \\ - \ 341 \\ \hline \end{array}$ ㉞ $\begin{array}{r} 57 \\ 87 \\ 106 \\ + \ 113 \\ \hline \end{array}$

Solve these problems.

㉟ Janet has three parrots. Her friend, Sara, said she had three times as many. Sara has eight parrots. Is Sara correct? Explain why or why not.

㊱ Marty's left shoe weighs 8 ounces. How much does his pair of shoes weigh if the right shoe weighs the same as the left shoe?

Making Charts and Graphs

Katie is making a chart and a graph to show the length of different numbers of ice-cream sticks.

Use a computer or other means to draw the chart. Then complete it. You may want to use graphing software to create the graph below.

	Number of Sticks	Total Length (centimeters)
1	1	11
2	2	■
3	3	■
4	4	■
5	5	■
6	6	■
7	7	■
8	8	■
9	9	■

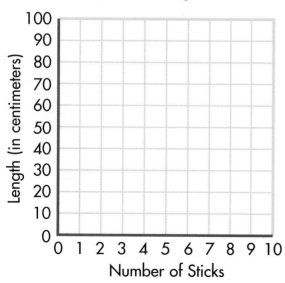

Stick Lengths

Now make a chart and a graph to show the length of different numbers of sticks.

Solve these problems.

⑩
$$\begin{array}{r} 6 \\ \times\ 5 \\ \hline \end{array}$$
⑪
$$\begin{array}{r} 8 \\ \times\ 7 \\ \hline \end{array}$$
⑫
$$\begin{array}{r} 9 \\ \times\ 9 \\ \hline \end{array}$$
⑬
$$\begin{array}{r} 8 \\ \times\ 0 \\ \hline \end{array}$$
⑭
$$\begin{array}{r} 8 \\ \times\ 3 \\ \hline \end{array}$$

⑮ $4\overline{)32}$ ⑯ $7\overline{)63}$ ⑰ $8\overline{)64}$ ⑱ $2\overline{)14}$ ⑲ $3\overline{)27}$

Divide. Solve for *n*.

⑳ $27 \div 9 = n$ ㉑ $20 \div 5 = n$ ㉒ $36 \div 6 = n$

㉓ $60 \div 10 = n$ ㉔ $30 \div 6 = n$ ㉕ $24 \div 3 = n$

㉖ $72 \div 8 = n$ ㉗ $50 \div 10 = n$ ㉘ $24 \div 4 = n$

Solve these problems. Watch the signs.

㉙
$$\begin{array}{r} 5 \\ +\ 4 \\ \hline \end{array}$$
㉚
$$\begin{array}{r} 7 \\ -\ 2 \\ \hline \end{array}$$
㉛
$$\begin{array}{r} 8 \\ +\ 3 \\ \hline \end{array}$$
㉜
$$\begin{array}{r} 6 \\ +\ 5 \\ \hline \end{array}$$
㉝
$$\begin{array}{r} 9 \\ -\ 8 \\ \hline \end{array}$$

㉞
$$\begin{array}{r} 16 \\ -\ 8 \\ \hline \end{array}$$
㉟
$$\begin{array}{r} 10 \\ +\ 8 \\ \hline \end{array}$$
㊱
$$\begin{array}{r} 9 \\ +\ 9 \\ \hline \end{array}$$
㊲
$$\begin{array}{r} 7 \\ -\ 6 \\ \hline \end{array}$$
㊳
$$\begin{array}{r} 8 \\ +\ 4 \\ \hline \end{array}$$

Solve.

㊴ Ms. Wray counted nine boxes of envelopes on each of seven shelves. How many boxes of envelopes are there?

㊵ Billy collects model airplanes. He bought two models each week for five weeks. How many airplanes did he buy during those five weeks?

Equalities and Inequalities

What is the right sign? Draw <, >, or = .

1 8 ● 7

2 5 × 7 ● 6 × 6

3 9 ● 5 + 5

4 6 × 8 ● 7 × 7

5 4 + 8 ● 10 + 2

6 7 × 8 ● 8 × 7

7 3 × 5 ● 4 × 6

8 12 ÷ 3 ● 24 ÷ 6

9 10 + 7 ● 9 + 9

10 9 × 6 ● 8 × 7

11 18 − 9 ● 13 − 3

12 5 × 9 ● 6 × 8

13 24 ÷ 3 ● 24 ÷ 4

14 7 + 2 ● 7 × 2

15 36 ÷ 9 ● 36 ÷ 6

16 15 ÷ 3 ● 15 ÷ 5

17 15 − 8 ● 12 − 5

18 9 × 2 ● 6 × 3

19 42 ÷ 7 ● 42 ÷ 6

20 20 − 5 ● 25 − 9

Talk about the Thinking Story "A Paneful Story (Part 1)."

In your Math Journal tell what strategies you used to choose the right sign in the problems above. Describe any shortcuts you used.

What is the right sign? Draw <, >, or = .

21 9 × 9 ⬤ 10 × 8

22 12 − 5 ⬤ 11 − 6

23 8 × 8 ⬤ 9 × 7

24 7 × 6 ⬤ 9 × 7

25 72 ÷ 8 ⬤ 48 ÷ 6

26 0 × 9 ⬤ 1 × 1

27 12 ÷ 4 ⬤ 24 ÷ 8

28 32 ÷ 8 ⬤ 35 ÷ 7

29 6 + 9 ⬤ 8 + 8

30 17 + 15 ⬤ 16 + 16

31 36 + 39 ⬤ 38 + 38

32 18 ÷ 3 ⬤ 36 ÷ 4

33 12 − 7 ⬤ 13 − 8

34 19 − 1 ⬤ 20 − 2

35 15 − 6 ⬤ 13 − 8

36 76 + 4 ⬤ 7 × 10

37 24 ÷ 4 ⬤ 48 ÷ 8

38 72 ÷ 8 ⬤ 72 ÷ 9

39 6 + 7 ⬤ 7 + 6

40 17 − 8 ⬤ 18 − 7

41 5 + 9 ⬤ 8 + 4

42 5 × 7 ⬤ 6 × 6

43 13 − 9 ⬤ 14 − 10

44 8 × 4 ⬤ 10 × 3

45 6 × 5 ⬤ 4 × 3

46 56 ÷ 8 ⬤ 36 ÷ 6

Fish never stop growing. The older they get, the bigger they grow.

◆ LESSON 91 Equalities and Inequalities

Each exercise below lists two objects and a way to compare them. Write a comparison using <, >, or =. If the two are so close you can't tell, write =.

Examples:

◆ gold watch and ruler (cost)

Compare the costs of a gold watch and a ruler. A gold watch costs more than a ruler, so you write:

gold watch > ruler

◆ gold watch and gold bracelet (length)

Compare the lengths of a gold watch and a gold bracelet. They are both about the same length, so you write:

gold watch = gold bracelet

47 bicycle and car (cost)

48 car and bicycle (weight)

49 brick and balloon (weight)

50 loaf of bread and football (length)

51 loaf of bread and football (cost)

52 car and truck (length)

53 sheet of paper and calculator (weight)

54 sheet of paper and calculator (cost)

55 adult human and adult pig (height)

56 adult human and adult giraffe (height)

C⬭⬭PERATIVE LEARNING

Try to Make an Inequality

Players:	**Two**
Materials:	**Two 0–5 cubes (red), two 5–10 cubes (blue)**
Object:	**To have the lower score**
Math Focus:	**Approximating sums, differences, products, and quotients; making equality and inequality statements**

RULES

1. Take turns rolling all four cubes and grouping the numbers rolled into two problems. Addition, subtraction, multiplication, and division are allowed.

2. The two problems must have the same answer or as close to the same answer as possible. For example, if you roll 2, 1, 9, and 6, you might write $2 + 1 = 9 - 6$.

3. A player's score for each turn is the difference between the two pairs of numbers.

4. Try to keep as low a score as possible. The first player to have a score of 5 loses.

Introducing the Decimal Point

You know that $5 equals 50 dimes or 500 cents. Five dimes equals 50¢ or $0.50. We can also write it as $0.5.

Solve these problems.

1 3 dimes = ___¢

2 $5 = ___ dimes

3 200 dimes = $ ___

4 200 dimes = ___ ¢

5 ___ dimes = $10

6 $___ = 80 dimes

7 $___ = 2 dimes

8 $4.20 = ___ dimes

9 17 dimes = $___

10 $___ = $8 and 7 dimes

11 If you have $8, how many dimes could you get for it at the bank?

12 If you have $7.60, how many dimes could you get?

13 If you take 253 dimes to the bank to exchange for one-dollar bills, how many one-dollar bills will you get? Will you have any dimes left over?

14 How many dimes could you get for 73¢? Would you have any cents left over?

Solve these problems. Make the least number possible in each case.

15 $8.47 = $___ and ___ dimes and ___¢

16 $___ = $7 and 15 dimes and 8¢

17 $___ = $5 and 24 dimes and 18¢

18 $4.56 = $___ and ___ dimes and ___¢

19 $17.93 = $___ and ___ dimes and ___¢

20 $___ = $43 and 9 dimes and 10¢

Solve these problems.

㉑ $4 and 5 dimes = ■ dimes

㉒ $1 and 0 dimes = ■ dimes

㉓ $ ■ and ■ dimes = 24 dimes

㉔ $8 and 0 dimes = ■ dimes

㉕ 37 dimes = $ ■ and ■ dimes

㉖ ■ dimes = $7 and 6 dimes

㉗ 5 dimes = $ ■ and ■ dimes

㉘ $9 and 4 dimes = ■ dimes

㉙ $1.1 = $ ■ and ■ dimes

㉚ $10 and 4 dimes = ■ dimes

㉛ $1.5 = $ ■ and ■ dimes

㉜ $10 and 6 dimes = $ ■

㉝ $4.5 = $ ■ and ■ dimes

㉞ $ ■ = $6 and 1 dime

㉟ $ ■ and ■ dimes = $9.2

㊱ $ ■ = $6 and 3 dimes

㊲ $13.7 = $ ■ and ■ dimes

㊳ $ ■ = $3 and 3 dimes

㊴ $10.5 = $ ■ and ■ dimes

㊵ $ ■ and ■ dimes = $8.00

㊶ There are $5 worth of dimes in a roll. How many dimes are

   a. in one roll? ■

   b. in two rolls? ■

Mid-Unit Review

The pictograph below shows the estimated number of people who lived in each of six states in 1990. Each stick figure stands for 1,000,000 people.

Use the graph to answer the questions.

State Populations

Rhode Island	
California	
New York	
Mississippi	
Arkansas	
Missouri	

❶ Which state had fewer than 2,000,000 people?

❷ Which state had the most people? About how many people did it have? Why is only part of the last figure shown?

❸ Which state had the fewest people? About how many people did it have?

❹ About how many people lived in New York?

❺ About how many people lived in Missouri?

❻ About how many people lived in Mississippi?

❼ About how many people lived in Rhode Island?

The line graph shows the growth of Jeremy's plant.

Use the graph to answer the questions.

8 How tall was the plant after one week?

9 In how many weeks did the plant grow to 7 inches tall?

10 How tall is the mature plant?

11 What was the change in height between week 1 and week 8?

12 How tall was the plant after eight weeks?

Plant Growth

Height (in inches)

Week

Choose the most sensible measure.

13 A kitten weighs about ▦ kilograms.

   a. 2000

   b. 200

   c. 2

14 A street lamp is about ▦ meters tall.

   a. 10

   b. 100

   c. 1000

15 An umbrella is about ▦ centimeters long.

   a. 8

   b. 80

   c. 800

16 A dictionary weighs about ▦ kilograms.

   a. 200

   b. 20

   c. 2

Give the temperature.

17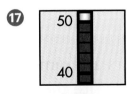

18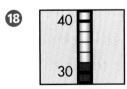

19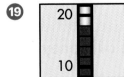

20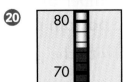

Dimes and Tenths

Dollars and Dimes Game

COOPERATIVE LEARNING

Players:	**Two**
Materials:	**Two 0–5 cubes (red), two 5–10 cubes (blue), a score form like the one on page 265**
Object:	**To make the greater total amount of money**
Math Focus:	**Addition facts and rewriting amounts of money (dollars and dimes)**

RULES

1. Take turns rolling all four cubes and adding the numbers rolled. For example, if you roll 10, 8, 5, and 1, your sum is 24.

2. Write this sum (the number of dimes) in the blank to the left of the first or the next available equal sign on the score form. For example, if your sum is 24, you would write:

   <u>24 dimes</u> = $ ___ and ___ dimes

3. Fill in the blanks to the right of the equal sign. You must write in a number less than 10 in the right-hand dimes blank.

   <u>24 dimes</u> = $ <u>2</u> and <u>4</u> dimes

4. After filling in all five lines on the score form, add to get the totals of the two right-hand columns.

5. Change the totals to the number of dollars and dimes (with the number of dimes less than 10). Write the new total in the bottom blank.

6. The player with the greater total amount of money is the winner.

Dollars and Dimes Game

____ dimes = $ ____ and ____ dimes

____ dimes = $ ____ and ____ dimes

____ dimes = $ ____ and ____ dimes

____ dimes = $ ____ and ____ dimes

____ dimes = $ ____ and ____ dimes

Totals: $ ____ and ____ dimes

Total money = $ ____ and ____ dimes

Divide.

1 $3\overline{)12}$ **2** $9\overline{)79}$ **3** $6\overline{)40}$ **4** $3\overline{)21}$ **5** $5\overline{)21}$

Solve.

Isaac has five $1 bills and 14 dimes.

6 Does Isaac have enough money to buy the bat?

7 Does he have enough money to buy two baseballs?

8 Does he have enough to buy the bat and two baseballs?

9 Isaac wants to buy three baseballs. How much more money does he need?

10 Which costs more, five baseballs or two bats?

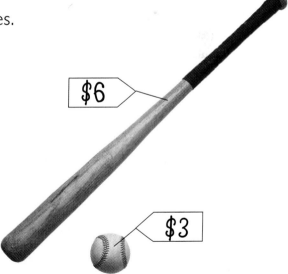

$6

$3

Decimal Points and Measurement

We can use the decimal point with measurements as well as with money.

With money we write $3.40 for three dollars and four dimes because a dime is one tenth of a dollar.

With measurement we write 3.4 meters for 3 meters and 4 decimeters because a decimeter is one tenth of a meter.

You can read 3.4 as "three and four tenths" or "three point four."

About 1 meter from the floor

About 10 decimeters from the floor

Answer these questions.

1. About how long is a decimeter? Draw a line on your paper about 1 decimeter long.

2. How many decimeters are there in a meter?

3. How many decimeters are there in 5 meters?

4. How many meters are there in 10 decimeters?

5. How many decimeters are there in 2.5 meters?

6. How many meters are there in 25 decimeters?

7. How many decimeters are there in 7.3 meters?

8. How many decimeters are there in 73 meters?

9. How many meters are there in 73 decimeters?

10. How many meters are there in 730 decimeters?

There are 10 centimeters in 1 decimeter.

    10 cm = 1 dm

There are 10 decimeters in 1 meter.

    10 dm = 1 m

Write the equivalent measures.

⑪ 2 m = ■ dm

⑫ 7 m and 4 dm = ■ m

⑬ 37 dm = ■ m and ■ dm

⑭ ■ m = 6 m and 1 dm

⑮ 40 m = ■ dm

⑯ ■ m = 10 m and 0 dm

⑰ 4.5 m = ■ m and ■ dm

⑱ 3000 dm = ■ m

⑲ ■ m and ■ dm = 9.2 m

⑳ 2 m and 7 dm = ■ m

㉑ ■ m and ■ dm = 12 m

㉒ ■ dm = 6.5 m

㉓ ■ dm = 100 m

㉔ 9 m = ■ dm

㉕ 4 m and 5 dm = ■ dm

㉖ 8.1 m = ■ m and ■ dm

㉗ ■ dm = 7 m and 6 dm

㉘ 200 dm = ■ m

㉙ 800 dm = ■ m

㉚ 25 m = ■ dm

㉛ 2 m and 3 dm = ■ m

㉜ 63 m = ■ dm

GAME

Play the "Metric Unit" game.

◆ **LESSON 94** Decimal Points and Measurement

Write the equivalent measures.

(33) 10 dm = ■ m

(34) 20 dm = ■ m

(35) 15 dm = ■ m

(36) 37 dm = ■ m

(37) ■ dm = 3.7 m

(38) 5.4 m = ■ dm

(39) 60 dm = ■ m

(40) 4.8 m = ■ dm

(41) 64 dm = ■ m

(42) 10 m = ■ dm

(43) 37 dm = ■ m and ■ dm

(44) ■ dm = 6 m and 2 dm

(45) ■ m = 6 m and 2 dm

(46) 6.8 m = ■ m and ■ dm

(47) 6.8 m = ■ dm

(48) 10.2 m = ■ m and ■ dm

(49) 20.2 m = ■ m and ■ dm

(50) 4 m and 3 dm = ■ dm

(51) 730 dm = ■ m

(52) ■ m = 11 m and 9 dm

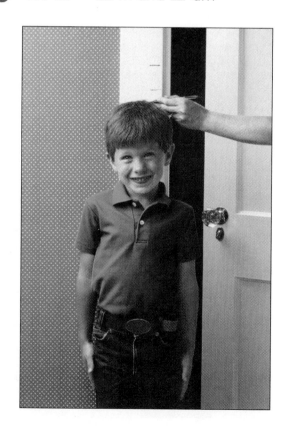

A **segment** is part of a line.

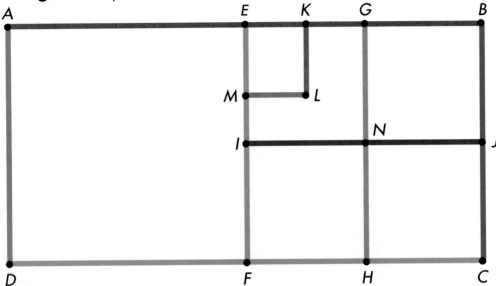

Look at the rectangle to answer the questions. Don't use your ruler yet!

53 About how many decimeters long is red segment *AB?*

54 About how many decimeters long is red segment *AE?*

55 What other segments of the figure are about as long as segment *AB?*

56 What other segments of the figure are about as long as segment *AE?*

57 There are 10 centimeters in a decimeter. About how many centimeters long is red segment *EB?*

58 About how many centimeters long is red segment *EG?*

59 About how many centimeters long is orange segment *EI?*

60 About how many centimeters long is pink segment *GH?*

61 About how many centimeters long is red segment *EK?*

62 About how many centimeters long is orange segment *EM?*

63 About how many centimeters long is red segment *KG?*

64 About how many centimeters long is orange segment *MI?*

65 Use a centimeter ruler to check your answers to questions 53–64.

Conversions: Meters and Centimeters

1 meter = 10 decimeters = 100 centimeters

Write the equivalent measures.

① 3 m = ■ cm

② 2000 cm = ■ m

③ 600 cm = ■ m

④ ■ cm = 10 m

⑤ 1000 cm = ■ m

⑥ ■ cm = 1 m

⑦ ■ cm = 9 m

⑧ ■ cm = 23 m

⑨ 100 cm = ■ m

⑩ 7 m = ■ cm

⑪ 1200 cm = ■ m

⑫ ■ m = 400 cm

⑬ 800 cm = ■ m

⑭ 300 cm = ■ m

⑮ ■ cm = 5 m

⑯ 200 cm = ■ m

Write the equivalent measures.

17 1 m and 73 cm = ▓ cm

18 4 m and ▓ cm = 452 cm

19 5 m and 43 cm = ▓ cm

20 ▓ m and ▓ cm = 925 cm

21 12 m and 17 cm = ▓ cm

22 22 m and 14 cm = ▓ cm

23 2 m and 10 cm = ▓ cm

24 ▓ m and 8 cm = 308 cm

25 2 m and 9 cm = ▓ cm

26 4 m and 5 cm = ▓ cm

27 ▓ m and ▓ cm = 1040 cm

28 ▓ m and ▓ cm = 636 cm

29 ▓ m and ▓ cm = 430 cm

30 8 m and 5 cm = ▓ cm

31 ▓ m and ▓ cm = 1234 cm

32 9 m and ▓ cm = 915 cm

33 ▓ m and 61 cm = 261 cm

34 ▓ m and 46 cm = 3146 cm

Multiply.

35 $\begin{array}{r} 6 \\ \times\ 100 \\ \hline \end{array}$

36 $\begin{array}{r} 8 \\ \times\ 7 \\ \hline \end{array}$

37 $\begin{array}{r} 10 \\ \times\ 5 \\ \hline \end{array}$

38 $\begin{array}{r} 9 \\ \times\ 3 \\ \hline \end{array}$

39 $\begin{array}{r} 100 \\ \times\ 2 \\ \hline \end{array}$

40 $\begin{array}{r} 5 \\ \times\ 8 \\ \hline \end{array}$

41 $\begin{array}{r} 2 \\ \times\ 4 \\ \hline \end{array}$

42 $\begin{array}{r} 5 \\ \times\ 100 \\ \hline \end{array}$

LESSON 96

Dollars and Cents

Write the equivalent amounts.

① 200¢ = $ ■

② ■ ¢ = $6 and 55¢

③ ■ ¢ = $10

④ ■ ¢ = $5

⑤ 1300¢ = $ ■

⑥ 2000¢ = $ ■

⑦ $1 and 73¢ = ■ ¢

⑧ ■ ¢ = $15

⑨ $ ■ and 69¢ = 269¢

⑩ $5 and ■ ¢ = 507¢

⑪ $7 and 81¢ = ■ ¢

⑫ $ ■ and ■ ¢ = 357¢

⑬ $5 and 10¢ = ■ ¢

⑭ $5 and 4¢ = ■ ¢

⑮ $ ■ and ■ ¢ = 807¢

⑯ $5 and 9¢ = ■ ¢

⑰ ■ ¢ = $6 and 5¢

⑱ $5 and 90¢ = ■ ¢

⑲ ■ ¢ = $6 and 50¢

⑳ $ ■ and ■ ¢ = 2034¢

㉑ $6 and 53¢ = ■ ¢

㉒ $ ■ and ■ ¢ = 322¢

㉓ Look at the items at the garage sale. Which pairs of items can be bought for less than $1?

Solve for *n*. Watch the signs.

㉔ $3 \times 9 = n$ ㉕ $4 \times 7 = n$ ㉖ $32 \div 4 = n$

㉗ $7 \times 5 = n$ ㉘ $63 \div 7 = n$ ㉙ $6 \times 6 = n$

㉚ $7 \times 8 = n$ ㉛ $72 \div 8 = n$ ㉜ $2 \times 5 = n$

㉝ $36 \div 4 = n$ ㉞ $60 \div 10 = n$ ㉟ $9 \times 9 = n$

㊱ $7 \times 6 = n$ ㊲ $6 \times 4 = n$ ㊳ $24 \div 3 = n$

㊴ $6 \times 8 = n$ ㊵ $12 \div 2 = n$ ㊶ $72 \div 9 = n$

Solve. Watch the signs.

㊷ $\begin{array}{r} 320 \\ -\ 205 \end{array}$ ㊸ $\begin{array}{r} 4230 \\ +\ 5985 \end{array}$ ㊹ $\begin{array}{r} 6050 \\ -\ 3296 \end{array}$ ㊺ $\begin{array}{r} 367 \\ 484 \\ 872 \\ +\ 906 \end{array}$

㊻ $\begin{array}{r} 763 \\ 105 \\ 342 \\ +\ 317 \end{array}$ ㊼ $\begin{array}{r} 8905 \\ -\ 4667 \end{array}$ ㊽ $\begin{array}{r} 591 \\ +\ 388 \end{array}$ ㊾ $\begin{array}{r} 6333 \\ +\ 7888 \end{array}$

Solve.

㊿ Dr. Tate took 18 hours to write his report. He worked on the report the same number of hours every day for six days. How many hours did he work on the report each day?

51 A truck driver unloaded 24 boxes. She made four equal stacks. How many boxes were in each stack?

LESSON 97

Rewriting Dollars and Cents

Rewrite to show less than 100¢. The first one has been done for you.

1. $1 and 120¢ = **$2** and **20¢**

2. $1 and 150¢ = $ ▣ and ▣ ¢

3. $1 and 250¢ = $ ▣ and ▣ ¢

4. $3 and 250¢ = $ ▣ and ▣ ¢

5. $10 and 129¢ = $ ▣ and ▣ ¢

6. $4 and 105¢ = $ ▣ and ▣ ¢

7. $4 and 205¢ = $ ▣ and ▣ ¢

8. $9 and 100¢ = $ ▣ and ▣ ¢

Solve.

Patti has a one-dollar bill and 350¢.

9. Does she have enough to buy two cans of tennis balls that cost $2 each?

10. Does she have enough to buy ten pens that cost 39¢ each?

11. Does she have enough money to buy a baseball cap that costs $6?

Talk about the Thinking Story "A Paneful Story (Part 2)."

Dollars and Cents Game

COOPERATIVE LEARNING

GAME

Players:	Two
Materials:	Two 0–5 cubes (red), two 5–10 cubes (blue), a score form like the one below for each player
Object:	To make a greater total amount of money
Math Focus:	Rewriting amounts of money to show less than 100 cents

RULES

1. Take turns rolling all four cubes and making two two-digit numbers.

2. Add the two two-digit numbers and write the total to the left of the first or the next available equal sign on your score form. For example, if your sum is 156, you would write: <u>156¢</u> = $____ and ____¢.

3. Fill in the blanks to the right of the equal sign. You must write less than 100 in the right-hand cents blank, like this: <u>156¢</u> = $ <u>1</u> and <u>56</u> ¢.

4. When the score card is filled in, add the number of dollars and cents beside "Totals" on the score form.

5. Change the totals to a number of dollars and cents, with the number of cents less than 100. For example, 162 cents would be changed to $1 and 62¢. Write the new total beside "Total money" on the score card.

6. The player with the greater total amount of money wins.

Score Card

____ ¢ = $ ____ and ____ ¢

____ ¢ = $ ____ and ____ ¢

____ ¢ = $ ____ and ____ ¢

____ ¢ = $ ____ and ____ ¢

Totals: $ ____ and ____ ¢

Total money = $ ____ and ____ ¢

Decimals: Tenths and Hundredths

This circle is divided into 100 equal parts.

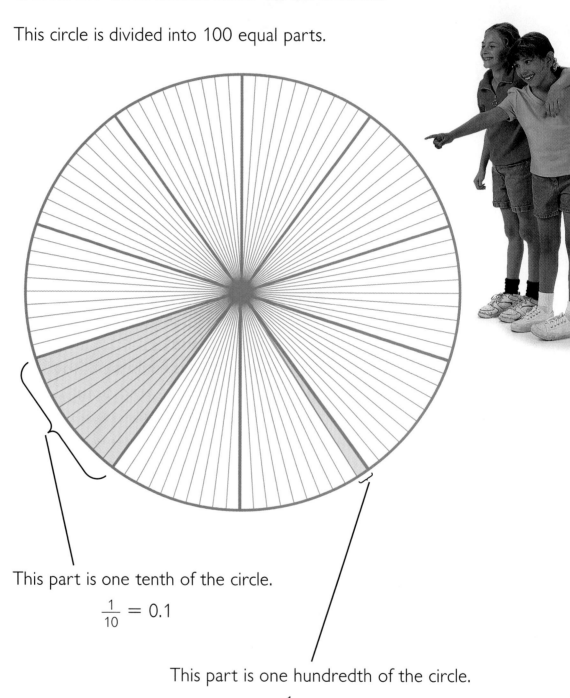

This part is one tenth of the circle.

$$\frac{1}{10} = 0.1$$

This part is one hundredth of the circle.

$$\frac{1}{100} = 0.01$$

Complete each statement.

There are 10 hundredths in 1 tenth.

$$0.10 = 0.1$$

1 1 dime =  cents

2 1 dm = ■ cm

3 There are ■ hundredths in 5 tenths.

4 0.5 = ■

5 5 dimes = ■ cents

6 5 dm = ■ cm

7 There are 80 hundredths in ■ tenths.

8 ■ = 0.80

9 ■ dimes = 80 cents

10 ■ dm = 80 cm

11 There are 30 hundredths in ■ tenths.

12 ■ = 0.30

13 ■ dimes = 30¢

14 ■ dm = 30 cm

15 There are 60 hundredths in ■ tenths.

16 ■ = 0.60

17 ■ dimes = 60¢

18 ■ dm = 60 cm

LESSON 99

Inequalities and Basic Operations Practice

What is the correct sign? Draw <, >, or =.

1 34 ● 46

2 12.1 ● 1.21

3 3.4 ● 4.6

4 70.04 ● 7.4

5 6.43 ● 6.5

6 5.4 ● 5.04

7 5.7 ● 5.70

8 3.7 ● 3.70

9 1 ● 0.1

10 2.10 ● 1.3

11 31.20 ● 31.26

12 8.0 ● 3.2

13 5.4 ● 50.4

14 14.34 ● 14.44

15 6.30 ● 7.2

16 0.5 ● 0.10

17 2.1 ● 1.21

18 1.05 ● 1.50

19 70.0 ● 7.00

20 4.36 ● 4.63

21 0.7 ● 1.02

22 9.9 ● 10.1

23 0.3 ● 0.03

24 81 ● 81.0

25 5.2 ● 5.08

26 3.31 ● 13.13

Number correct ▪

Solve these problems. Watch the signs.

27 6
× 7

28 4
× 8

29 9
− 6

30 7
× 3

31 5
− 2

32 7
× 8

33 4
+ 9

34 8
× 8

35 5
× 7

36 10
+ 6

37 634
+ 269

38 300
− 158

39 4724
+ 986

40 7100
− 600

41 3277
− 333

42 9588
− 8570

43 24 ÷ 8 = ■

44 18 − 9 = ■

45 17 ÷ 7 = ■

46 9 × 4 = ■

47 45 ÷ 5 = ■

48 2 × 4 = ■

49 6 × 9 = ■

50 17 − 8 = ■

51 40 ÷ 10 = ■

52 48 ÷ 6 = ■

53 10 × 8 = ■

54 4 × 10 = ■

GAME

Play the "Harder Rummage Sale" game.

Adding Decimals

If you had $3.86 and you earned $4.75 raking leaves, how much money would you have now? Add the two numbers to find out.

$3.86 + $4.75 = ?

$$\begin{array}{r} 3.86 \\ + \ 4.75 \\ \hline \end{array}$$
Line up the decimal points.

$$\begin{array}{r} {\scriptstyle 1\ 1} \\ 3.86 \\ + \ 4.75 \\ \hline \mathbf{8.61} \end{array}$$
Add.

6.39 + 2.4 = ?

$$\begin{array}{r} 6.39 \\ + \ 2.4 \\ \hline \end{array}$$
Line up the decimal points.

$$\begin{array}{r} 6.39 \\ + \ 2.40 \\ \hline \end{array}$$
If it helps, put in a 0 (because 2.4 and 2.40 have the same value).

$$\begin{array}{r} 6.39 \\ + \ 2.40 \\ \hline \mathbf{8.79} \end{array}$$
Add.

Add.

1　3.27
　　+ 2.48

2　7.63
　　+ 1.54

3　5.4
　　+ 2.55

4　8.31
　　+ 4.24

5　7.45
　　+ 6.7

6　1.30
　　+ 2.74

7　10.28
　　+ 17.94

8　12.34
　　+ 19.8

9　43.72
　　+ 56.28

10　2.4
　　+ 1.65

11　325.6
　　+ 35.3

12　98.6
　　+ 98.6

13 4.3 + 1.5 = ■

14 9 + 5.6 = ■

15 2.5 + 4 = ■

16 4.2 + 1.05 = ■

17 25.6 + 30.2 = ■

18 3.4 + 10.4 = ■

19 86.8 + 2.7 = ■

20 121.8 + 72.2 = ■

Solve.

21 Olga ran 100 meters in 14.3 seconds. Jenny ran the same distance, but 3.7 seconds slower. What was Jenny's time?

22 Bill wants to run 20 kilometers this week. Monday he ran 8.4 kilometers. Tuesday he ran 4.8 kilometers. How far has Bill run so far this week?

◆ LESSON 100 Adding Decimals

Solve these problems.

23 How much do the bicycle and the water bottle cost together?

$82.30

$10.41

24 Jason ran a lap around the track in 45.3 seconds. He ran a second lap in 53.8 seconds. How fast did he run the two laps together?

25 Lynda had $2.73. Then she earned $1.50. How much does she have now?

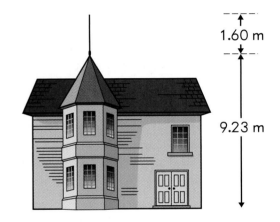

1.60 m

9.23 m

26 It is 9.23 meters from the ground to the top of the house. The antenna is 1.6 meters tall. How far is it from the ground to the top of the antenna?

27 Sunnie bought some apples for $2.36 and some pineapples for $12.95. How much did she spend all together?

28 Mr. Bourne drives to work and back each day. If he lives 76.54 kilometers from work, how far does he drive in a day?

29 Juanita counted her money. She had seven dimes and four cents. Then she earned $5.75 more. She wants to buy a toy that costs $6.50. Does she have enough money? If so, how much money will she have left? If not, how much more money does she need?

30 Building laws in Shasta say that a house cannot be more than 6.5 meters from front to back. Ms. Soto measured her house. It was exactly 5.75 meters from front to back. But she forgot to measure the small front porch. The porch floor sticks out 7 decimeters from the house. The porch railing sticks out another 4 centimeters. Does the house follow the law? If so, how much extra room does Ms. Soto have? If not, how far over the limit is the house?

5.75m   7dm 4cm

31 Sonia can usually jump about 2.6 meters. She marked a spot 2.6 meters from the starting line. On her first jump, she landed 53 cm past that mark. How far did she jump?

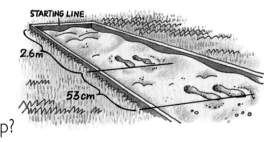

32 The next time Sonia jumped, she landed 53 centimeters short of the 2.6-meter mark. How far did she jump this time?

Subtracting Decimals

If you had $23.79 and you bought a book for $10.82, how much money would you have left? Subtract to find out.

$23.79 − $10.82 = **?**

$$
\begin{array}{r}
23.79 \\
-\ 10.82 \\
\end{array}
$$
Line up the decimal points.

$$
\begin{array}{r}
\overset{2\ \ 17}{2\cancel{3}.\cancel{7}9} \\
-\ 10.82 \\
\hline
\mathbf{12.97} \\
\end{array}
$$
Subtract.

4.6 − 3.25 = **?**

$$
\begin{array}{r}
4.6 \\
-\ 3.25 \\
\end{array}
$$
Line up the decimal points.

$$
\begin{array}{r}
4.6\mathbf{0} \\
-\ 3.25 \\
\end{array}
$$
If it helps, put in a 0 (because 4.6 and 4.60 have the same value).

$$
\begin{array}{r}
\overset{5\ 10}{4.\cancel{6}\cancel{0}} \\
-\ 3.25 \\
\hline
\mathbf{1.35} \\
\end{array}
$$
Subtract.

Subtract.

1.   12.73
    − 9.06

2.   5.45
    − 2.9

3.   10.00
    − 2.50

4.   43.85
    − 27.8

5.   63.5
    − 18.55

6.   2.05
    − 1.38

7.   5.09
    − 4.92

8.   6.43
    − 2.31

9.   4.7
    − 4

10. 10.00
    − 0.03

11. 17.4
    − 15.26

12. 12.07
    − 9.38

13. $7.0 - 3.5 = $ ■

14. $8.30 - 4.17 = $ ■

15. $11.7 - 2.9 = $ ■

16. $4.2 - 1.75 = $ ■

17. $8.03 - 4.17 = $ ■

18. $3.5 - 1.5 = $ ■

19. $5.6 - 1.43 = $ ■

20. $0.9 - 0.85 = $ ■

21. $12.2 - 6.6 = $ ■

22. $5.06 - 1.43 = $ ■

23. $0.42 - 0.39 = $ ■

24. $0.03 - 0.03 = $ ■

Solve.

25. On Monday Nikki bought a pair of sneakers for $42.99. On Tuesday the same sneakers went on sale for $40.50. How much would Nikki have saved if she had waited a day to buy the sneakers?

26. Agatha spent $3.43 for milk and bread. The bread cost $1.39. How much was the milk?

◆ LESSON 101 Subtracting Decimals

Choose the correct answer. Look for shortcuts.

㉗

$4.35 - 2.1 = \blacksquare$

a. 4.14
b. 2.25
c. 2.24

㉘

$106 - 5.43 = \blacksquare$

a. 437
b. 51.7
c. 100.57

㉙

$3.7 + 4.65 = \blacksquare$

a. 5.02
b. 7.35
c. 8.35

㉚

$3.74 + 8.79 = \blacksquare$

a. 11.53
b. 12.53
c. 13.53

㉛

$10.3 + 4.76 = \blacksquare$

a. 15.06
b. 57.9
c. 5.79

㉜

$8.79 - 3.74 = \blacksquare$

a. 5.05
b. 4.95
c. 4.05

㉝

$10.3 - 4.76 = \blacksquare$

a. 3.73
b. 5.54
c. 15.06

㉞

$73.2 - 6.47 = \blacksquare$

a. 8.5
b. 67.73
c. 66.73

㉟

$106 + 5.43 = \blacksquare$

a. 111.43
b. 160.3
c. 649

㊱

$73.2 + 6.47 = \blacksquare$

a. 79.67
b. 13.79
c. 137.9

In your Math Journal write about a shortcut you used to solve these problems.

REAL-WORLD CONNECTION

Solve these problems.

37 Ms. Swenson has a pole that is 2 meters long. She wants to cut it so that it is 1.55 meters long. How long a piece must she cut off?

38 Sid is saving his money to buy a football. It costs $12. He has $5.65 in his bank. How much more money does he need?

39 Mr. Rice bought some gum for 55 cents. He gave the storekeeper a $5 bill. How much change should the storekeeper give Mr. Rice?

40 Before today, Andrea had ridden her bicycle a total of 274.8 kilometers. Now she has ridden her bicycle a total of 275.4 kilometers. How far did Andrea ride today?

41 Sylvia weighed 52.3 kilograms. A month later she had gained 3.96 kilograms. How much does she weigh now?

42 Megan had $7.43. She bought a book. She had $1.48 left. How much did the book cost?

LESSON 102

Adding and Subtracting Decimals

Solve these problems. Look for problems that are alike.

①
```
   823
 − 159
```

②
```
   243
 +  61
```

③
```
   82.3
 − 15.9
```

④
```
   307
 − 180
```

⑤
```
   351
 +  39
```

⑥
```
   3.51
 + 0.39
```

⑦
```
   3.07
 − 1.8
```

⑧
```
   8.23
 − 1.59
```

⑨
```
   2.43
 + 0.61
```

⑩
```
   35.1
 +  3.9
```

⑪
```
   24.3
 +  6.1
```

⑫
```
   823
 − 159
```

⑬
```
   3.33
 + 0.61
```

⑭
```
    61
 + 243
```

⑮
```
   30.7
 − 18
```

⑯
```
   26.3
 + 58
```

⑰
```
   29.33
 −  6.72
```

⑱
```
   36.83
 − 19.17
```

⑲
```
    8.9
 + 12.33
```

⑳
```
   8.10
 − 6.87
```

In your Math Journal tell how looking for problems that are alike can help you solve the problems.

What is the right sign? Draw <, > or =.

㉑ 2.3 ● 2.7   **㉒** 22 ● 2.02   **㉓** 14.41 ● 14.14

㉔ 0.50 ● 1.2   **㉕** 1.51 ● 1.15   **㉖** 3.10 ● 31.0

㉗ 63 ● 7.4   **㉘** 3.5 ● 4.5   **㉙** 8.7 ● 8.70

㉚ 1.80 ● 1.08   **㉛** 3.5 ● 0.45   **㉜** 6.42 ● 6.49

㉝ 3.4 ● 3.07   **㉞** 10.1 ● 10.01   **㉟** 201 ● 20.1

㊱ 0.9 ● 4   **㊲** 0.2 ● 4.06   **㊳** 11 ● 0.111

㊴ 13.50 ● 13.47   **㊵** 5 ● 5.00   **㊶** 49.2 ● 149

㊷ 12 ● 12.0   **㊸** 42.40 ● 42.36   **㊹** 16.5 ● 12.8

㊺ 0.64 ● 1.0   **㊻** 3.10 ● 2.3   **㊼** 97.8 ● 89.3

㊽ 0.08 ● 3   **㊾** 21.1 ● 2.11   **㊿** 16 ● 16.0

GAME   **Play the "Store" game.**

103 Organizing Data

Mrs. Hartman's third-grade class recorded their ages in months. Here are the ages of all the students.

134	129	126	137	134	142	127	128	130	134
131	130	128	132	139	129	125	137	136	128
136	132	126	126	130	135	132	130	132	129

1 List the numbers in order from least to greatest.

2 What is the least number in your list?

3 What is the greatest number?

4 Which numbers appear most often?

Here are the students' scores on Mrs. Hartman's math test.

83	85	91	62	85	74	95	68	92	94
85	97	73	78	80	86	88	91	93	87
81	79	76	83	82	96	84	82	85	86

5 What is the lowest score?

6 What is the highest score?

7 What is the most common score?

In your Math Journal explain the method you used to sort the numbers in these problems. Share your method with the class.

In the chart below, the number 91 is written as 9 tens and 1 one. The number 83 is written as 8 tens and 3 ones. The number 85 is written as 8 tens and 5 ones. In the "8 tens" row the 3 stands for 83, and the 5 stands for 85. If you wanted to write another number 85 in the chart, you would write another 5 in the "8 tens" row under "Ones."

Tens	Ones
9	1
8	3, 5
7	
6	

◆ Copy the chart above and use the math scores on page 290 to complete it.

◆ Is it now easier to find the lowest, highest, and most common scores?

◆ Could you now easily put the scores in order from lowest to highest?

Measure the height in centimeters of each member of your class. Record the heights on a sheet of paper. Arrange the heights in order from shortest to tallest.

8 What is the shortest height on your list?

9 What is the tallest height?

10 What is the most common height?

LESSON
104

Applied Addition and Subtraction of Decimals

Solve these problems.

1 One book is 25 centimeters across. How many meters long is a row of five books?

25 cm

2 Each book at the garage sale costs 25¢. How much do five books cost?

Kelsey is 1.32 meters tall. Lindsay is 1.28 meters tall.

3 Who is taller?

4 How many meters taller?

5 How many centimeters taller?

6 Mr. Brown had $10. He spent some money at the football game. He has $5.73 left. How much did Mr. Brown spend?

Solve.

7 The sides of Mrs. Blake's lawn measure 10.5 meters, 12.6 meters, 11.9 meters, and 9.76 meters. How many meters of fencing does she need to surround her lawn?

Ms. Garza needs two boards, each 28.5 centimeters in length. She can buy boards that are 50 centimeters long.

8 How many boards will she need to buy?

9 When Ms. Garza cuts the boards she needs, how many boards will she have left? How long will they be?

Jeff's dog, Spot, weighs 9.75 pounds. Ahmad's dog, Rover, weighs 9.40 pounds.

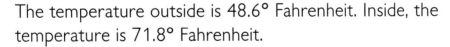

10 Which dog weighs more? How much more?

11 Jorge wants to buy a baseball mitt that costs $35.95. He only has $26.50. How much more does he need?

12 One lap around the block is 2.1 kilometers. How far is four laps?

The temperature outside is 48.6° Fahrenheit. Inside, the temperature is 71.8° Fahrenheit.

13 Is it colder inside or outside?

14 How much colder?

Make up at least three problems and write them in your Math Journal. Solve them. Use them in the next lesson to challenge the rest of the class.

Play the "Harder Checkbook" game.

Using Decimals

Solve these problems.

1. Wei made curtains for one window. She used 2.68 yards of cloth. How many yards of cloth will she need to make curtains for four more windows the same size?

2. Wei is buying 10.8 yards of cloth. The piece at the store is 14.5 yards long. What length of cloth will be left?

3. The cloth costs $35.26. Wei gave the storekeeper two $20 bills. How much change should Wei get?

4. Wei decided to buy 2 yards of fancy cloth to make a pillowcase. The fancy cloth costs $8.99 per yard. How much did Wei spend?

5. How much would she spend if she bought 3 yards of the fancy cloth?

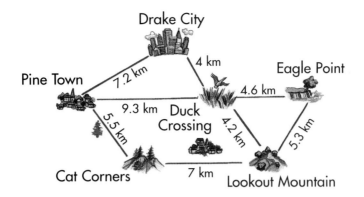

Solve.

6 How far is it from Pine Town to Duck Crossing?

7 How far is it from Pine Town to Eagle Point?

8 How far is it from Pine Town to Lookout Mountain if you go through Duck Crossing?

9 How far is it from Pine Town to Lookout Mountain if you go through Cat Corners?

10 If you go from Lookout Mountain to Pine Town, is it shorter to go through Duck Crossing or Cat Corners?

11 How much shorter?

12 Suppose you are going from Duck Crossing to Pine Town. How much farther would it be to go through Drake City?

13 What is the shortest route from Eagle Point to Cat Corners?

14 How many kilometers is that route?

15 If you left from Drake City and traveled 8.2 kilometers, which town would you end up in?

If a bird flew directly between Cat Corners and Duck Crossing, about how far would it fly? In your Math Journal tell how you got your answer.

Talk about the Thinking Story "Mosquito Lake."

◆ LESSON 105   Using Decimals

Solve these problems.

16 Mary saved 25¢ each week. After a while she began keeping a record of how much money she had. This is what she had for the past five weeks.

Week	1	2	3	4	5	6	7	8	9	10
Amount	$4.50	$4.75	$5.00	$5.25	$5.50	■	■	■	■	■

Mary wonders how much money she will have five weeks from now. Continue the pattern for five more weeks. Tell how much money Mary will have.

17 Selena earns some money each week, but she also spends some. Three weeks ago she had $7.10. Two weeks ago she had $6.75. Last week she had $6.40. This week she has only $6.05. At this rate, how much money will she have next week? How much money will she have the week after next?

18 Scott is putting books on his bookshelf. Each book is 5 centimeters thick. The bookshelf is 1.5 meters long. Scott wants to know how much space will be used by one book, two books, and so on. Copy and complete the table. How much space will Scott have used after 10 books?

Space on Scott's Bookshelf										
Number of Books	1	2	3	4	5	6	7	8	9	10
Space Used	0.05	0.1	0.15	0.2	0.25	0.3	0.35	■	■	■

Find the rule for each number series. Write four more numbers in each series.

19 1.4, 1.6, 1.8, 2.0, ■, ■, ■, ■, 3.0

20 $2, $2.50, $3, $3.50, ■, ■, ■, ■, $6

21 8.7, 8.3, 7.9, 7.5, ■, ■, ■, ■, 5.5

22 8.70, 8.35, 8, 7.65, ■, ■, ■, ■, 5.9

23 $9.05, $8.70, $8.35, $8, ■, ■, ■, ■, $6.25

24 $9, $8.65, $8.30, $7.95, ■, ■, ■, ■, $6.20

25 $9.45, $9.10, $8.75, $8.40, ■, ■, ■, ■, $6.65

26 5.9, 6.25, 6.6, 6.95, ■, ■, ■, ■, 8.7

27 5.85, 6.2, 6.55, 6.9, ■, ■, ■, ■, 8.65

28 1, 1.45, 1.9, 2.35, ■, ■, ■, ■, 4.6

29 3.14, 3.51, 3.88, 4.25, ■, ■, ■, ■, 6.1

30 6.4, 6.19, 5.98, 5.77, ■, ■, ■, ■, 4.72

Practicing Basic Operations

Solve these problems. Watch the signs.

1
```
   5.3
-  2.1
```

2
```
   5.47
-  3.6
```

3
```
   2.4
-  1.87
```

4
```
   4.71
+  5.62
```

5
```
   5.62
+  4.71
```

6
```
   5.62
-  4.71
```

7
```
   3.8
+  1.2
```

8
```
   4.07
-  3.7
```

9
```
   12.13
-   8.6
```

10 $5.81 - 3.28 = $ ■

11 $9.03 + 9.3 = $ ■

12 $2.66 - 1.7 = $ ■

13 $7.56 + 9.33 = $ ■

14 $4.2 - 1.75 = $ ■

15 $3.44 - 2.07 = $ ■

16 $5.4 + 8.17 = $ ■

17 $12.1 + 4.79 = $ ■

Number correct ■

Solve.

18 Each time Amy adds a book to her bookshelf, she records how much room is left on the shelf in centimeters. All her books are the same thickness. Copy and complete Amy's table.

Space on Amy's Bookshelf									
Number of Books	5	6	7	8	9	10	11	12	13
Space Left	1.03	0.99	0.95	0.91	0.87	0.83	■	■	■

Make up five problems using the map below and solve them. Write your problems in your Math Journal and explain how to solve them.

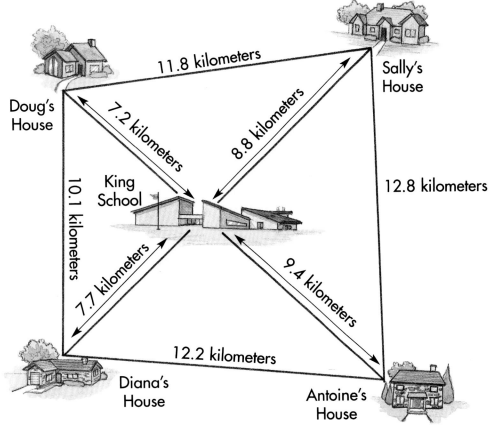

Fractions: Halves, Thirds, and Fourths

Listen as your teacher explains the "Coloring Halves, Thirds, and Fourths" activity.

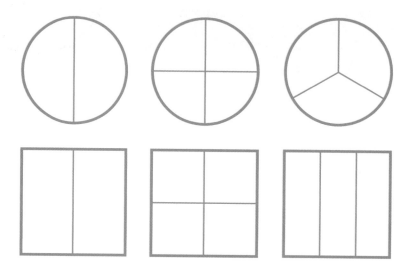

What fraction of each figure is colored? To find out, you count the number of parts (bottom number in a fraction) and the number of colored parts (top number in a fraction).

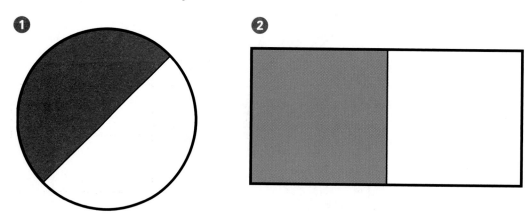

❶   ❷

What fraction of each figure is colored?

3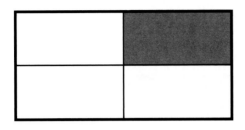

4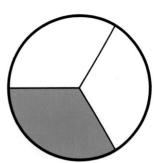

5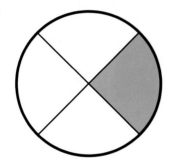

6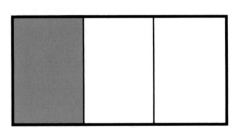

7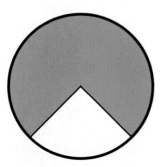

8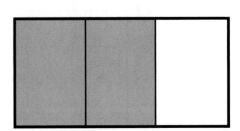

Fractions of Sets

Tell how many parts the rectangle or line segment is divided into. Tell how many dividing lines were drawn. The first one has been done for you.

	Number of Parts	Number of Dividing Lines
1	2	1
2	■	■
3	■	■
4	■	■
5	■	■
6	■	■
7	■	■
8	■	■

Answer these questions.

9 Which is bigger, $\frac{1}{2}$ of the cake or $\frac{1}{3}$ of the cake?

10 Which is bigger, $\frac{1}{2}$ of the pie or $\frac{1}{5}$ of the pie?

11 Which is bigger, $\frac{1}{3}$ of the loaf of bread or $\frac{1}{5}$ of the loaf?

12 Which is bigger, $\frac{1}{3}$ of the pizza or $\frac{1}{4}$ of the pizza?

13 Which is bigger, $\frac{1}{2}$ of the muffin or $\frac{1}{4}$ of the muffin?

14 Which is bigger, $\frac{1}{4}$ of the apple or $\frac{1}{2}$ of the apple?

15 Which is bigger, $\frac{1}{5}$ of the banana or $\frac{1}{2}$ of the banana?

16 Which is bigger, $\frac{1}{3}$ of the sandwich or $\frac{1}{4}$ of the sandwich?

In your Math Journal tell how you got your answer to problem 16.

◆ **LESSON 108** **Fractions of Sets**

What fraction is colored?

17

18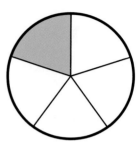

19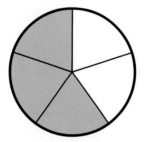

20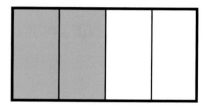

21

22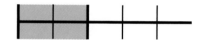

23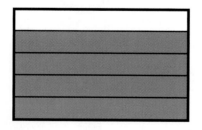

24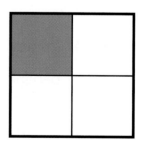

 **Play the "Fraction" game.**

Answer these questions.

25 Which picture is $\frac{2}{3}$ shaded? Explain why the other pictures don't show $\frac{2}{3}$.

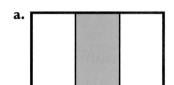

26 Which picture is $\frac{3}{5}$ shaded? Explain why the other pictures don't show $\frac{3}{5}$.

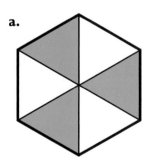
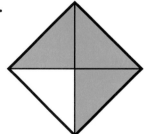
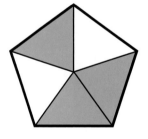

27 Which picture is $\frac{1}{6}$ shaded? Explain why the other pictures don't show $\frac{1}{6}$.

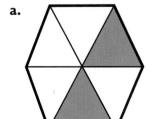
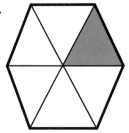

Mixed Numbers

Sometimes we use fractions for numbers greater than 1. For example, Matt baked three whole pies. He served half a pie. He still had two whole pies and another half-pie left. He has two and one half, or $2\frac{1}{2}$, pies left. If he had served only $\frac{1}{4}$ of a pie, he would have $2\frac{3}{4}$ pies left.

We call numbers like $2\frac{1}{2}$ and $2\frac{3}{4}$ **mixed numbers** because they mix whole numbers and fractions.

Copy each number line. Write in the missing numbers for the colored points. Use fractions, whole numbers, and mixed numbers.

1

0　$\frac{1}{2}$　1　　　　4　　5　　　　7

2
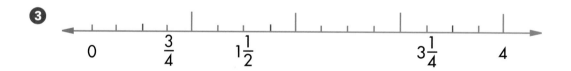
0　　$\frac{2}{3}$　1　　　3　　$3\frac{2}{3}$　　　5

3

0　　$\frac{3}{4}$　　$1\frac{1}{2}$　　　　$3\frac{1}{4}$　　4

4

0　　$\frac{3}{5}$　1　　　　$3\frac{3}{5}$　　$5\frac{1}{5}$　6

Remember that in a number sentence, the greater number is on the side of the sign with the larger opening.

Copy and replace the ● with <, >, or = to make a true statement.

5 $5 \bullet 5\frac{2}{3}$

6 $2\frac{4}{5} \bullet 2\frac{3}{4}$

7 $4\frac{1}{2} \bullet 3\frac{1}{3}$

8 $5\frac{4}{5} \bullet 5\frac{3}{4}$

9 $1\frac{1}{2} \bullet 1\frac{3}{4}$

10 $5\frac{4}{5} \bullet 6\frac{3}{4}$

11 $\frac{3}{5} \bullet 1\frac{1}{5}$

12 $5\frac{4}{5} \bullet 4\frac{3}{4}$

13 $\frac{4}{5} \bullet \frac{3}{4}$

14 $6\frac{2}{5} \bullet 6\frac{3}{4}$

15 $7\frac{2}{3} \bullet 8\frac{3}{4}$

16 $\frac{2}{3} \bullet \frac{3}{4}$

17 $7\frac{2}{3} \bullet 7\frac{3}{4}$

18 $5\frac{2}{3} \bullet 5\frac{3}{4}$

19 $7\frac{2}{3} \bullet 6\frac{3}{4}$

20 $3\frac{1}{5} \bullet 2\frac{3}{5}$

Solve.

21 Margaret has three boxes of green pens and $\frac{3}{4}$ of a box of red pens. How many boxes of pens does she have?

22 Natasha has three boxes of green pens and $\frac{1}{2}$ box of red pens. How many boxes of pens does she have?

23 Who has more pens?

In your Math Journal write instructions for how to decide which mixed number is greater. What do you look at first? Then what?

LESSON 110

Practice with Fractions of Sets

You may use manipulatives to act out these problems.

Rosalie divided 15 coins into 3 equal piles.

1 How many coins are there in each pile?

2 $\frac{1}{3}$ of 15 is ▪.

She divided 10 coins into 5 equal piles.

3 Draw the 5 piles.

4 How many coins are there in each pile?

5 $\frac{1}{5}$ of 10 is ▪.

6 $\frac{1}{4}$ of 16 is ▪.   **7** $\frac{1}{3}$ of 9 = ▪.

   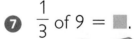

8 $\frac{1}{4}$ of 12 is ▪.   **9** $\frac{1}{2}$ of 12 is ▪.

10 $\frac{1}{5}$ of 15 is ▪.   **11** $\frac{2}{5}$ of 15 is ▪.

Use the picture to help answer the questions.
You may also use coins or other objects.

12 How many stars are there?

13 $\frac{1}{2}$ of 12 is ■   **14** ■ is $\frac{5}{6}$ of 12   **15** $\frac{1}{3}$ of 12 is ■

16 $\frac{6}{6}$ of 12 is ■   **17** $\frac{1}{4}$ of 12 is ■   **18** $\frac{2}{12}$ of 12 is ■

19 $\frac{1}{6}$ of 12 is ■   **20** $\frac{3}{12}$ of 12 is ■   **21** $\frac{1}{12}$ of 12 is ■

22 $\frac{4}{12}$ of 12 is ■   **23** $\frac{2}{2}$ of 12 is ■   **24** $\frac{5}{12}$ of 12 is ■

25 $\frac{2}{3}$ of 12 is ■   **26** $\frac{6}{12}$ of 12 is ■   **27** $\frac{3}{3}$ of 12 is ■

28 $\frac{7}{12}$ of 12 is ■   **29** $\frac{2}{4}$ of 12 is ■   **30** ■ is $\frac{8}{12}$ of 12

31 ■ is $\frac{3}{4}$ of 12   **32** ■ is $\frac{9}{12}$ of 12   **33** ■ is $\frac{4}{4}$ of 12

34 $\frac{10}{12}$ of 12 is ■   **35** ■ is $\frac{2}{6}$ of 12   **36** $\frac{11}{12}$ of 12 is ■

37 ■ is $\frac{3}{6}$ of 12   **38** $\frac{12}{12}$ of 12 is ■   **39** ■ is $\frac{4}{6}$ of 12

40 Compare your answers to questions 16, 23, 27, 33, and 38. Write a sentence about what these problems have in common.

41 Compare your answers to questions 13, 26, 29, and 37. Write a sentence about these problems.

42 Look for other patterns. Tell what problems follow a pattern. Explain the pattern.

Fractions: Numerators Greater Than 1

To find out what fraction of each circle is colored, count the total number of parts. This is the bottom number (denominator). Then count the number of colored parts. This is the top number (numerator).

What fraction of each circle is colored?

1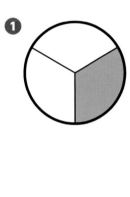

2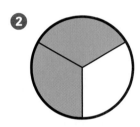

3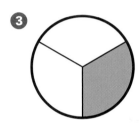

4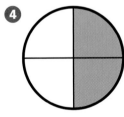

5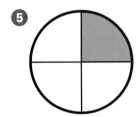

6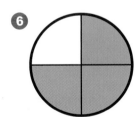

7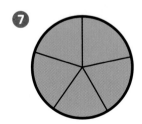

8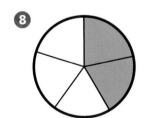

9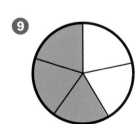

10 Copy or trace this figure four times. Color $\frac{1}{4}$ in four different ways.

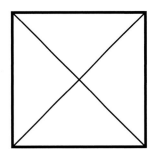

11 Copy or trace this figure six times. Color $\frac{2}{4}$ in six different ways.

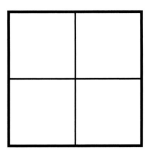

12 Copy or trace this figure four times. Color $\frac{3}{4}$ in four different ways.

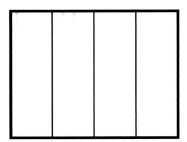

Answer these questions. You may use manipulatives to help.

13 $\frac{1}{4}$ of 12 is ■.

14 $\frac{2}{4}$ of 12 is ■.

15 ■ is $\frac{3}{4}$ of 12.

16 ■ is $\frac{4}{4}$ of 12.

 **Do the "Pouring Fractions" activity.**

 **In your Math Journal describe another strategy you could use to fill $\frac{1}{3}$ of the glass jar.**

◆ **LESSON 111** Fractions: Numerators Greater Than 1

What fraction is colored?

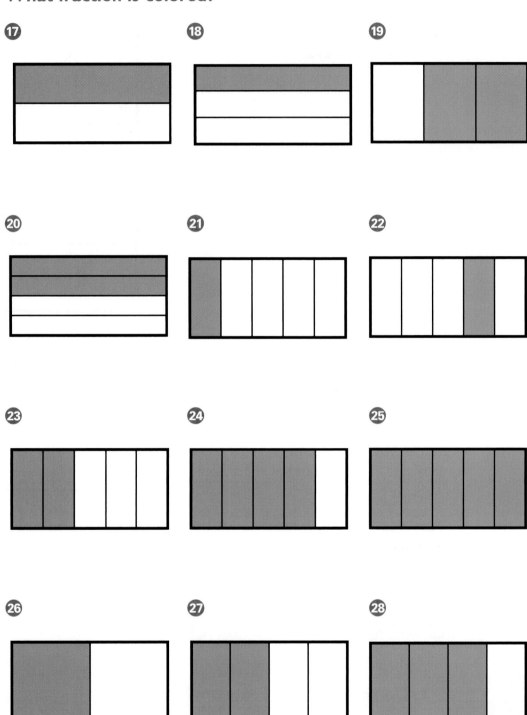

⑰

⑱

⑲

⑳

㉑

㉒

㉓

㉔

㉕

㉖

㉗

㉘

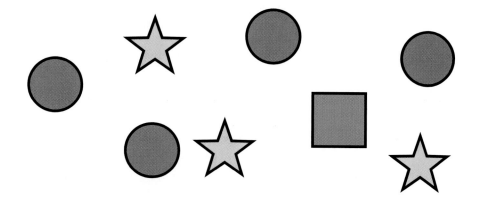

Use the picture to answer the questions.

29 What fraction of the set is stars?

30 What fraction of the set is circles?

31 What fraction of the set is squares?

32 What fraction of the set includes all the stars and all the circles?

33 What fraction of the set is **not** squares?

34 What fraction of the set is **not** circles?

35 What fraction of the set includes all the stars, circles, and squares?

36 What fraction of the set includes **no** stars, circles, or squares?

37 Make your own picture like the one above and write three problems about it. Solve the problems, then share them with the class.

LESSON 112

Halves through Fifths: Practice

Solve.

1 What is the area of the rectangle?

■ square centimeters

2 cm

5 cm

2 Copy or trace the outside of the rectangle. Color $\frac{1}{2}$ of it.

3 What is the area of the part you colored?

■ square centimeters

Remember:
To find the area of a rectangle you multiply the length by the width.

4 What is $\frac{1}{2}$ of 10?

Use manipulatives to help you solve these problems. Work down each column.

5 $\frac{1}{4}$ of 20 is ■.

6 $\frac{2}{4}$ of 20 is ■.

7 $\frac{3}{4}$ of 20 is ■.

8 $\frac{4}{4}$ of 20 is ■.

9 $\frac{1}{2}$ of 10 is ■.

10 $\frac{2}{2}$ of 10 is ■.

11 $\frac{1}{5}$ of 30 is ■.

12 $\frac{3}{5}$ of 30 is ■.

13 $\frac{1}{3}$ of 30 is ■.

14 $\frac{2}{3}$ of 30 is ■.

15 $\frac{1}{4}$ of 40 is ■.

16 $\frac{1}{2}$ of 40 is ■.

Talk about the Thinking Story "The Easy Way and the Breezy Way."

Solve these problems.

17 In Michael's class, $\frac{1}{3}$ of the students are boys. What fraction of the students are girls?

There are 20 students in Bev's class; $\frac{1}{2}$ of them are girls.

18 How many girls are in Bev's class?

19 How many boys are in Bev's class?

20 Julius lives 30 kilometers from where he works. He has driven $\frac{1}{3}$ of the way there. How many kilometers has he driven?

21 There are 60 minutes in one hour. How many minutes are there in $\frac{1}{4}$ of an hour?

22 How many minutes are there in $\frac{1}{2}$ of an hour?

23 Keiko and her four friends want to share a pizza equally. What fraction of the pizza should each person get?

Fractions: Sixths Through Tenths

Remember, the denominator (bottom number) is the total number of parts and the numerator (top number) is the number of colored parts.

What fraction is colored?

1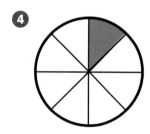

2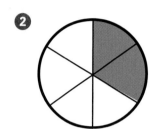

3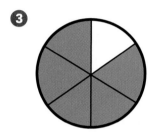

4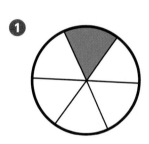

5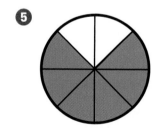

6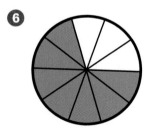

7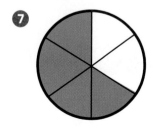

8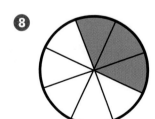

9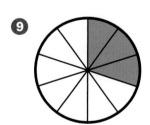

You may use manipulatives to help you solve these problems. Work down the page.

10. $\frac{1}{6}$ of 12 is ■.
11. $\frac{1}{6}$ of 18 is ■.
12. $\frac{2}{6}$ of 12 is ■.
13. $\frac{5}{6}$ of 18 is ■.
14. $\frac{1}{7}$ of 14 is ■.
15. $\frac{2}{7}$ of 14 is ■.
16. $\frac{3}{7}$ of 14 is ■.
17. $\frac{1}{8}$ of 24 is ■.
18. $\frac{2}{8}$ of 24 is ■.
19. $\frac{3}{8}$ of 24 is ■.
20. $\frac{4}{8}$ of 24 is ■.
21. $\frac{1}{4}$ of 24 is ■.
22. $\frac{3}{4}$ of 24 is ■.
23. $\frac{1}{9}$ of 18 is ■.
24. $\frac{2}{9}$ of 18 is ■.
25. $\frac{3}{9}$ of 18 is ■.
26. $\frac{1}{3}$ of 18 is ■.
27. $\frac{1}{10}$ of 30 is ■.
28. $\frac{2}{10}$ of 30 is ■.
29. $\frac{3}{10}$ of 30 is ■.
30. $\frac{1}{10}$ of 20 is ■.
31. $\frac{5}{10}$ of 20 is ■.
32. $\frac{1}{5}$ of 25 is ■.
33. $\frac{2}{5}$ of 25 is ■.
34. $\frac{3}{5}$ of 25 is ■.
35. $\frac{1}{4}$ of 40 is ■.
36. $\frac{2}{4}$ of 40 is ■.
37. $\frac{1}{9}$ of 27 is ■.
38. $\frac{4}{5}$ of 25 is ■.
39. $\frac{2}{9}$ of 27 is ■.
40. $\frac{3}{4}$ of 40 is ■.
41. $\frac{3}{9}$ of 27 is ■.
42. $\frac{1}{3}$ of 27 is ■.

Equivalent Fractions

The same amount can have more than one name.
Look at these pictures.

What fraction is colored?

❶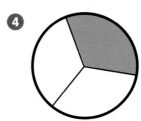

❷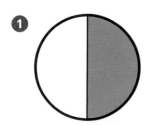

❸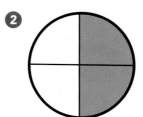

❹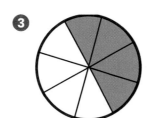

❺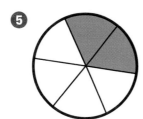

❻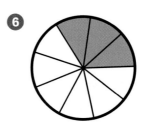

❼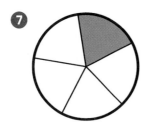

❽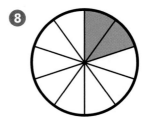

 **Do the "Folding Halves, Fourths, and Eighths" activity.**

What fraction is colored?

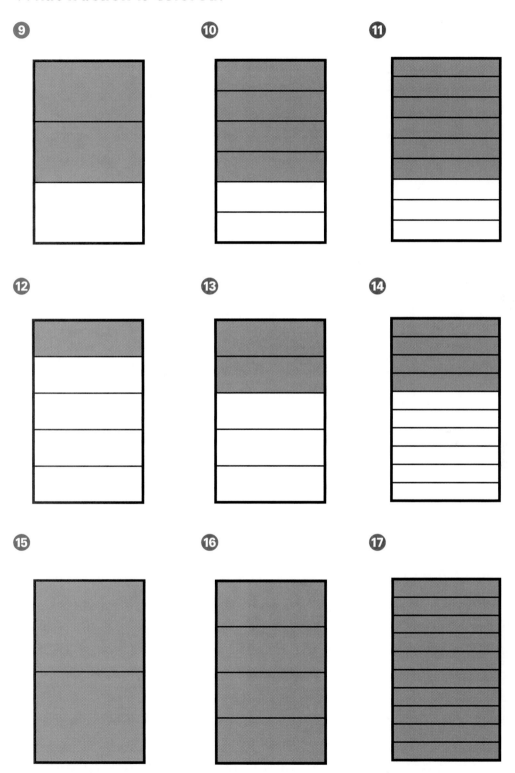

9

10

11

12

13

14

15

16

17

◆ LESSON 114   Equivalent Fractions

Copy each statement and replace the ● with <, >, or = to make a true statement. The picture may help you.

18. $\frac{1}{3}$ ● $\frac{1}{2}$ 19. $\frac{1}{2}$ ● $\frac{2}{5}$ 20. $\frac{2}{3}$ ● $\frac{2}{2}$

21. $\frac{1}{3}$ ● $\frac{1}{4}$ 22. $\frac{1}{2}$ ● $\frac{3}{5}$ 23. $\frac{2}{4}$ ● $\frac{1}{3}$

24. $\frac{1}{3}$ ● $\frac{1}{5}$ 25. $\frac{2}{4}$ ● $\frac{3}{5}$ 26. $\frac{3}{4}$ ● $\frac{1}{5}$

27. $\frac{1}{2}$ ● $\frac{1}{4}$ 28. $\frac{2}{4}$ ● $\frac{2}{5}$ 29. $\frac{1}{4}$ ● $\frac{1}{5}$

30. $\frac{1}{2}$ ● $\frac{2}{4}$ 31. $\frac{2}{4}$ ● $\frac{2}{3}$ 32. $\frac{4}{5}$ ● $\frac{4}{4}$

33. $\frac{1}{2}$ ● $\frac{2}{3}$ 34. $\frac{2}{4}$ ● $\frac{1}{3}$ 35. $\frac{1}{3}$ ● $\frac{1}{3}$

36. $\frac{1}{2}$ ● $\frac{1}{5}$ 37. $\frac{3}{3}$ ● $\frac{4}{5}$ 38. $\frac{4}{5}$ ● $\frac{2}{4}$

Solve.

39. Denise has to keep at least $500 in her bank account. She has $836.33 in her account now. If she withdraws $335.80, will she have at least $500 in her account?

Solve for *n*. Watch the signs.

⓵⓪ $6 \times 3 = n$　　　⓵① $27 \div 9 = n$

⓵② $9 \times 7 = n$　　　⓵③ $7 \times 8 = n$

⓵④ $40 \div 5 = n$　　　⓵⑤ $30 \div 10 = n$

⓵⑥ $6 \times 9 = n$　　　⓵⑦ $5 \times 7 = n$

⓵⑧ $48 \div 6 = n$　　　⓵⑨ $28 \div 4 = n$

Add or subtract.

⑤⓪
```
   505
 − 228
```

⑤①
```
   674
 + 793
```

⑤②
```
   4050
 − 2175
```

⑤③
```
   3200
   2750
 + 1675
```

⑤④
```
   3.05
 + 0.68
```

⑤⑤
```
   3.7
 + 1.85
```

⑤⑥
```
   25.40
 −  8.6
```

⑤⑦
```
   12.6
 −  4.35
```

⑤⑧ $6.2 + 5.4 = \blacksquare$　⑤⑨ $10.5 - 2.5 = \blacksquare$　⑥⓪ $13.2 - 4.6 = \blacksquare$

⑥① $3 - 1.5 = \blacksquare$　⑥② $3 + 1.5 = \blacksquare$　⑥③ $4.5 - 2 = \blacksquare$

⑥④ $12.2 - 6.6 = \blacksquare$　⑥⑤ $5.3 - 3.3 = \blacksquare$　⑥⑥ $17.3 + 8.5 = \blacksquare$

LESSON 115

Equivalent Fractions and Time

When two fractions name the same amount we call them **equivalent fractions**.

What fraction is colored?

1   **2**    **3**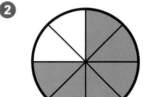

4 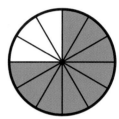   **5** 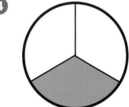   **6**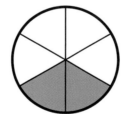

7 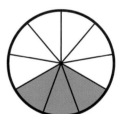   **8** 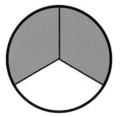   **9**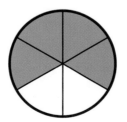

How many minutes?

10 1 hour = ▦ minutes

11 $\frac{1}{2}$ of an hour = ▦ minutes

12 $\frac{2}{2}$ of an hour = ▦ minutes

13 $\frac{2}{4}$ of an hour = ▦ minutes

14 $\frac{3}{4}$ of an hour = ▦ minutes

15 $\frac{4}{4}$ of an hour = ▦ minutes

16 $\frac{1}{3}$ of an hour = ▦ minutes

17 $\frac{2}{3}$ of an hour = ▦ minutes

18 $\frac{3}{3}$ of an hour = ▦ minutes

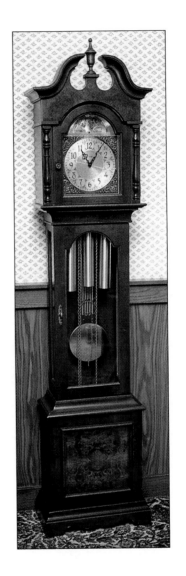

Which is longer?

19 $\frac{1}{2}$ of an hour or $\frac{2}{4}$ of an hour?

20 $\frac{1}{2}$ of an hour or $\frac{1}{4}$ of an hour?

21 $\frac{1}{2}$ of an hour or $\frac{3}{4}$ of an hour?

22 $\frac{2}{2}$ of an hour or $\frac{1}{1}$ of an hour?

23 $\frac{2}{2}$ of an hour or $\frac{4}{4}$ of an hour?

24 $\frac{2}{4}$ of an hour or $\frac{2}{3}$ of an hour?

Unit 3 Review

Solve for *n*. Watch the signs.

1 $6 \times 7 = n$ **2** $3 \times 1 = n$ **3** $8 \times 9 = n$

4 $8 \times 0 = n$ **5** $49 \div 7 = n$ **6** $28 \div 4 = n$

Lesson 99

7 $8 + 9 = n$ **8** $16 - 7 = n$ **9** $6 \times 8 = n$

10 $15 - 8 = n$ **11** $4 \times 5 = n$ **12** $8 \times 7 = n$

Solve these problems. Watch the signs.

Lesson 99

13
$$\begin{array}{r} 8 \\ \times\ 8 \\ \hline \end{array}$$

14
$$\begin{array}{r} 5 \\ +\ 10 \\ \hline \end{array}$$

15
$$\begin{array}{r} 8 \\ \times\ 4 \\ \hline \end{array}$$

16
$$\begin{array}{r} 6 \\ -\ 3 \\ \hline \end{array}$$

17
$$\begin{array}{r} 9 \\ +\ 5 \\ \hline \end{array}$$

What is the right sign? Draw <, >, or =.

Lessons 91, 99

18 2.54 ● 2.70   **19** 2.5 ● 2.50   **20** 0.6 ● 0.45

21 6.67 ● 16.67   **22** 12.1 ● 1.21   **23** 10.5 ● 2.05

24 1.05 ● 1.4   **25** 35.6 ● 40.2   **26** 41.1 ● 41.01

Solve these problems. Watch the signs.

Lesson 100

27.
$$587 + 369$$

28.
$$5.87 + 3.69$$

29.
$$587 - 369$$

30.
$$5.87 - 3.69$$

31.
$$53.20 + 4.78$$

32.
$$26.10 - 13.05$$

33.
$$3.45 + 6.8$$

34.
$$4.6 - 3.15$$

Solve these problems.

Lessons 95, 98, 100, 101

35. $65.30 - 22.21 = \blacksquare$

36. $2.5 \text{ m} = \blacksquare \text{ cm}$

37. $12.8 - 4.6 = \blacksquare$

38. $628¢ = \$ \blacksquare$

39. $1.08 + 1.08 = \blacksquare$

40. $\$4.05 = \blacksquare ¢$

41. $32.6 - 24.25 = \blacksquare$

42. $\$ \blacksquare = 706¢$

43. $21 + 7.5 = \blacksquare$

44. $6 \text{ m} = \blacksquare \text{ dm}$

45. $3 \text{ m} = \blacksquare \text{ cm}$

46. $76 \text{ dm} = \blacksquare \text{ m}$

47. $628 \text{ cm} = \blacksquare \text{ m}$

48. $\blacksquare \text{ dm} = 44.8 \text{ m}$

49. $\blacksquare \text{ cm} = 5.71 \text{ m}$

50. $\blacksquare \text{ cm} = 11 \text{ dm}$

51. $12 + 13.8 = \blacksquare$

52. $\$ \blacksquare = 865¢$

53. $10 \text{ m} = \blacksquare \text{ dm}$

54. $22.64 - 12.75 = \blacksquare$

◆ **LESSON 116   Unit 3 Review**

Solve these problems.

55 The book cost $8.76. Ms. Colson gave the storekeeper a $10 bill. How much change should she get?

56 Jim earned $2.50 today. Now he has $4.75. How much did he have before?

57 Two boxes are stacked together. Each box is 1.5 m tall. How tall is the stack?

58 Danny saved $2.63 last week. He saved $3.49 this week. How much did he save in the two weeks?

59 In October, 7.65 cm of rain fell. In November, 4.38 cm of rain fell. How much did it rain during these two months?

60 Martin has $697.60. He wants to buy a computer and some software. If he spends $435.00 on a computer, how much money will he have left for software?

Try to Make an Inequality

GAME

Players:	**Two**
Materials:	**Two 0–5 cubes (red), two 5–10 cubes (blue)**
Object:	**To fill in an inequality statement correctly**
Math Focus:	**Mental math, basic facts (all four operations), and using relation signs (>, <)**

RULES

1. The first player writes an inequality sign (> or <) and rolls all four cubes.

2. The second player chooses one of the four numbers rolled and one of the four basic operations ($+$, $-$, $\times$, $\div$) and writes them on one side of the inequality sign.

3. The first player tries to make a true statement using the remaining three numbers and any of the four basic operations.

4. The statement must have two numbers and an operation sign on each side of the relation sign.

5. Fractions are not allowed, and neither are division problems with remainders. The division operation cannot be used if it would force the other player to break this rule.

6. If the first player makes a true statement, he or she wins the round. If not, the second player wins the round.

7. Players take turns being first.

SAMPLE GAME

Player 1 writes > and rolls 6, 2, 3, and 8. Player 2 writes $\div$ and 3 to the left of the relation sign. Player 1 must write $6 \div 3$ to the left of the sign, because 8 or 2 would give a remainder. Player 1 must now use 8 and 2 on the right side of the relation sign. Player 1 cannot make a combination of those numbers that is less than $6 \div 3$, so Player 2 wins the round.

Unit Test

Solve for *n*. Watch the signs.

1 $5 \times 6 = n$

2 $12 - 7 = n$

3 $8 \times 8 = n$

4 $2 \times 9 = n$

5 $6 \div 3 = n$

6 $7 \times 8 = n$

7 $4 + 9 = n$

8 $56 \div 8 = n$

9 $3 \times 8 = n$

10 $10 \times 5 = n$

What is the right sign? Draw <, >, or =.

11 3.9 ● 4.3

12 1.05 ● 1.3

13 46.3 ● 46.0

14 0.8 ● 6

15 22.3 ● 2.23

16 0.11 ● 1.0

17 7.2 ● 7.20

18 0.48 ● 0.61

19 8.02 ● 8.1

20 15.7 ● 10.0

21 1.5 ● 1.5

22 10.0 ● .01

Solve these problems. Watch the signs. Use shortcuts when you can.

㉓　　43
　　+ 26

㉔　　63
　　− 29

㉕　　63
　　− 28

㉖　　47
　　+ 86

㉗　　102
　　−　83

㉘　　275
　　+ 125

㉙　　2843
　　+ 1376

㉚　　2843
　　− 1376

㉛　　4.6
　　+ 2.3

㉜　　5.8
　　− 2.4

㉝　　2.5
　　+ 2.5

㉞　　17.05
　　+ 24.7

㉟　　58
　　− 24

㊱　　40.1
　　− 26.0

㊲　　28.43
　　− 13.76

㊳　　6.3
　　− 2.6

㊳⁹ $3.46 - 1.72 = \blacksquare$　　　　**㊵** $4.70 + 10.26 = \blacksquare$

㊶ $6.2 - 3.05 = \blacksquare$　　　　**㊷** $11.7 - 4.8 = \blacksquare$

㊸ $7.02 - 6.1 = \blacksquare$　　　　**㊹** $1.8 + 0.95 = \blacksquare$

㊺ $4.99 + 6.54 = \blacksquare$　　　　**㊻** $5.38 - 4.4 = \blacksquare$

◆ **Unit 3 Test**

What fraction is colored?

47

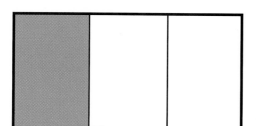

48

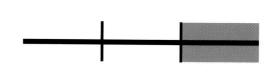

49

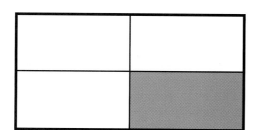

50

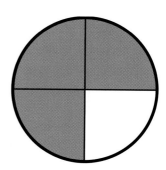

51

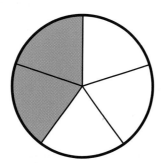

52

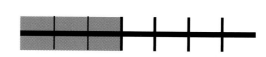

Copy or trace each figure. Color the fractions shown.

53 $\frac{1}{2}$

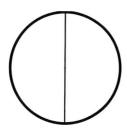

54 $\frac{3}{4}$

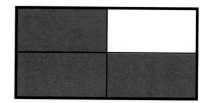

Solve these problems.

55. 300 cm = ■ m

56. ■ cm = 4.28 m

57. 300 cents = $ ■

58. 136 cents = $ ■

59. 6.06 m = ■ dm

60. 318 dm = ■ m

61. Nails cost 5¢ each. How much do six nails cost?

62. At 5¢ each, how much do ten nails cost?

63. Kareem paid 36¢ for four hooks. How much does one hook cost?

64. Nuts are 5¢ each, and bolts are 3¢ each. How many pairs of nuts and bolts can Corinne buy with 34¢?

65. If Corinne bought only nuts with her 34¢, how many could she buy?

66. Would she have enough money left over to buy two bolts?

67. How much more money would Corinne need to buy six nuts and three bolts?

◆ Unit 3 Test

Solve.

68. Jared bought a postcard that cost 46¢. He gave the storekeeper a $5 bill. How much change should he get?

69. How much do the glove and the bat cost together?

70. How much more than the bat does the glove cost?

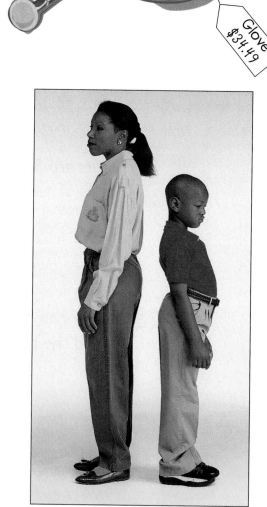

Bat $26.89

Glove $34.49

71. Allison lives 2.5 kilometers from school. She rode her bicycle there and back. How far did she ride?

Mrs. Hayes is 1.70 meters tall. Tyrone is 1.16 meters tall.

72. Who is taller?

73. How much taller?

74. The Quinn's garage door is 7 feet wide. What is the width of the door in inches?

Look at each thermometer.

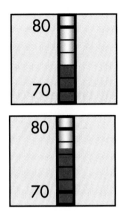

75 What is the temperature?

76 What is the temperature?

The pictograph shows 1990 census figures for Massachusetts and Illinois. Each figure stands for 1,000,000 people.

| Massachusetts | 🚶🚶🚶🚶🚶🚶 |
| Illinois | 🚶🚶🚶🚶🚶🚶🚶🚶🚶🚶🚶 |

77 About what was the population of Massachusetts?

78 About what was the population of Illinois?

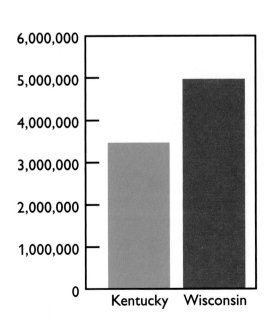

The bar graph shows 1990 census figures for Kentucky and Wisconsin.

79 About what was the population of Kentucky?

80 About what was the population of Wisconsin?

Extend Your Thinking

Solve these problems. Try to find a pattern.

1 $1 + 3 = \blacksquare$

2 $1 + 3 + 5 = \blacksquare$

3 $1 + 3 + 5 + 7 = \blacksquare$

4 $1 + 3 + 5 + 7 + 9 = \blacksquare$

5 $1 + 3 + 5 + 7 + 9 + 11 = \blacksquare$

6 $1 + 3 + 5 + 7 + 9 + 11 + 13 = \blacksquare$

7 $1 + 3 + 5 + 7 + 9 + 11 + 13 + 15 = \blacksquare$

8 $1 + 3 + 5 + 7 + 9 + 11 + 13 + 15 + 17 = \blacksquare$

Multiply.

9 $2 \times 2 = \blacksquare$ **10** $6 \times 6 = \blacksquare$

11 $3 \times 3 = \blacksquare$ **12** $7 \times 7 = \blacksquare$

13 $4 \times 4 = \blacksquare$ **14** $8 \times 8 = \blacksquare$

15 $5 \times 5 = \blacksquare$ **16** $9 \times 9 = \blacksquare$

◆ Look at your work on page 334. How many numbers did you add in problem 8? What was the sum of those numbers? What is 9 × 9?

Look at the last addend in each series and the number of addends in the series.

Last addend	3	5	7	9	11	13	15	17
Number of addends	2	3	4	5	6	7	8	9

◆ What is the pattern?

Use what you learned to predict each answer below. You can replace the dots with the numbers that belong there. Or you can figure out how many addends there would be and use that information to find the sum.

⑰ 1 + 3 + 5 + ... + 19 = ▨

⑱ 1 + 3 + 5 + 7 + 9 + ... + 27 + 29 = ▨

⑲ 1 + 3 + 5 + ... + 97 + 99 = ▨

⑳ 1 + 3 + 5 + ... + 197 + 199 = ▨

㉑ Write a sentence or two about how you can find the sum of a series of odd numbers beginning with 1.

㉒ Check your answers to problems 17 and 18 with a calculator. Were you right?

How Accurate?

The students in Mr. Smith's third-grade class tried an experiment. They wanted to know how accurate the weights on food labels are. They started with a 5-pound bag of potatoes and a 5-pound bag of rice.

◆ Do you think a 5-pound bag of potatoes weighs exactly 5 pounds?

◆ Do you think a 5-pound bag of rice weighs exactly 5 pounds?

◆ Would it be more difficult for a packer to make a bag of potatoes or a bag of rice weigh exactly 5 pounds? Why?

Talk about other foods and make two lists.

FOODS THAT PROBABLY WEIGH EXACTLY AS LABELED	FOODS THAT PROBABLY WEIGH APPROXIMATELY AS LABELED
rice	potatoes

Work in small groups. Make a stack of paper until you get it as close to 2 pounds as possible.

Now make a stack of math books. Adjust the number of books until you get as close to 2 pounds as possible.

In your Math Journal write about your group's experience. Why is it easier to place some things in packages of equal weight? Why is it more difficult for other items?

UNIT 4

Geometry

UNDERSTANDING GEOMETRIC RELATIONSHIPS

- **points, lines, angles, and figures**

- **congruency and symmetry**

- **multidigit multiplication**

- **multiplication of decimals**

- **multidigit addition and subtraction**

Astronomers use math . . .

Astronomers use geometry to study the stars, planets, constellations, and galaxies. They know that the Big Dipper points to the North Star at a certain angle. Points, lines, and angles seen through a telescope are analyzed to gather information.

LESSON 118

Volume

How many cubes? Count the cubes in an orderly manner. You may want to use cubes to build the solid figures if you need help.

1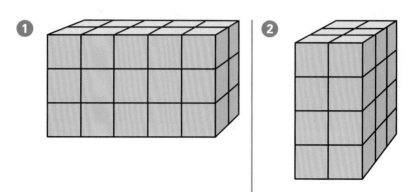

2

3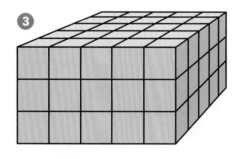

4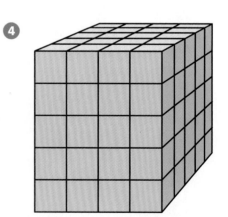

How many cubes?

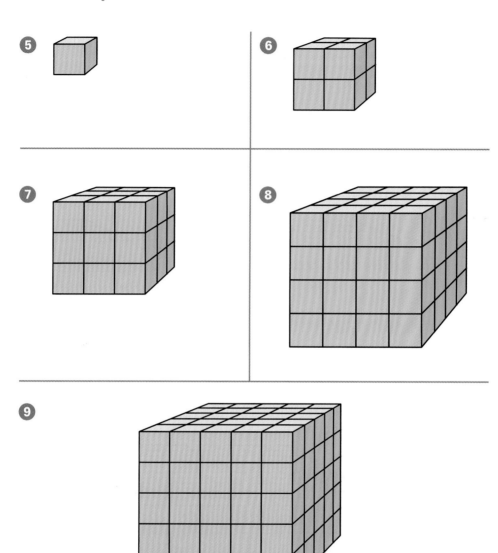

⑤

⑥

⑦

⑧

⑨

 Do the "Pouring Fractions" activity.

 In your Math Journal record your estimate for the "Pouring Fractions" activity. Then record your measurement. Was there a difference? How much?

Metric Units

Volume is often measured in cubic units—that is, how many cubes of the same size fit into the space being measured.

The **cubic centimeter** is a unit of volume. This cube has a volume of 1 cubic centimeter.

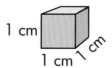

1 cm

1 cm   1 cm

Find out how many of these cubes are in each box. Then give the volume of the box.

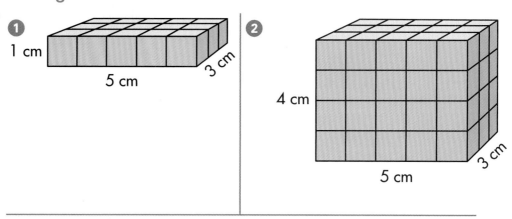

1   1 cm   5 cm   3 cm

2   4 cm   5 cm   3 cm

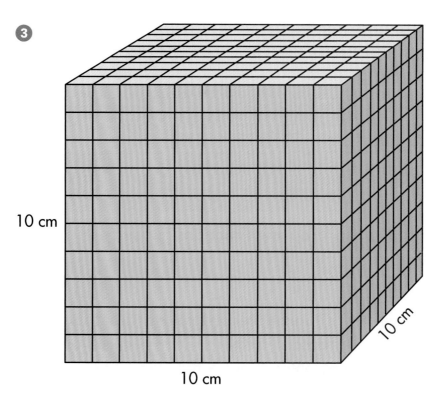

3   10 cm   10 cm   10 cm

The **liter** and **milliliter** are units of volume.

There are 1000 milliliters in 1 liter.

1000 mL = 1 L

1 milliliter is about the same volume as 1 cubic centimeter.

Write the equivalent amounts.

④ 1 L = ▦ mL

⑤ ▦ L = 1000 mL

⑥ 2 L = ▦ mL

⑦ ▦ L = 3000 mL

⑧ 7 L = ▦ mL

⑨ ▦ L = 5000 mL

⑩ 4 L = ▦ mL

⑪ ▦ L = 8000 mL

◆ **LESSON 119** Metric Units

Write the name of the unit that makes sense.
Use *milliliters* or *liters*.

12 About 250 ■ of juice

13 About 10 ■ of water

14 About 100 ■ of perfume

15 About 1 ■ of stew

16 About 2 ■ of soda

Do the "Estimating and Measuring Volume" activity.

**Write the unit that makes sense. Use *cm, m, km,*
mL, L, or *kg.***

⑰ runs about 10 ___ in one hour.

⑱ holds about 800 ___ of water.

⑲ weighs about 35 ___.

⑳ is about 120 ___ tall.

㉑ is about 5 ___ tall.

㉒ drinks about 2 ___ of water
each day.

Customary Units

The **cup, pint, quart,** and **gallon** are units of volume usually used for liquids.

There are 2 cups in 1 pint.

There are 2 pints in 1 quart.

There are 4 quarts in 1 gallon.

Write the equivalent amounts.

1 1 quart = ■ cups

2 $\frac{1}{2}$ gallon = ■ pints

3 2 quarts = ■ cups

4 $\frac{1}{2}$ gallon = ■ quarts

5 1 gallon = ■ cups

6 $\frac{1}{4}$ gallon = ■ quarts

7 1 gallon = ■ pints

8 8 pints = ■ quarts

Which unit makes more sense?

9 About 1 (gallon, cup)

10 About $\frac{1}{2}$ (gallon, pint)

11 About 1 (quart, cup)

12 About 2 (gallons, cups)

 Do the "Estimating and Measuring Volume" activity.

 In your Math Journal record your estimate for the "Estimating and Measuring Volume" activity. Then record your measurement. Was there a difference? How much?

◆ **LESSON 120 Customary Units**

Write the unit that makes sense. Use *cups, pints, quarts, inches, feet, miles,* or *pounds.*

⑬  can run about 6 ____ in one hour.

⑭ 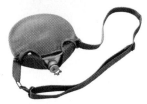 holds about 3 ____ of water.

⑮  weighs about 80 ____.

⑯  is about 8 ____ tall.

⑰  is about 18 ____ tall.

⑱  drinks about 2 ____ of water each day.

Solve for *n*. Watch the signs.

⑲ $5 \times 8 = n$ ⑳ $3 \times 4 = n$ ㉑ $27 \div 3 = n$

㉒ $56 \div 7 = n$ ㉓ $40 \div 5 = n$ ㉔ $5 \times 5 = n$

㉕ $6 \times 7 = n$ ㉖ $4 \times 7 = n$ ㉗ $9 \times 6 = n$

㉘ $3 \times 9 = n$ ㉙ $8 \times 100 = n$ ㉚ $24 \div 3 = n$

Solve these problems. Watch the signs.

㉛ $8\overline{)48}$ ㉜ $6\overline{)54}$ ㉝ $2\overline{)12}$ ㉞ $2\overline{)14}$ ㉟ $6\overline{)42}$

㊱ $\begin{array}{r} 8 \\ \times\, 3 \\ \hline \end{array}$ ㊲ $\begin{array}{r} 5 \\ \times\, 2 \\ \hline \end{array}$ ㊳ $\begin{array}{r} 8 \\ \times\, 4 \\ \hline \end{array}$ ㊴ $\begin{array}{r} 7 \\ \times\, 5 \\ \hline \end{array}$ ㊵ $\begin{array}{r} 9 \\ \times\, 7 \\ \hline \end{array}$

㊶ $\begin{array}{r} 543 \\ -\,261 \\ \hline \end{array}$ ㊷ $\begin{array}{r} 3.12 \\ -\,1.59 \\ \hline \end{array}$ ㊸ $\begin{array}{r} 207 \\ -\,138 \\ \hline \end{array}$ ㊹ $\begin{array}{r} 426 \\ 512 \\ +\,394 \\ \hline \end{array}$ ㊺ $\begin{array}{r} 254 \\ 167 \\ +\,598 \\ \hline \end{array}$

SOCIAL STUDIES CONNECTION

Roman Numerals

Have you ever seen a clock or watch with Roman numerals? These numerals were first used by the Romans about 2500 years ago.

I = 1

V = 5

X = 10

L = 50

C = 100

D = 500

M = 1000

The number 6 can be written as 5 plus 1; or VI. The number 9 can be written as 1 less than 10; or IX.

Write the Arabic numeral for each of these Roman numerals.

① III   ② XV   ③ XXVII

④ V   ⑤ XVI   ⑥ XXIX

⑦ X   ⑧ IX   ⑨ LXIX

⑩ XX   ⑪ XIX   ⑫ CC

⑬ C   ⑭ LX   ⑮ CCL

⑯ L   ⑰ LXII   ⑱ CCLVII

Write the Roman numeral for each Arabic numeral.

19 5   **20** 10   **21** 20

22 50   **23** 88   **24** 89

25 101   **26** 150   **27** 600

28 2000   **29** 2500   **30** 4999

Solve. Remember to subtract lesser Roman numerals that come before greater Roman numerals.

31 At the end of movies, the year in which the movie was first shown is often given in Roman numerals. Jamie went to see a movie with his parents yesterday. The date shown at the end was MCMXCV. How many years ago was the movie first shown?

32 Mrs. Merrill drives by City Hall every day. She sees the Roman numerals MDCCCLXXXIX on the cornerstone of the building. What is this date in Arabic numerals?

33 On the Statue of Liberty there is a date 113 years earlier than the date on City Hall in question 32. Write the date on the Statue of Liberty in Roman numerals.

34 The date on the Liberty Bell is MDCCLIII. What is that date in Arabic numerals?

In your Math Journal list some reasons why Roman numerals are used less often than Arabic numerals.

◆ **LESSON 121 Roman Numerals**

COOPERATIVE LEARNING

Roman Numeral Game

GAME

Players:	**Two**
Materials:	**Game board; 23 play dimes or other markers; two 0–5 cubes (red) and two 5–10 cubes (blue)**
Object:	**To get the most markers**
Math Focus:	**Recognizing equivalent Roman and Arabic numerals and mental arithmetic**

RULES

1. Cover each circle on the game board with a play dime or marker. You should be able to see the Roman numerals, but not the Arabic numerals.

2. Take turns rolling all four cubes. Make a number by using any combination of addition, subtraction, multiplication, and division with all four numbers rolled. For example, if you roll 4, 7, 8, and 3, you could make the number 12 in this way:

$$[8 \div 4] + 7 + 3 = 12$$

3. After you make a number, pick up the marker under the Roman numeral for the number you made. If you are correct, you keep the marker. If you are incorrect, you replace the marker.

4. If a player makes a number that is not on the board, or a number whose marker has already been taken, the player loses that turn.

5. The player with more markers at the end of the game is the winner.

ROMAN NUMERAL GAME BOARD

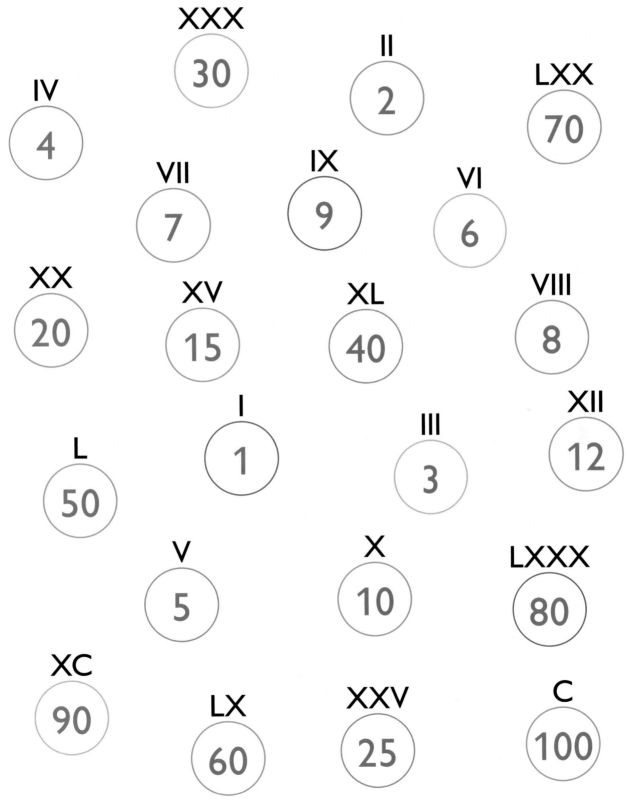

XXX
30

II
2

LXX
70

IV
4

VII
7

IX
9

VI
6

XX
20

XV
15

XL
40

VIII
8

I
1

III
3

XII
12

L
50

V
5

X
10

LXXX
80

XC
90

LX
60

XXV
25

C
100

LESSON

122

Making Predictions

COOPERATIVE LEARNING **Do the "Guess the Marker" activity.**

Solve for *n*. Watch the signs.

1 $2 + 5 = n$

2 $17 - 8 = n$

3 $8 - 6 = n$

4 $7 - 4 = n$

5 $17 - 9 = n$

6 $14 - 6 = n$

7 $7 + 4 = n$

8 $12 - 8 = n$

9 $11 - 7 = n$

10 $15 - 8 = n$

11 $12 + 8 = n$

12 $8 + 7 = n$

13 $15 - 7 = n$

14 $4 + 9 = n$

15 $17 - 5 = n$

16 $10 + 6 = n$

17 $13 - 6 = n$

18 $12 + 3 = n$

19 $9 + 6 = n$

20 $16 - 6 = n$

21 $12 - 3 = n$

22 $15 - 6 = n$

23 $8 + 6 = n$

24 $11 + 6 = n$

MATH JOURNAL

Suppose you are playing "Guess the Marker" and after the first four markers have been drawn the chart shows: Ⓡ Ⓡ R W. In your Math Journal tell how many markers of each color are left in the can. What would you guess next? Why?

Multiply.

25　　6
　　× 5

26　　7
　　× 4

27　　8
　　× 6

28　　5
　　× 5

29　　4
　　× 3

30　　9
　　× 2

31　　9
　　× 9

32　　6
　　× 7

33　　8
　　× 7

34　　3
　　× 2

35　　3
　　× 6

36　　4
　　× 4

37　　7
　　× 5

38　　2
　　× 8

39　　6
　　× 5

Divide.

40 5)25　　**41** 6)30　　**42** 7)28　　**43** 9)81　　**44** 8)64

45 10)30　　**46** 4)28　　**47** 6)36　　**48** 2)12　　**49** 7)49

50 5)10　　**51** 4)32　　**52** 3)27　　**53** 8)32　　**54** 6)18

55 3)12　　**56** 7)56　　**57** 5)30　　**58** 6)24　　**59** 4)20

LESSON 123

Predicting the Outcome

Solve these problems. Watch the signs. Use shortcuts when you can.

1
$$652$$
$$+ \ 208$$

2
$$7571$$
$$- \ 3651$$

3
$$857$$
$$+ \ 632$$

4
$$300$$
$$- \ 175$$

5
$$6319$$
$$+ \ \ 765$$

6
$$891$$
$$- \ 606$$

7
$$783$$
$$+ \ 169$$

8
$$4197$$
$$- \ 3636$$

9
$$927$$
$$+ \ 631$$

10
$$7265$$
$$+ \ 8319$$

11
$$200$$
$$- \ 199$$

12
$$50,000$$
$$- \ 49,999$$

13
$$400$$
$$- \ 390$$

14
$$340$$
$$+ \ \ 10$$

15
$$600$$
$$- \ 300$$

16
$$470$$
$$- \ 460$$

17
$$25$$
$$25$$
$$25$$
$$+ \ 25$$

18
$$50$$
$$50$$
$$50$$
$$+ \ 50$$

 Do the "Which Sum Will Win?" activity.

Look at the graph below.

Cody and Rachel are rolling a 0–5 Number Cube and a 5–10 Number Cube. Rachel is keeping a tally of the number of rolls. Cody is using a graph to keep track of how many times each sum is rolled. This is Cody's graph after seven rolls.

19 Which sum will reach the top of the graph first? Explain your prediction.

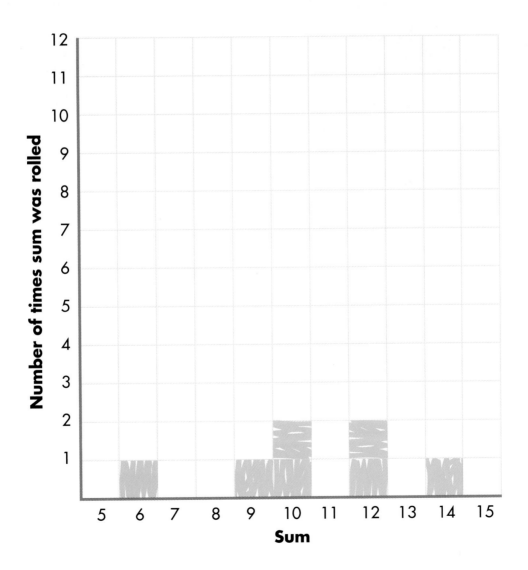

Probability and Predictions

There are 40 markers in the can. Bruce's class is trying to figure out how many red markers and how many white markers are in the can. Mrs. Hoffman is taking samples from the can. After each sample of 10 markers, Bruce can change his prediction. This is Bruce's record after the first sample of 10.

First sample

Color	Number
Red	3
White	7

First prediction

Color	Number
Red	10
White	30

Use a computer or other means to draw charts like Bruce's. Keep a record when you try to predict what is in the can.

Second sample

Color	Number
Red	
White	

Second prediction

Color	Number
Red	
White	

Third sample

Color	Number
Red	
White	

Third prediction

Color	Number
Red	
White	

Actual number of markers

Color	Number
Red	
White	

Solve these problems.

1 How much will four boxes of paper clips cost?

2 How much will seven erasers cost?

3 How much will six pencils cost?

4 How much will three pencils and two erasers cost?

5 How much will two pieces of colored chalk, three erasers, and four pencils cost?

6 How much will three erasers and one box of paper clips cost?

7 How much will two erasers, eight pencils, and one piece of colored chalk cost?

LESSON 125

Scale Drawings

Scale drawings are a different size from, but with the same shape as, the original object.

Clara's class made this scale drawing. Each side of a square on the graph paper represents 1 meter in length.

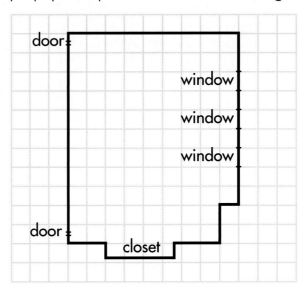

Answer these questions.

1. About how wide is Clara's classroom?

2. About how long is Clara's classroom?

3. About how wide is the closet in Clara's classroom?

On a sheet of graph paper, make a scale drawing of your classroom. In your Math Journal compare your classroom to Clara's. Which is larger?

Solve for *n*. Watch the signs.

4. $8 \times 0 = n$

5. $10 \times 4 = n$

6. $3 \times 3 = n$

7. $4 \times 3 = n$

8. $90 \div 10 = n$

9. $30 \div 10 = n$

10. $7 \times 8 = n$

11. $24 \div 8 = n$

12. $7 \times 6 = n$

13. $16 \div 4 = n$

14. $8 \times 6 = n$

15. $12 \div 3 = n$

16. $5 \div 5 = n$

17. $63 \div 9 = n$

18. $81 \div 9 = n$

19. $9 \times 1 = n$

20. $6 \times 9 = n$

21. $27 \div 9 = n$

22. $7 \times 6 = n$

23. $7 \times 7 = n$

24. $30 \div 5 = n$

25. $28 \div 4 = n$

26. $18 \div 2 = n$

27. $5 \times 5 = n$

28. $15 \div 3 = n$

29. $56 \div 8 = n$

30. $7 \times 10 = n$

31. $8 \times 9 = n$

32. $9 \times 3 = n$

33. $6 \times 6 = n$

Talk about the Thinking Story "Muddle the Engineer."

Reading Scale Drawings

Sam's group made a scale drawing of the top of a table.

Answer these questions.

1. How long is the table that Sam's group drew?
2. How wide is it?
3. How long is the drawing of the table?

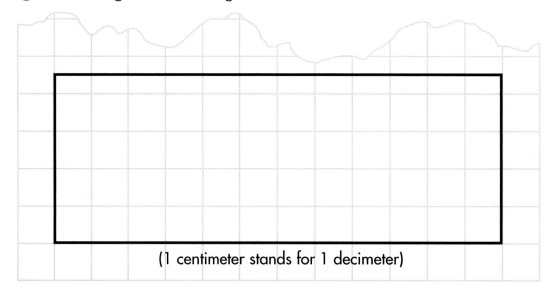

(1 centimeter stands for 1 decimeter)

4. How wide is it?

On a sheet of graph paper, make a scale drawing of two things in your classroom.

Solve for _n_. Watch the signs.

5 $6 \times 4 = n$ **6** $18 \div 9 = n$ **7** $4 \div 2 = n$

8 $35 \div 7 = n$ **9** $42 \div 6 = n$ **10** $56 \div 7 = n$

11 $4 \times 5 = n$ **12** $9 \times 6 = n$ **13** $10 \times 5 = n$

14 $14 \div 2 = n$ **15** $8 \times 6 = n$ **16** $28 \div 4 = n$

17 $8 \times 8 = n$ **18** $10 \div 1 = n$ **19** $3 \times 5 = n$

20
$$\begin{array}{r} 7.5 \\ -\ 2.5 \\ \hline \end{array}$$

21
$$\begin{array}{r} 10.8 \\ +\ 4.4 \\ \hline \end{array}$$

22
$$\begin{array}{r} 6.5 \\ -\ 3.25 \\ \hline \end{array}$$

23
$$\begin{array}{r} 8.45 \\ +\ 3.6 \\ \hline \end{array}$$

Multiply. Solve for _n_.

24 $7 \times 10 = n$ **25** $5 \times 10 = n$ **26** $11 \times 100 = n$

27 $7 \times 100 = n$ **28** $10 \times 25 = n$ **29** $2 \times 10 = n$

30 $10 \times 10 = n$ **31** $100 \times 13 = n$ **32** $20 \times 100 = n$

33 $100 \times 10 = n$ **34** $40 \times 10 = n$ **35** $10 \times 6 = n$

Solve these problems.

36 There are 12 eggs in a carton. At Mini's Diner they use ten cartons of eggs every day. How many eggs do they use in one day?

37 How many eggs do they use in ten days?

LESSON 127

Points, Lines, and Angles

Point to where the two lines will meet.

1

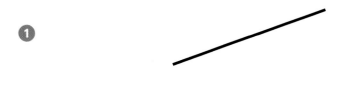

2

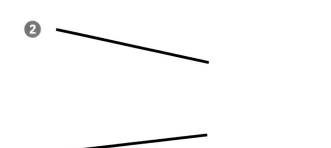

3

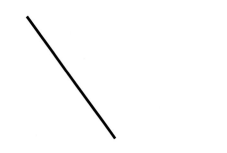

Answer these questions.

4 Where will these two lines meet? How do you know?

5 Where will these two lines meet? How do you know?

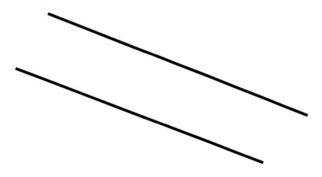

6 Where will these two lines meet? How do you know?

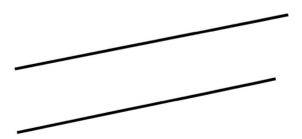

In your Math Journal tell how the lines in problems 4, 5, and 6 differ from the lines in problems 1, 2, and 3.

◆ LESSON 127 Points, Lines, and Angles

A **line segment** is a part of a line with two endpoints.

●────────────────● is a line segment.

An **angle** is formed where two lines meet.

∠ is an angle.

For each figure, count the number of line segments. Count the number of angles. Write your answers. When you finish, talk about your answers with other students. If you have different answers, try to decide why.

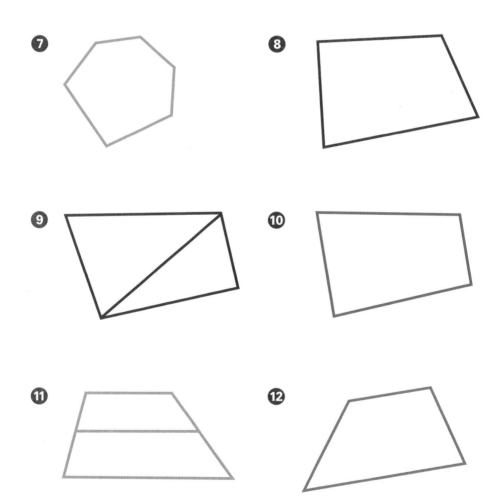

❼

❽

❾

❿

⓫

⓬

Solve for *n*. Watch the signs.

⑬ $6 \times 3 = n$

⑭ $50 \div 10 = n$

⑮ $48 \div 8 = n$

⑯ $5 \times 5 = n$

⑰ $9 \times 8 = n$

⑱ $16 - 9 = n$

⑲ $24 \div 6 = n$

⑳ $10 + 7 = n$

㉑ $8 \times 7 = n$

㉒ $9 \times 9 = n$

㉓ $36 \div 6 = n$

㉔ $17 - 9 = n$

㉕ $3 \times 5 = n$

㉖ $9 - 8 = n$

㉗ $42 \div 7 = n$

㉘ $4 + 8 = n$

㉙ $9 \times 4 = n$

㉚ $56 \div 7 = n$

Solve these problems.

㉛ Robbie had borrowed six books from the library. He returned the books he had borrowed and the books Scott had borrowed. Robbie returned 15 books all together. How many books had Scott borrowed?

㉜ Mr. Goldman has 382 envelopes. He needs 600 envelopes. How many more envelopes does he need?

㉝ Mr. Goldman's sister gave him four packs of envelopes. Each pack has 100 envelopes. Does Mr. Goldman have enough envelopes now?

㉞ How many extra envelopes does Mr. Goldman have?

Do the "Angles of a Triangle" activity.

LESSON 128

Four-Sided Figures

Figures that have four sides are called **quadrilaterals.**
Squares, rectangles, parallelograms, and trapezoids are
special quadrilaterals.

Write the name of each figure.

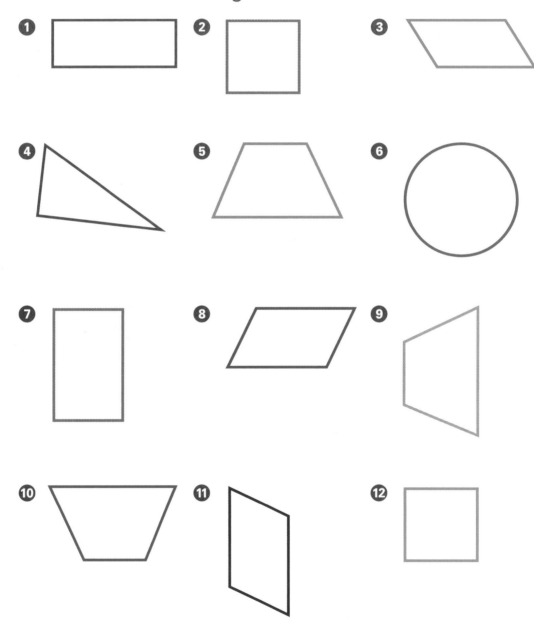

How many special figures can you find in the picture?

⑬ Squares ■

⑭ Rectangles ■

⑮ Parallelograms ■

⑯ Trapezoids ■

⑰ Circles ■

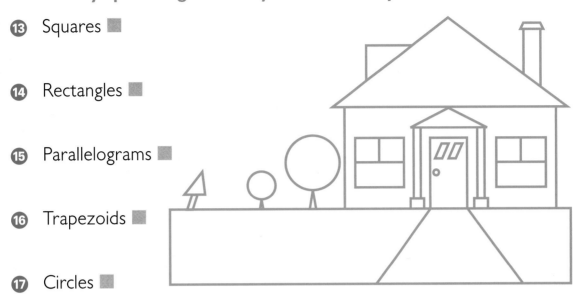

Predict what shape comes next.

⑱ △○□△○□△○□ __△__

⑲ □⌂△△△□⌂△△ __□__

⑳ □□○□□○□ __○__

 **Do the "Road Sign Shapes" activity.**

Circles: Exploring Distances

Carmen made a dartboard. She played a game with Julia.

Find the score for each dart. Measure the distance from each dart to the center.

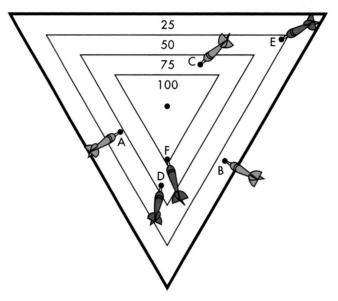

Carmen		
Dart	**Score**	**Distance from Center**
A	■	■ cm
B	■	■ cm
C	■	■ cm
Total	■	■ cm

Julia		
Dart	**Score**	**Distance from Center**
D	■	■ cm
E	■	■ cm
F	■	■ cm
Total	■	■ cm

1 Who had a higher score?

2 Which player do you think had more skill?

3 How would you design a dartboard?

Solve for *n*. Watch the signs.

④ $6 \times 5 = n$ ⑤ $5 \times 5 = n$ ⑥ $5 \times 7 = n$

⑦ $27 \div 3 = n$ ⑧ $14 \div 2 = n$ ⑨ $40 \div 10 = n$

⑩ $9 \times 6 = n$ ⑪ $9 \times 8 = n$ ⑫ $18 \div 3 = n$

⑬ $8 \times 7 = n$ ⑭ $24 \div 6 = n$ ⑮ $4 \times 4 = n$

⑯ $64 \div 8 = n$ ⑰ $3 \times 8 = n$ ⑱ $2 \times 3 = n$

⑲ $16 \div 4 = n$ ⑳ $6 \times 7 = n$ ㉑ $12 \div 1 = n$

㉒ $7 \times 9 = n$ ㉓ $20 \div 5 = n$ ㉔ $8 \times 10 = n$

㉕ $10 \times 6 = n$ ㉖ $7 \times 7 = n$ ㉗ $5 \times 9 = n$

Do the "Making Target Games" activity.

In your Math Journal draw your target game. Describe its shape.

LESSON 130

Circles: Diameter and Radius

A **diameter** of a circle is a line segment that passes through the center of the circle and whose endpoints are on the circle. A **radius** of a circle is a line segment that has one endpoint on the center of the circle and the other on the circle. The plural of *radius* is *radii*.

Solve these problems.

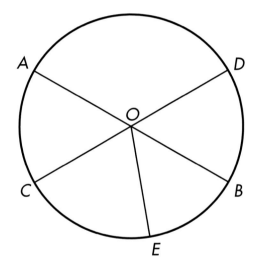

1. Diameter *AB* is ▒ centimeters long.

2. Diameter *CD* is ▒ centimeters long.

3. Radius *OE* is ▒ centimeters long.

4. Radius *OB* is ▒ centimeters long.

 **Do the "Making and Measuring Circles" activity.**

Measurements of My Circle

Length of Diameters	Length of Radii

Multiply.

⑤　　6
　　× 8

⑥　　7
　　× 7

⑦　　4
　　× 3

⑧　　2
　　× 9

⑨　　10
　　× 8

⑩　　5
　　× 7

⑪　　6
　　× 3

⑫　　7
　　× 9

⑬　　4
　　× 7

⑭　　8
　　× 5

⑮　　7
　　× 1

⑯　　3
　　× 8

⑰　　9
　　× 9

⑱　　4
　　× 5

⑲　　7
　　× 6

Add.

⑳　　37
　　49
　　63
　+ 218

㉑　　92
　　137
　　300
　+ 180

㉒　　3695
　　2780
　+ 1500

㉓　　106
　　127
　+ 159

Subtract.

㉔　　172
　− 30

㉕　　679
　− 297

㉖　　301
　− 137

㉗　　46
　− 39

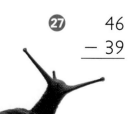

A garden snail has more than **14,000** teeth.
They are arranged in **135** rows of **105** each.
Human adults have about **32** teeth.

Congruency

Two figures are **congruent** if they are the same shape and same size. You can check to see if two figures are congruent by tracing one and seeing if the tracing fits on top of the other figure. Flip the tracing paper over to see that these two triangles are congruent.

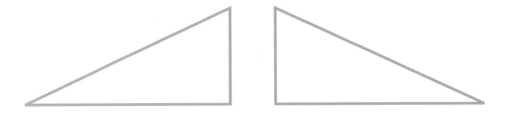

Look at the figures. Use tracing paper to help you see which are congruent.

① List each pair of congruent figures.

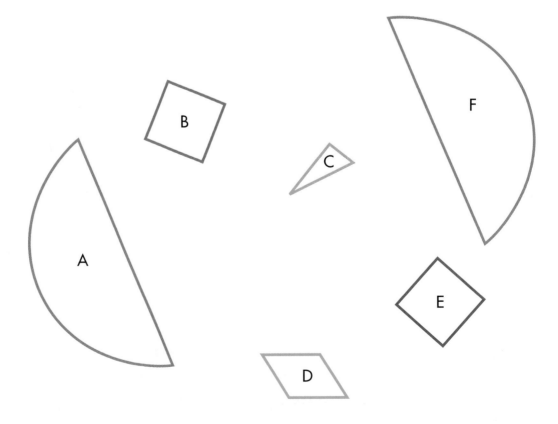

2 List each pair of congruent figures.

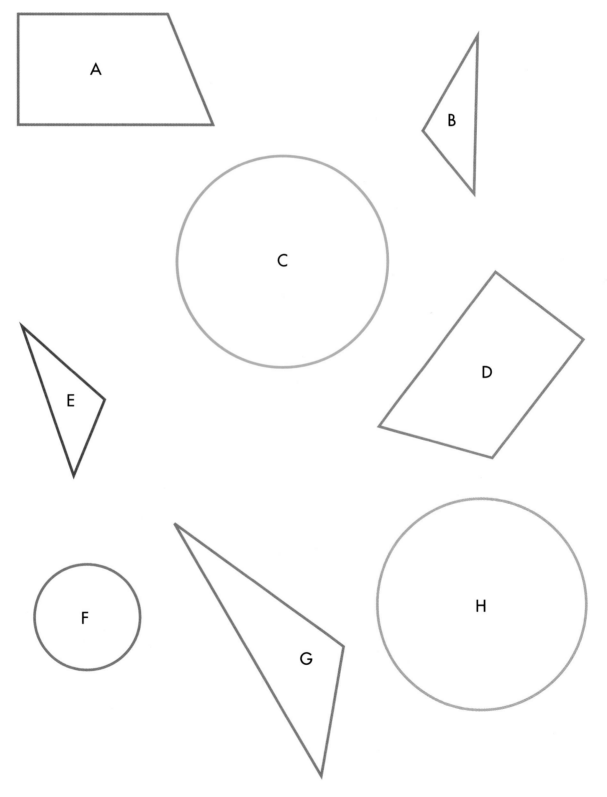

Lines of Symmetry

An object is **symmetrical** if it looks the same on one side of a line as it does on the other. If you can trace the part of a figure on one side of a line and flip the tracing so it fits on the other half of the figure, the figure is symmetrical at that line. The flip line is the **line of symmetry**. All lines of symmetry have been drawn in the following figures. Notice there is no line of symmetry for the third figure.

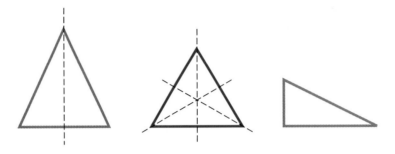

Copy the figures on your paper. Use a second color to draw all the lines of symmetry.

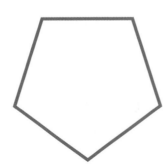

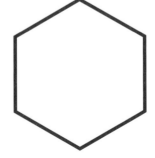

Copy the letters and figures on your paper. Draw all lines of symmetry in a different color.

5 A **6** E **7** 8 **8** W **9** C

10 F **11** H **12** M **13** N **14** X

Is the dotted line a line of symmetry? Write *yes* or *no*.

15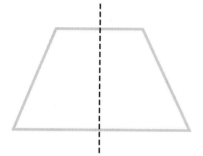

16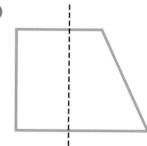

17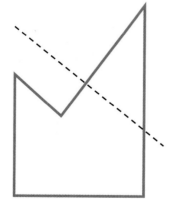

18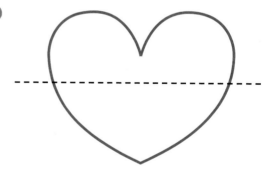

19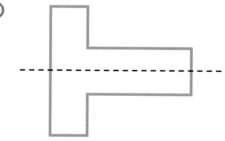

20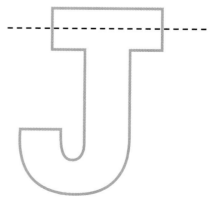

Three-Dimensional Figures

Look at the pictures of the solid objects. How many do you recognize? List some things that look like each object.

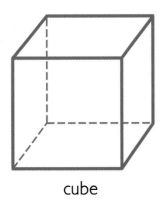

cube

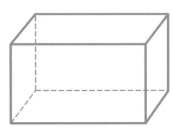

box or rectangular prism

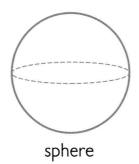

sphere

cylinder

triangular pyramid

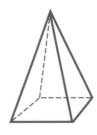

square pyramid

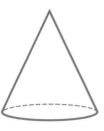

cone

The line segments in a solid figure are called **edges.** The corners or points where edges meet are called **vertices** (one is called a **vertex**). The polygons in a solid figure are called **faces.**

Answer these questions.

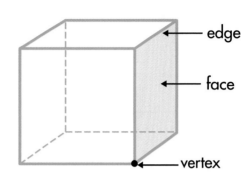

edge

face

vertex

1 How many faces does a cube have?

2 How many edges does a cube have?

3 How many vertices does a cube have?

4 How many faces does a box or rectangular prism have?

5 How many edges does a box or rectangular prism have?

6 How many vertices does a box or rectangular prism have?

7 How many faces does a triangular pyramid have?

8 How many edges does a triangular pyramid have?

9 How many vertices does a triangular pyramid have?

10 Use a computer or a piece of paper to copy and complete the chart.

Figure	Number of Faces	Number of Vertices	Number of Edges
Cube	6	8	12
Box	■	■	■
Triangular pyramid	4	■	■
Square pyramid	■	5	■

LESSON 134

Area

Find the area of these figures.

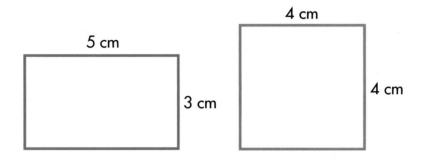

① ◼ square centimeters   ② ◼ square centimeters

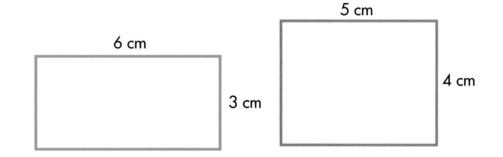

③ ◼ square centimeters   ④ ◼ square centimeters

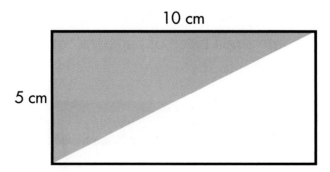

⑤ Area of the whole rectangle = ◼ square centimeters

⑥ Area of the orange triangle = ◼ square centimeters

Multiply.

7   6
   × 5

8   8
   × 3

9   9
   × 7

10   7
   × 8

11   4
   × 5

12   7
   × 3

13   5
   × 2

14   10
   × 1

15   2
   × 8

16   9
   × 6

17 $1 \times 1 = $ ■

18 $2 \times 2 = $ ■

19 $3 \times 3 = $ ■

20 $4 \times 4 = $ ■

21 $5 \times 5 = $ ■

22 $6 \times 6 = $ ■

23 $7 \times 7 = $ ■

24 $8 \times 8 = $ ■

25 $9 \times 9 = $ ■

26 $10 \times 10 = $ ■

27 $3 \times 4 = $ ■

28 $7 \times 6 = $ ■

29 $9 \times 10 = $ ■

30 $3 \times 2 = $ ■

31 $8 \times 9 = $ ■

Solve these problems.

It takes about five seconds for the sound of thunder to travel 1 mile.

32 About how far can the sound of thunder travel in one minute?

33 About how long would it take for the sound of thunder to travel 5 miles?

Talk about the Thinking Story "A Chancy Birthday Party."

UNIT 4

Mid-Unit Review

How many cubes?

①

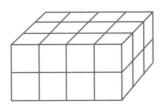

②

Give the volume of each box.

③

④

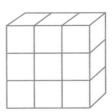

Solve.

⑤ 4 L = ____ mL

⑥ ____ L = 1000 mL

⑦ 6 L = ____ mL

⑧ ____ L = 9000 mL

Choose the unit that makes sense. Write _mL_ or _L_.

⑨

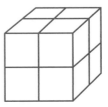

About 200 ____ of tea

⑩

About 4 ____ of laundry soap

Choose the unit that makes sense. Write _cm, m, km,_ or _kg._

⑪

weighs about 15 ____.

⑫

jogs about 5 ____ in a half hour.

Solve these problems.

⑬ 2 quarts = ____ pints

⑭ $\frac{1}{2}$ gallon = ____ cups

⑮ 8 pints = ____ gallon(s)

⑯ 1 quart = ____ cups

Which unit makes more sense?

⑰

About 1 <u>(quart, gallon)</u>

⑱

About $\frac{1}{2}$ <u>(gallon, pint)</u>

Choose the unit that makes sense. Write *inches, feet, miles,* or *pounds.*

⑲ A banana is about 7 ____ long.

⑳ Jason lives 2 ____ from school.

Write the Arabic numeral for each Roman numeral.

㉑ XXIV

㉒ LXXVII

㉓ CLIX

㉔ MM

Write the Roman numeral for each Arabic numeral.

㉕ 29

㉖ 54

㉗ 135

㉘ 1016

Multiply.

㉙ 3
  × 7

㉚ 8
  × 5

㉛ 4
  × 6

㉜ 9
  × 7

Write the name of each figure.

㉝

㉞

㉟

Applying Multiplication Skills

Robin was going shopping at the hardware store. She made a chart of what she needed to buy.

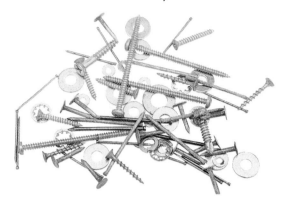

Solve these problems.

1 Write the missing amounts.

Item	Number Needed	Unit Price	Amount of Money Needed
Screws	3	10¢	■
Washers	6	8¢	■
Nails	2	9¢	■
Tacks	4	5¢	■

2 How much money will Robin need all together?

3 If Robin gives the shopkeeper $2, how much change will she get?

4 Suppose Robin wants to buy twice as many of each item. How much money will she need?

Solve these problems.

Ms. Gomez wants to buy a carpet for her living room. The floor is a rectangle that is 7 meters long and 5 meters wide. The carpet costs $10 a square meter.

5 How many square meters of carpet will Ms. Gomez need?

6 How much will that cost?

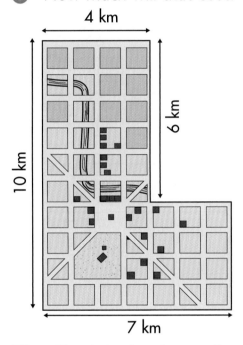

Ellen City is in the shape of an L. Copy or trace the map. Then draw a line to divide Ellen City into two rectangles.

7 What is the area of one of the rectangles?

8 What is the area of the other rectangle?

9 What is the total area of Ellen City?

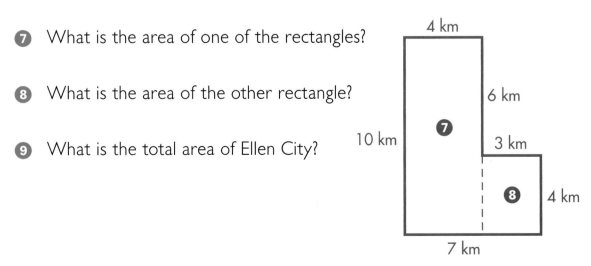

Multiplying Two-Digit Numbers

If you wanted to know the area of a rectangle that was 27 units long and 4 units wide, you would multiply 27 × 4.

$$27 \times 4 = \underline{\ ?\ }$$

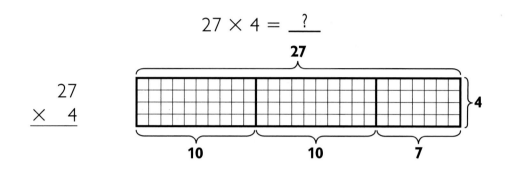

$$\begin{array}{r} 27 \\ \times\ 4 \\ \end{array}$$

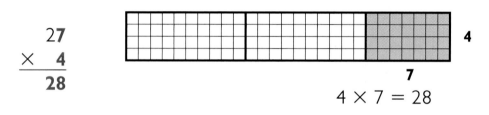

$$\begin{array}{r} 27 \\ \times\ 4 \\ \hline 28 \\ \end{array}$$

$$4 \times 7 = 28$$

$$\begin{array}{r} 27 \\ \times\ 4 \\ \hline 28 \\ 80 \\ \end{array}$$

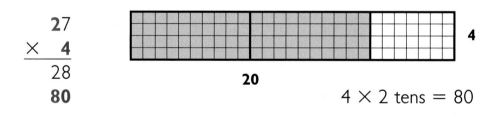

$$4 \times 2 \text{ tens} = 80$$

$$\begin{array}{r} 27 \\ \times\ 4 \\ \hline 28 \\ 80 \\ \hline 108 \\ \end{array}$$

$$28 + 80 = 108$$

Multiply. You may draw pictures to help. Talk about whether your answers are reasonable.

1. 35
× 4

2. 28
× 7

3. 48
× 1

4. 15
× 6

5. 83
× 9

6. 90
× 8

7. 72
× 5

8. 45
× 2

9. 67
× 3

10. 41
× 5

11. 45
× 8

12. 80
× 7

13. 26
× 4

14. 32
× 8

15. 74
× 6

16. 52
× 5

17. 19
× 3

18. 87
× 6

19. 61
× 6

20. 22
× 9

21. 57
× 2

22. 12
× 8

23. 45
× 3

24. 45
× 9

Using Two-Digit Multiplication

Roll a Problem Game

Players:	**Two or more**
Materials:	**One 0–5 cube (red)**
Object:	**To get the greatest product**
Math Focus:	**Multiplying two-digit numbers by one-digit numbers, place value, and mathematical reasoning**

RULES

1. Use blanks to outline a multiplication problem on your paper like this:

$$\frac{\begin{array}{r} \underline{}\ \underline{} \\ \times\ \underline{} \end{array}}{}$$

2. The first player rolls the cube three times.

3. Each time the cube is rolled, write that number in one of the blanks in your outline.

4. When all the blanks have been filled in, find the product of the two numbers.

5. The player with the greatest product wins the round.

ANOTHER WAY TO PLAY THIS GAME

Use a 5–10 cube (blue). If you roll a 10, roll again.

Multiply.

①	83 × 5	②	47 × 5	③	26 × 1	④	76 × 5	⑤	11 × 4

⑥	38 × 5	⑦	29 × 7	⑧	26 × 0	⑨	30 × 8	⑩	30 × 9

⑪	58 × 9	⑫	62 × 6	⑬	55 × 3	⑭	91 × 4	⑮	90 × 4

Solve these problems.

⑯ Brenda and Joe put 1 cup of popcorn kernels in their popcorn maker. About 8 cups of popcorn came out. How many cups of popcorn would 15 cups of kernels make?

⑰ The cafeteria at Rosie's school uses 6 quarts of cooking oil every day. How many quarts are used in 16 days? How many gallons is that?

In your Math Journal write two more story problems like the ones above and solve them. Share them with the class.

Multiplying Two-Digit Numbers: Applications

Solve these problems.

1 Melissa saves $3 each month. Will she save enough in one year to buy a $26.95 tape player?

2 How many horseshoes are needed to shoe 13 horses?

3 Mr. Segal can finish a 1-kilometer race in three minutes. How long do you think it would take him to finish a 10-kilometer race?

4 There are 15 slices of bread in a loaf. How many slices are there in four loaves?

Talk about the Thinking Story "A Sticky Problem."

Solve.

5 Liza goes to ballet class twice a week. The class is in a building 17 miles from her house. How many miles does Liza travel to ballet class and back each week?

6 Angie earns $8.00 an hour working at a grocery store. How much does she earn in 40 hours?

Students from Los Amigos School are going on a field trip. There are 350 people going. Each bus can seat 45 people.

7 How many people can seven buses seat?

8 How many buses should the school use?

9 It costs $92 to rent one bus for a day. How much will it cost to rent eight buses?

10 If the school rents eight buses, how many extra seats will there be?

11 Suppose that each person going on the trip pays $1. Will that be enough to pay for eight buses?

Multiplying Three-Digit Numbers

What is the area of a room that is 134 units long and 8 units wide? To find out, multiply 134 by 8.

$$134 \times 8 = \underline{}$$

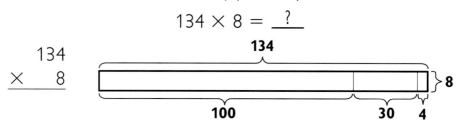

$$\begin{array}{r} 134 \\ \times\ \ 8 \\ \hline \end{array}$$

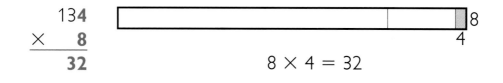

$$\begin{array}{r} 134 \\ \times\ \ 8 \\ \hline 32 \end{array}$$

$8 \times 4 = 32$

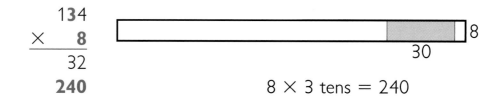

$$\begin{array}{r} 134 \\ \times\ \ 8 \\ \hline 32 \\ 240 \end{array}$$

$8 \times 3 \text{ tens} = 240$

$$\begin{array}{r} 134 \\ \times\ \ 8 \\ \hline 32 \\ 240 \\ 800 \end{array}$$

$8 \times 1 \text{ hundred} = 800$

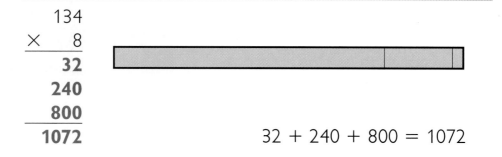

$$\begin{array}{r} 134 \\ \times\ \ 8 \\ \hline 32 \\ 240 \\ 800 \\ \hline 1072 \end{array}$$

$32 + 240 + 800 = 1072$

Multiply. Use shortcuts where possible. Compare and discuss your methods. Which are easiest?

1
```
  247
×   3
```

2
```
  108
×   7
```

3
```
  596
×   8
```

4
```
  111
×   6
```

5
```
  432
×   4
```

6
```
  909
×   9
```

7
```
  356
×   6
```

8
```
  732
×   0
```

9
```
  480
×   5
```

10
```
  379
×   2
```

11
```
  876
×   1
```

12
```
  380
×   6
```

13
```
  282
×   9
```

14
```
  250
×   4
```

15
```
  611
×   5
```

16
```
  222
×   3
```

17
```
  308
×   2
```

18
```
  297
×   8
```

19
```
  912
×   4
```

20
```
  140
×   7
```

In your Math Journal tell about a shortcut you took to solve these problems.

Practice Multiplying Three-Digit Numbers

Multiply. Use shortcuts when possible.

1　　555
　　×　　7

2　　204
　　×　　6

3　　373
　　×　　7

4　　250
　　×　　4

5　　694
　　×　　9

6　　447
　　×　　8

7　　109
　　×　　2

8　　311
　　×　　9

9　　378
　　×　　3

10　　984
　　×　　1

11　　800
　　×　　7

12　　900
　　×　　6

13　　700
　　×　　5

14　　451
　　×　　3

15　　532
　　×　　8

16　　750
　　×　　2

17　　840
　　×　　1

18　　664
　　×　　6

19　　479
　　×　　5

20　　728
　　×　　7

Solve these problems. Watch the signs.

㉑
```
   475
 + 362
```

㉒
```
   312
 + 769
```

㉓
```
   52.35
 - 27.26
```

㉔
```
   61.2
 -  8.5
```

㉕
```
   847
 - 285
```

㉖
```
   668
 + 488
```

㉗
```
   23.4
 - 19.3
```

㉘
```
   73.48
 + 24.70
```

Divide.

㉙ $6\overline{)48}$ ㉚ $7\overline{)42}$ ㉛ $8\overline{)48}$ ㉜ $5\overline{)30}$

㉝ $9\overline{)18}$ ㉞ $3\overline{)27}$ ㉟ $2\overline{)20}$ ㊱ $3\overline{)24}$

㊲ $2\overline{)18}$ ㊳ $4\overline{)16}$ ㊴ $7\overline{)63}$ ㊵ $7\overline{)21}$

㊶ $8\overline{)40}$ ㊷ $8\overline{)64}$ ㊸ $4\overline{)32}$ ㊹ $8\overline{)32}$

㊺ $7\overline{)49}$ ㊻ $8\overline{)24}$ ㊼ $6\overline{)42}$ ㊽ $4\overline{)36}$

㊾ $5\overline{)45}$ ㊿ $6\overline{)30}$ 51 $3\overline{)18}$ 52 $5\overline{)15}$

53 $8\overline{)56}$ 54 $9\overline{)81}$ 55 $3\overline{)21}$ 56 $4\overline{)28}$

FANTASTIC FACT

An average nine-year-old has about 75,000 hairs on his or her head. Each hair grows about 5 inches per year.

◆ **LESSON 140** Practice Multiplying
Three-Digit Numbers

Roll Four Multiplication Game

Players: Two
Materials: Two 0–5 cubes (red), two 5–10 cubes (blue)
Object: To get the greater product
Math Focus: Place value and multiplying three-digit numbers by one-digit numbers

RULES

1. Take turns rolling all four cubes. If a 10 is rolled, roll that cube again.

2. Combine the numbers you roll to make a three-digit by one-digit multiplication problem. You must use the least number rolled as the multiplier.

If you rolled: These are some problems you could make:

8 7 3 5

$$\begin{array}{r} 875 \\ \times\ \ \ 3 \end{array} \qquad \begin{array}{r} 857 \\ \times\ \ \ 3 \end{array} \qquad \begin{array}{r} 758 \\ \times\ \ \ 3 \end{array} \qquad \begin{array}{r} 587 \\ \times\ \ \ 3 \end{array}$$

3. Calculate the product. The player with the greater product wins.

SAMPLE GAME

Terri rolled **4**, **2**, **7**, and **8**.
She made this problem:

$$\begin{array}{r} 874 \\ \times\ \ \ 2 \end{array}$$

Earl rolled **3**, **0**, **6**, and **5**.
He made this problem:

$$\begin{array}{r} 653 \\ \times\ \ \ 0 \end{array}$$

Terri's product was 1748, and Earl's product was 0.
Terri won the round.

Solve.

57 Each shelf is 123 cm long. If you put six of them together, end to end, what will their total length be? Will they fit along a library wall that is 7.5 meters long?

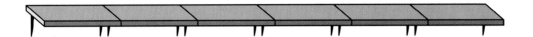

58 Seven wrestlers each weigh about 129 pounds. How much do they weigh all together?

59 The same seven wrestlers can each jump a puddle that is 129 cm across. How wide a puddle can they jump together?

60 Canoes cost $349. How much will eight canoes cost? If you have $2500 to spend, can you get a canoe for each of the eight members of your family?

61 Canoes are on sale this week for $299 each. How much will eight of them cost this week? Will you be able to buy eight canoes if you have $2500? If not, how much more do you need? If you can buy them, how much money will you have left over?

Multiplying Three-Digit Numbers: Applications

Solve.

① Muffin eats about 250 grams of dog food each day. About how many grams does he eat in seven days?

② Ms. Chen earns about $325 each week. About how much money does she earn in four weeks?

③ If an eighth of a kilogram of cheese costs 93¢, how many cents will 1 kilogram cost?

④ Write that amount in dollars and cents.

⑤ The Nuts and Bolts Factory makes 534 bolts in one hour. How many bolts are made in eight hours?

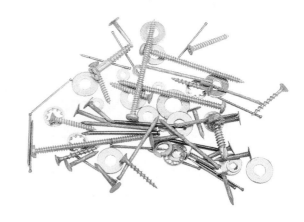

Solve.

6 The Brown Cow Dairy Company produces 450 gallons of milk each day. How much milk does it produce in seven days?

7 There are 356 children at Hidden Hollow camp. The kitchen staff prepares breakfast, lunch, and dinner for each child. How many meals are prepared for the children every day?

Adam wanted to know about how many hours he spent doing certain things each year. He made some estimates and wrote them in a chart.

8 Write the missing amounts.

Activity	Hours Each Day	Number of Days Each Year	Hours Each Year
Sleeping	8	365	▪
Eating	2	365	▪
Reading at home	2	250	▪
Being in school	5	180	▪
Watching television	1	175	▪

9 Does Adam spend more time eating or reading each year?

10 Does Adam spend more time sleeping than he spends doing all the other activities put together?

11 About how many hours do you spend reading each year?

◆ LESSON 141 Multiplying Three-Digit Numbers: Applications

Solve.

Most years have 365 days. Leap years have 366 days. Leap years come every four years. In a leap year, February has 29 days instead of 28 days. The years 1988, 1992, 1996, and 2000 are leap years.

			FEBRUARY			
SUNDAY	MONDAY	TUESDAY	WEDNESDAY	THURSDAY	FRIDAY	SATURDAY
				1	2	3
4	5	6	7	8	9	10
11	12	13	14	15	16	17
18	19	20	21	22	23	24
25	26	27	28	29		

12 Alonzo has owned his dog for exactly three years. One of those years was a leap year. How many days has Alonzo had his dog?

13 Ruth is exactly six years old. She has lived through one leap year. How many days old is Ruth?

14 Arnie is exactly six years old. He has lived through two leap years. How many days old is Arnie?

15 Mohammed just had his second birthday. Could he have been alive during a leap year? Explain your answer.

16 Bridget was born exactly four years before her cousin Angie. One of those years was a leap year. Bridget is how many days older than her cousin?

17 **Challenge:** Figure out how many days old you are. You may use a calendar to see how many days it is to your next birthday or how many days it has been since your last birthday. Compare results with your friends.

GAME

Cube 100 Game

Players:	Two or more
Materials:	Two 0–5 cubes (red), two 5–10 cubes (blue)
Object:	To score as close to 100 as possible without going over
Math Focus:	Adding, multiplying one- and two-digit numbers by one-digit numbers, and place value

RULES

1. Roll the cubes one at a time, adding the numbers as you roll.

2. After any roll, instead of adding that number you may multiply it by the sum of the previous numbers. But then your turn is over.

3. The player with the score closest to, but not over, 100 wins the round.

SAMPLE GAME

Wendy rolled 6, then 3.

She added: $6 + 3 = 9$

Then she rolled 9.

She multiplied: $9 \times 9 = 81$

She stopped after three rolls.

Wendy's score was 81.

Todd rolled 5, then 5.

He added: $5 + 5 = 10$

Then he rolled 6.

He added again: $10 + 6 = 16$

He rolled 6 again.

He multiplied: $16 \times 6 = 96$

Todd's score was 96.

Todd won the round.

LESSON
142

Multiplying Two- and Three-Digit Numbers

Multiply.

①   37
    × 5

②   43
    × 8

③   60
    × 6

④   364
    × 9

⑤   102
    × 9

⑥   841
    × 3

⑦   560
    × 2

⑧   367
    × 4

⑨   35
    × 8

⑩   205
    × 7

⑪   76
    × 3

⑫   311
    × 5

⑬   420
    × 7

⑭   82
    × 8

⑮   333
    × 6

⑯   125
    × 4

⑰   43
    × 7

⑱   58
    × 9

⑲   198
    × 3

⑳   707
    × 6

THINKING
STORY

Talk about the Thinking Story "Everyone Knows Mr. Muddle."

Tina wanted to buy a CD player, so she tried to figure out how much money she could save in one year. Tina and her friend made a chart to help her.

Use a computer or other means to draw the chart. You may use spreadsheet software to calculate the amounts.

Save This Much Each Day	Amount Saved in One Year (365 days)	
	Cents	Dollars and Cents
㉑ 1¢	■	■
㉒ 2¢	■	■
㉓ 3¢	■	■
㉔ 4¢	■	■
㉕ 5¢	■	■
㉖ 6¢	■	■
㉗ 7¢	■	■
㉘ 8¢	■	■
㉙ 9¢	■	■
㉚ 10¢	■	■

Solve these problems.

㉛ If Tina wants to buy a $50.00 CD player in one year's time, how much money will she have to save every day?

㉜ If she wants to buy a CD player that costs $73.00, how much will she have to save each day to buy it in one year's time?

LESSON 143

ALGEBRA READINESS

Exploring Exponents

Solve these problems.

1 How many shells?

$3 + 8 = \blacksquare$

2 How many pennies?

$8 + 8 + 8 = \blacksquare$

$3 \times 8 = \blacksquare$

3 How many balls?

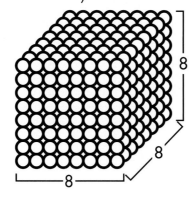

$8 + 8 + 8 + 8 + \ldots$

$8 \times 8 \times 8 = \blacksquare$

$8^3 = \blacksquare$

4 You know that for all numbers n and m, $n + m = m + n$. Here are some examples.

a. $4 + 2 = \blacksquare$ $2 + 4 = \blacksquare$

b. $7 + 9 = \blacksquare$ $9 + 7 = \blacksquare$

c. $283 + 5 = \blacksquare$ $5 + 283 = \blacksquare$

⑤ You know that for all numbers n and m, $n \times m = m \times n$. Here are some examples.

a. $4 \times 2 = $ ▦ $2 \times 4 = $ ▦

b. $7 \times 9 = $ ▦ $9 \times 7 = $ ▦

c. $283 \times 5 = $ ▦ $5 \times 283 = $ ▦

Is it true that for all numbers n and m, $n^m = m^n$?

To find out, solve these problems. Use a calculator.

⑥ $5^7 = $ ▦ $7^5 = $ ▦

⑦ $2^5 = $ ▦ $5^2 = $ ▦

⑧ $3^5 = $ ▦ $5^3 = $ ▦

⑨ $2^3 = $ ▦ $3^2 = $ ▦

⑩ $2^4 = $ ▦ $4^2 = $ ▦

⑪ $1^{10} = $ ▦ $10^1 = $ ▦

⑫ $3^6 = $ ▦ $6^3 = $ ▦

Use exponents to complete these number sentences.

⑬ $2 \times 2 \times 2 \times 2 \times 2 \times 2 = $ ▦

⑭ $3 \times 3 \times 3 = $ ▦

⑮ $6 \times 6 \times 6 \times 6 = $ ▦

⑯ $7 \times 7 = $ ▦

⑰ $4 \times 4 \times 4 \times 4 \times 4 \times 4 \times 4 = $ ▦

⑱ $5 \times 5 \times 5 \times 5 = $ ▦

LESSON
144

Multiplying Two-Digit Numbers by Two-Digit Numbers

What is the area of a garden that is 34 units long and 26 units wide? To find out, multiply 34 by 26.

$$34 \times 26 = \underline{\ ?\ }$$

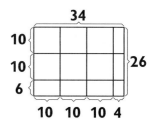

```
   34
 × 26
```

```
   34
 × 26
   24
```

$6 \times 4 = 24$

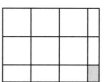

```
   34
 × 26
   24
  180
```

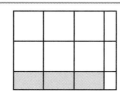

$6 \times 3 \text{ tens} = 180$

```
   34
 × 26
   24
  180
   80
```

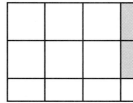

$2 \text{ tens} \times 4 = 80$

```
   34
 × 26
   24
  180
   80
  600
  884
```

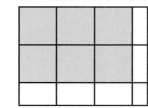

$2 \text{ tens} \times 3 \text{ tens} = 600$

406 • Geometry

Multiply. You may draw pictures to help. Discuss your answers.

1 25
× 25

2 74
× 38

3 56
× 22

4 49
× 22

5 44
× 51

6 91
× 34

7 81
× 18

8 75
× 75

9 35
× 44

10 72
× 54

11 24
× 57

12 64
× 28

13 45
× 14

14 79
× 21

15 17
× 29

16 12
× 12

17 17
× 36

18 41
× 29

19 57
× 11

20 49
× 13

Solve.

21 Each gymnastics team at the tournament has 15 team members. There are 13 teams at the tournament. How many gymnasts are there?

22 Each newspaper carrier delivers 65 newspapers every day. There are 28 carriers. How many newspapers do they deliver each day all together?

Practice Multiplying Two-Digit Numbers by Two-Digit Numbers

Multiply. Solve for *n*.

① $3 \times 6 = n$　　**②** $8 \times 7 = n$　　**③** $4 \times 3 = n$

④ $7 \times 4 = n$　　**⑤** $7 \times 8 = n$　　**⑥** $8 \times 2 = n$

⑦ $8 \times 1 = n$　　**⑧** $10 \times 10 = n$　　**⑨** $9 \times 2 = n$

⑩ $6 \times 0 = n$　　**⑪** $9 \times 7 = n$　　**⑫** $6 \times 6 = n$

⑬ $3 \times 9 = n$　　**⑭** $9 \times 8 = n$　　**⑮** $4 \times 2 = n$

⑯ $6 \times 7 = n$　　**⑰** $9 \times 9 = n$　　**⑱** $5 \times 8 = n$

Multiply.

⑲ 40 × 40	⑳ 41 × 39	㉑ 35 × 35	㉒ 30 × 30	㉓ 14 × 33
㉔ 25 × 25	㉕ 63 × 73	㉖ 43 × 31	㉗ 28 × 25	㉘ 76 × 22
㉙ 29 × 26	㉚ 65 × 80	㉛ 46 × 47	㉜ 62 × 27	㉝ 62 × 92

Multiply.

34 31
× 31

35 32
× 30

36 88
× 12

37 88
× 10

38 88
× 8

39 53
× 50

40 56
× 50

41 72
× 11

42 72
× 22

43 72
× 33

Solve these problems. Use shortcuts when you can. Remember to watch the signs.

44 3542
− 2542

45 7810
+ 3689

46 6005
− 2147

47 2121
+ 2879

48 2394
− 1475

49 1000
+ 1000

50 9999
+ 9999

51 3260
− 1979

52 Greenville and Fulton are both straight ahead. How far apart are the two towns?

Greenville 15 Km
Fulton   25 Km

LESSON 146

Multiply: Two-Digit Numbers by Two-Digit Numbers

Solve these problems.

1. There are 12 eggs in each carton. How many eggs are there in 12 cartons?

2. Each carton of eggs costs 98¢. How much do 12 cartons cost?

3. Write that amount in dollars and cents.

4. There are 24 cans of soup in each carton. How many cans are there in 12 cartons?

5. There are 60 minutes in one hour. How many minutes are there in 24 hours?

6. There are 60 seconds in one minute. How many seconds are there in one hour?

7 The Bella Theater has 26 rows of seats. There are 22 seats in each row. How many seats are in the theater?

8 Brianna had 15 quarters. How many cents is that worth?

9 Write that amount in dollars and cents.

10 There are 24 classes in Lincoln School. There are about 25 students in each class. About how many students are in the school?

11 The manager of a clothing store wanted to sell 3000 caps. There are 80 caps in a case. He sold 27 cases. Did the manager meet his goal?

12 How many months old are you?

13 Each box is 11 centimeters thick. Can Mr. Walker fit one stack of 14 boxes under the table?

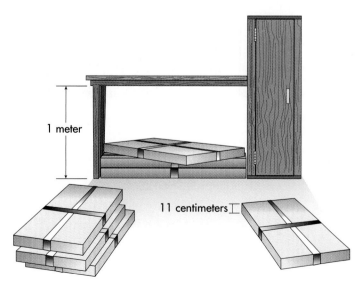

1 meter

11 centimeters

◆ LESSON 146 Multiply: Two-Digit Numbers by Two-Digit Numbers

Solve these problems.

Ashley earned $12 each month for a whole year.

14 How much did she earn that year?

15 Ashley put her earnings in the bank each month. At the end of the year she had $147.50. How much interest did she get from the bank?

There are 24 hours in one day.

16 April has 30 days. How many hours are there in April?

17 May has 31 days. How many hours are there in May?

18 Rani's classroom is 13 meters long. How many decimeters is that?

19 Pablo's table is 22 decimeters long. How many centimeters is that?

Portia and Willy and Manolita and Marcus were standing in a big circle with their arms outstretched and fingertips touching. Marcus wanted to know how big the circle was. He was very careful and measured everybody's arm down to the fingertips. Each arm was about 50 centimeters long.

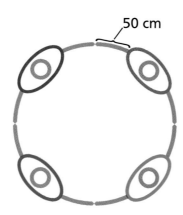

50 cm

20 If you add the lengths of all the arms together, how long will that be?

Marcus said, "This circle is 400 centimeters around."

21 Is Marcus right?

22 Why not?

23 In a small group, act out the problem. How big was the circle you made?

"This is a fine day for flying kites," said Manolita. "My kite is all the way out, as far as my string will reach."

"So is mine," said Willy.

"But that is impossible," said Manolita. "Your string is longer than mine, but my kite is higher than yours."

24 Is that really impossible? Draw a picture to show how it could happen.

Multiplying Decimals by Whole Numbers

When you multiply a decimal by a whole number, remember to place the decimal point in the answer.

Solve.

1 One book costs 347 cents. How many cents do eight books cost?

2 One book costs $3.47. How much do eight books cost?

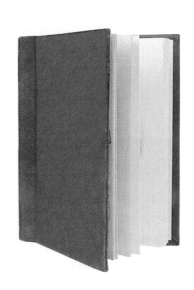

3 Each table is 127 centimeters long. How many centimeters long are six tables placed end to end?

4 Each table is 1.27 meters long. How many meters long are six tables placed end to end?

5 One ticket to the movie costs $5.25. How much do four tickets cost?

6 One lap around the racetrack is 1.25 miles. How many miles is six laps?

Multiply.

7　2.43　**8**　3.02　**9**　4.25　**10**　1.75　**11**　4.42
　　× 5　　　× 7　　　× 4　　　× 5　　　× 6

12　6.33　**13**　4.5　**14**　3.7　**15**　7.5　**16**　2.43
　　× 3　　　× 6　　　× 9　　　× 4　　　× 7

17　3.00　**18**　2.5　**19**　1.25　**20**　3.2　**21**　8.1
　　× 8　　　× 4　　　× 8　　　× 7　　　× 2

22　13.61　**23**　8.12　**24**　7.33　**25**　5.8　**26**　5.02
　　× 5　　　× 2　　　× 9　　　× 6　　　× 6

27　1.48　**28**　3.1　**29**　9.9　**30**　1.3　**31**　1.08
　　× 3　　　× 2　　　× 6　　　× 8　　　× 2

32　2.04　**33**　1.01　**34**　2.29　**35**　3.47　**36**　5.9
　　× 5　　　× 9　　　× 4　　　× 7　　　× 4

Approximating Multiplication

What is the right sign? Draw <, >, or =.

1 243 ● 342

2 7 × 3.45 ● 7 × 4

3 25 × 25 ● 24 × 25

4 20 × 30 ● 6 × 100

5 38 × 27 ● 27 × 38

6 81 × 81 ● 82 × 82

7 7 × 345 ● 7 × 3.45

8 9.99 × 76 ● 10 × 76

9 30 × 40 ● 12 × 100

10 11 × 9 ● 110 × 9

11 25 × 35 ● 6 × 100

12 10 × 60 ● 100 × 6

13 43 × 47 ● 42 × 66

14 12.1 × 10 ● 12.01

15 19 × 12 ● 11 × 11

16 64 × 66 ● 65 × 67

17 87 × 28 ● 82 × 87

18 8 × 10.1 ● 801

19 46.1 × 17 ● 64 × 17

20 3.4 × 12 ● 34 × 12

$9.98

$8.98

$1.98

$6.97

$3.95

$8.98

Solve these problems.

Mrs. Ferroni wants to buy the same present for each of her seven grandchildren. About how many dollars will she need if she buys each grandchild . . .

21 a model airplane?

22 a T-shirt?

23 a football?

24 a storybook?

25 a poster?

26 a paint set?

27 Whitman Elementary School has 34 buses. Each bus seats 45 students. Does the school have enough buses to seat 2000 students?

28 How many more students could be seated if the school bought 11 more buses? Would there be enough buses for each of the 2000 students to have a seat?

29 If a snail can travel 23 inches in an hour, how many inches can it travel in one day?

◆ **LESSON 148** Approximating
Multiplication

COOPERATIVE LEARNING

Tell the Truth Multiplication Game

Players:	**Two**
Materials:	**A score form, two 0–5 cubes (red) and two 5–10 cubes (blue), a pencil**
Object:	**To make a true inequality statement**
Math Focus:	**Recognizing true and false inequality statements involving multiplication**

RULES

1. The first player makes one of these score forms on a sheet of paper:

   ____ < ____   or   ____ > ____

2. The first player chooses any two cubes, rolls them, and writes the product (for example, 3×8) on either side of the inequality sign on the score form.

3. The second player chooses any two cubes, rolls them, and writes the product (for example, 3×5) on the other side of the inequality sign. The second player has no choice about where to write the product.

4. If the resulting inequality statement is true, the second player wins the round. If the statement is false, the first player wins the round. If the products are equal, the statement is false and the first player wins the round.

5. Take turns being the first player.

Copy each problem and write <, >, or =. Look for shortcuts.

30 31 × 43 ■ 30 × 42

31 8471 − 471 ■ 8147 − 47

32 174 + 861 ■ 175 + 860

33 61 × 52 ■ 59 × 51

34 7 × 8 ■ 6 × 9

35 33 + 44 ■ 3000 + 344

36 83 × 94 ■ 84 × 94

37 84 × 87 ■ 83 × 87

38 2001 + 593 ■ 2000 + 594

39 2664 + 3654 ■ 2604 + 3604

40 7083 − 5461 ■ 7085 − 5463

41 21 × 59 ■ 20 × 60

42 783 − 561 ■ 785 − 559

43 5 × 7 ■ 8 × 4

44 479 × 365 ■ 481 × 366

45 1500 + 154 ■ 1503 + 151

46 47 × 83 ■ 40 × 90

47 37 × 28 ■ 74 × 14

48 100 × 5 ■ 100 × 20

49 27 + 15 ■ 21 + 75

Solve these problems.

Hannah wants to give small gifts to the nine children who come to her birthday party. She wants everyone to have the same kind of gift. She has $12 to spend. Party hats cost 57¢ each. Noisemakers cost 48¢ each. Flags cost $1.24 each.

50 Does Hannah have enough money to buy nine flags?

51 Does Hannah have enough money to buy nine noisemakers?

52 Does she have enough to buy nine party hats?

53 Does Hannah have enough money to buy a party hat and a noisemaker for every child who comes to the party?

Approximating Answers

In each problem, two of the answers are clearly wrong and one is correct. Choose the correct answer.

1 $57 + 92 =$
a. 86
b. 37
c. 149

2 $1001 - 900 =$
a. 253
b. 300
c. 101

3 $320 + 430 =$
a. 841
b. 750
c. 940

4 $8135 + 1200 =$
a. 9335
b. 8450
c. 4375

5 $63 - 28 =$
a. 35
b. 152
c. 63

6 $6437 - 2375$
a. 9999
b. 2075
c. 4062

7 $21.1 + 36.2 =$
a. 573
b. 57.3
c. 18.7

8 $55.2 + 37.4 =$
a. 9.26
b. 926
c. 92.6

9 $9 - 4.5 =$
a. 13.5
b. 8.55
c. 4.5

10 $3.15 + 6.78 =$
a. 9.93
b. 99.3
c. 993

In each problem, two of the answers are clearly wrong and one is correct. Choose the correct answer.

⑪ $20 \times 45 =$
a. 90
b. 900
c. 9000

⑫ $34 \times 3 =$
a. 1020
b. 75
c. 102

⑬ $63 \times 2 =$
a. 126
b. 315
c. 33

⑭ $59 \times 3 =$
a. 197
b. 177
c. 77

⑮ $19 \times 19 =$
a. 361
b. 523
c. 190

⑯ $36 \times 90 =$
a. 2751
b. 1025
c. 3240

⑰ $325 \times 3 =$
a. 555
b. 78
c. 975

⑱ $80 \times 7 =$
a. 560
b. 750
c. 870

⑲ $31 \times 29 =$
a. 60
b. 899
c. 6009

⑳ $6 \times 20 =$
a. 120
b. 12
c. 720

㉑ $152 \times 8 =$
a. 1216
b. 250
c. 2016

㉒ $464 \times 4 =$
a. 2666
b. 1856
c. 4006

◆ **LESSON 149 Approximating Answers**

Solve these problems.

23 Diana has a $10 bill. Does she have enough to buy four baseballs?

24 There are 42 rows of seats in the auditorium. There are 31 seats in each row. Are there enough seats for 1000 people?

25 Mr. Martinez paid $100 for a box of 50 T-shirts. Will he make money if he sells the shirts for $1.89 each?

26 James can type 52 words per minute. Can he type a 3000-word paper in an hour?

27 Tickets to the art museum cost $5.80 each for students. Mr. Booker is taking 17 students to the museum. Is $150 enough to pay for the students' tickets?

THINKING STORY

Talk about the Thinking Story "Mr. Muddle's Time Machine (Part 1)."

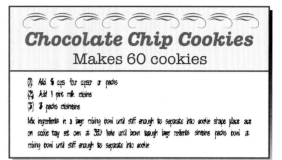

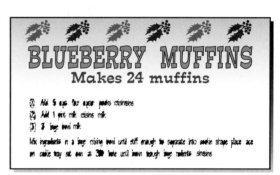

Solve these problems.

28 Mr. Blosser made oatmeal raisin cookies for his class of 26 students. He baked two batches of cookies. Does he have enough for each student in his class to have two cookies?

29 Pumpkin muffins sell for 35¢ each at the school bake sale. How much will one dozen pumpkin muffins cost?

30 Ms. Fong wants to buy muffins at the bake sale. Pumpkin muffins cost 35¢. Blueberry muffins cost 45¢. Ms. Fong has $2. How can she buy five muffins? How much money will she have left?

31 The recipe for chocolate chip cookies calls for two eggs for each batch. How many eggs are needed to make 180 cookies?

32 Each batch of chocolate chip cookies contains 12 ounces of chocolate chips. Could you make three batches of cookies with 35 ounces of chocolate chips? Explain.

Unit 4   Lesson 149 • **423**

Counting to One Million

Count up. Fill in the missing numbers.

1 | 97 | 98 | ■ | ■ | ■ | ■ | 103 |

2 | 997 | 998 | ■ | ■ | ■ | 1002 |

3 | 9999 | 10,000 | ■ | ■ | 10,003 |

4 | 10,998 | ■ | ■ | ■ | 11,002 |

5 | 100,998 | ■ | ■ | 101,001 |

6 | 900,997 | ■ | ■ | 901,000 |

7 | 909,998 | ■ | ■ | 910,001 |

8 | 999,998 | ■ | ■ | 1,000,001 |

Use a computer or other means to copy and fill in the chart.

Distance in Meters	Distance in Centimeters
1	■
10	■
100	■
1000	■

There are 100,000 centimeters in 1 kilometer. How many centimeters are there in 10 kilometers?

How many kilometers is 1,000,000 centimeters?

◆ About how long is 1 centimeter?

◆ About how long is 10 kilometers?

◆ Can you think of a place that is 10 kilometers from your school?

FANTASTIC FACT

Students spend about 1,000,000 minutes in school from kindergarten through 12th grade.

◆ **LESSON 150   Counting to One Million**

*In the last lesson your teacher read the first part
of this story to you. Now read this part yourself.*

Mr. Muddle's Time Machine

Part 2

The next day Mr. Muddle bought two hands for his clock. They were both the same length and looked exactly alike. He put the hands on carefully. "There," he said, "this clock looks better than most. There's something uneven about most clocks."

One afternoon Marcus and Manolita stopped by to see how Mr. Muddle's time machine was working. "The clock works just fine," said Mr. Muddle. "Listen to it tick. But sometimes I can't tell what time it is. Look at it now."

One hand was pointing at 11. The other hand was pointing at 4. "It could be almost any time," said Mr. Muddle. "I can't tell."

"It's not that bad," said Marcus. "There are only two different times it could be."

"And I think I know which is the right time," said Manolita.

Work in groups. Discuss your answers and how you figured them out. Then compare your answers with those of other groups.

1 Why is it hard to tell what time it is with Mr. Muddle's clock?

2 Look at the clock in the picture. What are the two times that it could be?

3 Which of these is the right time? Look for a clue in the story.

Adding Multidigit Numbers

Add.

1　 6
　　+ 8

2　 7
　　+ 2

3　 8
　　+ 6

4　 2
　　+ 9

5　 7
　　+ 7

6　 36
　　+ 72

7　 85
　　+ 97

8　 346
　　+ 763

9　 602
　　+ 147

10　 7218
　　+ 6318

11　 3190
　　+ 2530

12　 65,151
　　+ 37,629

13　 8,745,648
　　+ 6,639,425

14　 12,795,000
　　+ 36,312,128

15　 7,667,357
　　+ 591,628

16　 219,994,336
　　+ 618,430,828

17　 14,352,476
　　+ 27,264,818

18　 452,663,347
　　+ 834,952,563

Solve.

19 In the number 80,151,761, which digit is in the millions place? Which digit is in the ten thousands place? Which digit is in the ten millions place?

Use a computer or other means to copy and fill in the chart.

Amount in Dollars	Amount in Cents
1	100
10	▪
100	▪
1000	▪
10,000	▪

◆ What can you buy for 1 cent?

◆ What can you buy for 1,000,000 cents?

Use a computer or other means to copy and fill in the chart.

Number of Pennies	Weight
1	About **4** grams
10	About ▪ grams
100	About ▪ grams
1000	About ▪ grams
10,000	About ▪ grams

◆ About how many pennies do you think you can carry?

◆ **LESSON 151 Adding Multidigit Numbers**

You read Part 2 of this story in the last lesson.
Read on to find out what happens next.

Mr. Muddle's Time Machine

Part 3

One day Loretta the letter carrier stopped to talk to Mr. and Mrs. Muddle. Mr. Muddle asked Loretta to look at her watch to see what time it was. "It's either a little after one or a little after two," Mr. Muddle said, "but I can't tell which."

Mr. Muddle showed his clock to Loretta. He noticed that the hands had moved a bit since the last time he had looked. Now the clock looked like this:

"Now I'm really confused," said Mr. Muddle. "It could be either a quarter after two or ten minutes after three."

"I think I can figure this out," said Loretta. "You told me that just a few minutes ago it was either a little after one or a little after two. Right?"

"Right," said Mr. Muddle.

"Well then, it couldn't be after three o'clock now," said Loretta.

Work in groups. Discuss your answers and how you figured them out. Then compare your answers with those of other groups.

❶ What time was it?

❷ How did Loretta know what time it was?

❸ In the picture of Mr. Muddle's clock, which hand is the minute hand?

Subtracting Multidigit Numbers

LESSON 152

Subtract.

1
```
   14
 −  7
```

2
```
    8
 −  2
```

3
```
   16
 −  8
```

4
```
   17
 −  9
```

5
```
   13
 −  7
```

6
```
   94
 − 36
```

7
```
   75
 − 28
```

8
```
   420
 − 105
```

9
```
   657
 − 348
```

10
```
   8675
 − 4382
```

11
```
   9400
 − 3250
```

12
```
   4307
 − 2632
```

13
```
   97,520
 − 86,672
```

14
```
   3,642,758
 − 2,642,635
```

15
```
   14,756,821
 − 13,647,945
```

16
```
   74,685,300
 − 28,400,524
```

17
```
   8,372,463
 − 1,377,469
```

18
```
   2,077,560
 −   84,102
```

THINKING STORY

Talk about the Thinking Story "Mr. Muddle's Time Machine (Part 4)."

The largest city in the state of New York is New York City. New York City is divided into five parts called boroughs. They are the Bronx, Brooklyn, Manhattan, Queens, and Staten Island. The populations of the five boroughs according to the 1990 census are shown.

1990 Population of New York City's Boroughs	
Bronx	1,203,789
Brooklyn	2,300,664
Manhattan	1,487,536
Queens	1,951,598
Staten Island	378,977
Total:	7,322,564

Answer these questions.

19 Which of New York City's boroughs had the most people?

20 Which of the boroughs had the fewest people?

21 What was the difference in population between Brooklyn and Staten Island?

22 The 1990 population of the whole state of New York was 17,990,455. How many people who lived in New York State did not live in New York City in 1990?

ASSESSMENT

Unit 4 Review

Give the volume of these boxes.

Lessons 118, 119

1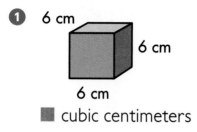
6 cm
6 cm
6 cm
■ cubic centimeters

2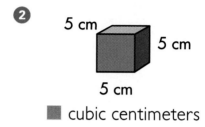
5 cm
5 cm
5 cm
■ cubic centimeters

Solve these problems.

Lessons 119, 120

3 2 quarts = ■ cups **4** $\frac{1}{2}$ gallon = ■ pints **5** ■ mL = 3 L

6 1 L = ■ mL **7** 1 gallon = ■ quarts **8** 2 L = ■ mL

Solve for *n*. Watch the signs.

9 $48 \div 8 = n$ **10** $36 \div 6 = n$ **11** $8 \times 7 = n$

Lesson 120 **12** $27 \div 3 = n$ **13** $64 \div 8 = n$ **14** $7 \times 2 = n$

Count the line segments and angles in these figures.

Lesson 127

15  ■ line segments
■ angles

16 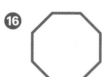 ■ line segments
■ angles

Name each figure. Write *square, rectangle, parallellogram,* or *trapezoid.*

Lesson 128

17

18

19

434 • Geometry

Multiply.

Lessons
136, 137,
139, 140,
144, 145

㉑
```
   35
×   7
```

㉑
```
  375
×   6
```

㉒
```
   34
× 25
```

㉓
```
   60
× 40
```

㉔
```
   68
× 33
```

㉕
```
  179
×   5
```

㉖
```
   86
×   9
```

㉗
```
   19
× 54
```

Solve these problems. Watch the signs.

Lessons
151, 152

㉘
```
  7241
+ 3689
```

㉙
```
  8703
− 2694
```

㉚
```
  3948
+ 2817
```

㉛
```
   7,652,871,999
+ 10,743,426,000
```

㉜
```
  90,300
− 31,120
```

Solve.

Lesson 119

㉝ A baseball that was hit to Sharon landed about 10 meters in front of the center field fence. About how far was the ball hit?

Lesson 138

㉞ There are 24 rows of seats in the theater. Each row has 32 seats. Are there enough seats in the theater for 600 people?

Lesson 147

㉟ The rental fee for each video is $1.28. How much does it cost to rent five videos?

Unit Test

Multiply.

1 $3 \times 3 \times 3 =$ ■   **2** $5 \times 5 \times 5 =$ ■   **3** $7 \times 7 \times 7 =$ ■

4 $2 \times 2 \times 2 \times 2 =$ ■ **5** $8 \times 8 \times 8 =$ ■   **6** $6 \times 6 \times 6 =$ ■

Solve these problems.

7 1 gallon = ■ quarts **8** ■ pints = 2 quarts **9** 3 quarts = ■ cups

10 4000 mL = ■ L   **11** ■ L = 6000 mL   **12** ■ mL = 5 L

Name each figure. Write *square, rectangle,* *parallellogram,* **or** *trapezoid.*

13    **14**

15    **16**

17    **18**

Solve these problems. Watch the signs.

19
$$\begin{array}{r} 45 \\ +\ 36 \\ \hline \end{array}$$

20
$$\begin{array}{r} 62 \\ -\ 28 \\ \hline \end{array}$$

21
$$\begin{array}{r} 703 \\ -\ 249 \\ \hline \end{array}$$

22
$$\begin{array}{r} 346 \\ +\ 679 \\ \hline \end{array}$$

23
$$\begin{array}{r} 8{,}704{,}956 \\ +\ 4{,}283{,}504 \\ \hline \end{array}$$

24
$$\begin{array}{r} 12{,}048{,}759 \\ -\ 9{,}237{,}825 \\ \hline \end{array}$$

25
$$\begin{array}{r} 4{,}347{,}031 \\ +\ 3{,}681{,}928 \\ \hline \end{array}$$

26
$$\begin{array}{r} 5{,}216{,}802 \\ -\ 994{,}365 \\ \hline \end{array}$$

What fraction is colored?

27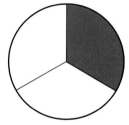

28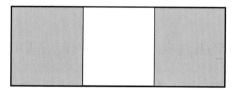

29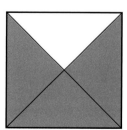

30

◆ **Unit 4 Test**

Multiply.

31 $7 \times 8 = \blacksquare$

32 $3 \times 3 = \blacksquare$

33 $7 \times 4 = \blacksquare$

34 $3 \times 6 = \blacksquare$

35 $6 \times 3 = \blacksquare$

36 $5 \times 5 = \blacksquare$

37 $8 \times 8 = \blacksquare$

38 $5 \times 6 = \blacksquare$

39 $6 \times 9 = \blacksquare$

Divide.

40 $56 \div 7 = \blacksquare$

41 $30 \div 3 = \blacksquare$

42 $49 \div 7 = \blacksquare$

43 $24 \div 4 = \blacksquare$

44 $24 \div 6 = \blacksquare$

45 $32 \div 8 = \blacksquare$

46 $30 \div 5 = \blacksquare$

47 $35 \div 7 = \blacksquare$

48 $63 \div 7 = \blacksquare$

What is the right sign? Draw <, >, or =.

49 43 ● 37

50 1.08 ● 1.4

51 45 ● 54

52 98 ● 106

53 32.6 ● 12.9

54 3.0 ● 3

55 6.2 ● 3.9

56 7.3 ● 7.30

57 29.1 ● 28.7

58 63.08 ● 63.10

59 4.2 ● 2.1

60 1.50 ● 1.05

61 21.6 ● 2.16

62 108 ● 98

63 23 ● 32

64 108 ● 180

65 16 ● 16.5

66 9.80 ● 9.8

Solve these problems. Watch the signs.

⑥⑦
```
   3.42
 + 1.98
```

⑥⑧
```
   8.6
 - 4.8
```

⑥⑨
```
  16.85
 + 8.4
```

⑦⓪
```
   7.7
 - 3.55
```

⑦①
```
  67
× 5
```

⑦②
```
  241
×   6
```

⑦③
```
  507
×   9
```

⑦④
```
  801
×   3
```

⑦⑤
```
  43
× 58
```

⑦⑥
```
  45
× 45
```

⑦⑦
```
  4.67
×    3
```

⑦⑧
```
  11.4
×    9
```

Solve.

⑦⑨ What is the area of this rectangle?

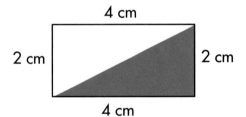

4 cm

2 cm   2 cm

4 cm

⑧⓪ What is the area of the blue triangle?

Draw all lines of symmetry.

⑧①

⑧②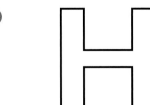

◆ **Unit 4 Test**

Solve.

83 Each pen costs 20¢.
How much do four pens cost?

Tami is 135 centimeters tall.

Kay is 128 centimeters tall.

84 Who is taller?

85 How much taller?

86 There are 20 rows of seats
in the room. There are 30
seats in each row. How many
seats are in the room?

There are 36 cookies to share among the students in the class.
How many cookies does each student receive if there are

87 six students in the class?

88 nine students in the class?

89 36 students in the class?

90 18 students in the class?

A Message from the Authors

Can you break the code?

14 15 23   20 8 1 20   25 15 21   8 1 22 5

6 9 14 9 19 8 5 4   15 21 18   2 15 15 11,   23 5

8 15 16 5   25 15 21   8 1 22 5   12 5 1 18 14 5 4

20 15   5 14 10 15 25   13 1 20 8 5 13 1 20 9 3 19

1 14 4   6 15 21 14 4   9 20   20 15   2 5   21 19 5 6 21 12.

19 20 5 16 8 5 14   23 9 12 12 15 21 7 8 2 25

3 1 18 12   2 5 18 5 9 20 5 18

16 5 20 5 18   8 9 12 20 15 14

10 15 19 5 16 8   18 21 2 9 14 19 20 5 9 14

LESSON
154

Extend Your Thinking

Use this code to answer the questions.

GEOGRAPHY
CONNECTION

A	B	C	D	E	F	G	H	I	J	K	L	M
21	14	1	25	9	17	26	10	23	18	3	11	19

N	O	P	Q	R	S	T	U	V	W	X	Y	Z
4	7	16	15	8	24	6	22	13	2	12	20	5

1 What shell could trap a man?

13×2 $47 - 24$ 3×7 $2 + 2$ $42 \div 7$

1×1 $6 + 5$ 7×3 $11 + 8$

2 What animal lives the longest?

3×2 $3 + 4$ $10 - 2$

$54 \div 9$ $49 \div 7$ $18 + 5$ 8×3 $8 + 1$

3 What is the world's most poisonous snake?

$12 + 12$ $19 - 10$ 3×7

$18 + 6$ $16 - 12$ $17 + 4$ 3×1 $45 \div 5$

Solve each problem. Use the chart to decode the answers.

GEOGRAPHY CONNECTION

A	B	C	D	E	F	G	H	I	J	K	L	M
21	14	1	25	9	17	26	10	23	18	3	11	19

N	O	P	Q	R	S	T	U	V	W	X	Y	Z
4	7	16	15	8	24	6	22	13	2	12	20	5

④ Which of the United States is farthest north?

7 × 3   22 − 11   3 × 7

67 − 43   3 ÷ 1   9 + 12

⑤ Which of the United States is farthest south?

100 ÷ 10   15 + 6   12 ÷ 6

26 − 5   9 + 14   11 + 12

⑥ Which of the United States is farthest west?

92 − 71   4 + 7   6 + 15

12 × 2   24 ÷ 8   17 + 4

UNIT
4
WRAP-UP

Finding Frequent Numbers

On page 357 you tried an experiment with a 0–5 cube and a 5–10 cube. Do you remember that when you rolled the two cubes some totals seemed to come up more often than others? Which sums were most common? Which sums were least common?

In this project, you will try a similar experiment. Work with two other students. Roll three 0–5 cubes. Add the three numbers together. What are the possible sums? Is it possible to get a sum of 0? Is it possible to get a sum of 15? Is it possible to get a sum of 16?

Which sums do you think will be most common? Which will be least common? About how many more times do you think you will get a total of 7 than of 0?

Work in pairs. Use three 0–5 cubes (red). Play a game in which one person wins if the total is 6, 7, 8, or 9. The other person wins if the total is any of the other 12 numbers. How much of an advantage do you think the second player has?

Make a graph like the one below. Roll the three cubes 25 times. Record the sums on the graph. Then, as a class, add the numbers from each group's graph. Make a class bar graph. What do you see? Can you explain what happened?

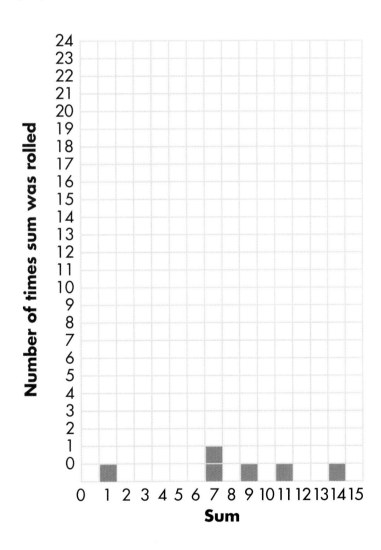

Cumulative Review
Use after Lesson 4.

Find the numbers that are written twice.

1 Start at 56.

59 61 57 62 66 65 60 63 67 58 60 62 56 64

2 Start at 269.

277 271 278 272 276 269 273 275 270 273
272 274

Write the number.

3 Four hundred twenty-six

4 Thirty-five

5 One hundred four

6 Seventy

Count up or down. Fill in the missing numbers.

7 8   9   ▪   ▪   ▪   13   ▪   ▪

8 23   22   21   ▪   ▪   ▪   17   ▪

9 96   97   ▪   ▪   ▪   101   ▪   103

10 354 353 352 ▪   ▪   ▪   348   ▪

11 ▪   ▪   671 672 673 ▪   ▪   ▪

Write the numbers in words.

12 80

13 49

14 117

15 651

16 926

17 308

Count up or down. Fill in the missing numbers.

18 998   999   ▪   ▪   ▪   1003

19 3057 3058   ▪   ▪   ▪   3062

20 5432 5431   ▪   ▪   5428   ▪

Cumulative Review
Use after Lesson 7.

The graph shows the number of cousins that students in Sam's class have. Use the graph to answer the questions below.

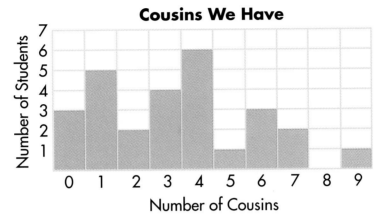

Cousins We Have

① What is the greatest number of cousins anyone in the class has?

② What is the most common number of cousins?

③ How many students have three cousins?

④ How many students have no cousins?

⑤ How many more students have four cousins than have seven cousins?

Use the number 34,785.

⑥ What digit is in the hundreds place?

⑦ Name the place with the digit 8 in it.

⑧ What digit is in the ones place?

⑨ What digit is in the thousands place?

⑩ Name the place with the digit 3 in it.

Solve these problems. Watch the signs.

⑪	⑫	⑬	⑭	⑮
7 + 3	8 + 4	5 + 9	10 − 6	13 − 8

Cumulative Review
Use after Lesson 9.

Match each word problem with a number problem.
Then solve the problems.

1. Rey has four cats. He used to have nine cats. How many cats did he give away?

2. Celeste is nine years old. Daniel is four years older. How old is Daniel?

3. Five kids want to play baseball. They need nine players for a team. How many more kids are needed?

4. Some birds sat in a tree. After five flew off, there were still nine birds in the tree. How many birds were there at first?

a.	b.	c.	d.
9	9	5	■
+ 4	− ■	+ ■	− 5
■	4	9	9

Solve these problems. Watch the signs.

5.   4   6.   13   7.   9   8.   10   9.   5
  + 7   − 7   + 3   − 3   + 8
   ■   ■   ■   ■   ■

10.   7   11.   18   12.   12   13.   8   14.   14
   + 9   − 9   − 5   + 7   − 6
    ■   ■   ■   ■   ■

15.   3   16.   15   17.   10   18.   17   19.   0
   + 9   − 9   + 6   − 10   + 4
    ■   ■   ■   ■   ■

Write the words as numerals.

20. Five thousand nine hundred sixty-two   21. eighty-two

22. Four hundred twelve   23. one hundred one

24. Six hundred three   25. three hundred

Cumulative Review
Use after Lesson 12.

Use the map to answer questions 1 and 2.

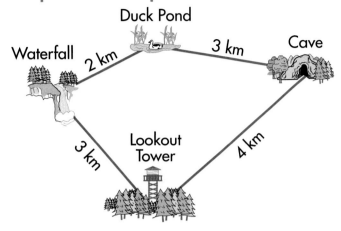

1. How far is it from the lookout tower to the cave?

2. How much farther is it from the cave to the duck pond than from the duck pond to the waterfall?

Solve these problems. Watch the signs.

3. 10 + 5 − 8 = ■
4. 17 − 9 − 6 + 10 + 3 = ■
5. 13 − 5 + 4 = ■
6. 4 + 6 − 8 + 10 = ■
7. 6 + 6 + 6 − 10 − 4 = ■
8. 7 + 7 − 3 + 9 = ■

Tell which numbers are odd.

9. 3 10 17 20 35 44 60

Add or subtract.

10.
$$8 + 8$$

11.
$$9 + 5$$

12.
$$15 - 9$$

13.
$$11 - 7$$

Write the standard name for each of these.

14. 5 tens and 6 = ■
15. 7 tens and 17 = ■

Cumulative Review
Use after Lesson 16.

Solve these problems. Watch the signs.

①
$$\begin{array}{r} 60 \\ +\ 30 \\ \hline \end{array}$$

②
$$\begin{array}{r} 90 \\ +\ 50 \\ \hline \end{array}$$

③
$$\begin{array}{r} 65 \\ -\ 36 \\ \hline \end{array}$$

④
$$\begin{array}{r} 83 \\ -\ 75 \\ \hline \end{array}$$

⑤
$$\begin{array}{r} 50 \\ -\ 27 \\ \hline \end{array}$$

⑥
$$\begin{array}{r} 80 \\ +\ 60 \\ \hline \end{array}$$

⑦
$$\begin{array}{r} 41 \\ -\ 19 \\ \hline \end{array}$$

⑧
$$\begin{array}{r} 50 \\ +\ 70 \\ \hline \end{array}$$

⑨
$$\begin{array}{r} 34 \\ +\ 57 \\ \hline \end{array}$$

⑩
$$\begin{array}{r} 93 \\ -\ 60 \\ \hline \end{array}$$

⑪
$$\begin{array}{r} 81 \\ +\ 16 \\ \hline \end{array}$$

⑫
$$\begin{array}{r} 35 \\ +\ 45 \\ \hline \end{array}$$

⑬
$$\begin{array}{r} 72 \\ -\ 54 \\ \hline \end{array}$$

⑭
$$\begin{array}{r} 24 \\ -\ 19 \\ \hline \end{array}$$

⑮
$$\begin{array}{r} 36 \\ -\ 28 \\ \hline \end{array}$$

Rewrite to show ten more ones.

⑯ 36 = ■ tens and ■

⑰ 90 = ■ tens and ■

⑱ 18 = ■ tens and ■

⑲ 63 = ■ tens and ■

Rewrite to show ten more tens.

⑳ 350 = ■ hundreds and ■ tens

㉑ 890 = ■ hundreds and ■ tens

㉒ 130 = ■ hundreds and ■ tens

㉓ 660 = ■ hundreds and ■ tens

Fill in the missing numbers.

㉔ 3, 6, 9, ■, ■, ■

㉕ 77, 66, 55, ■, ■, ■

㉖ 21, 23, 25, ■, ■, ■

㉗ 260, 270, 280, ■, ■, ■

Rewrite to show no hundreds. Then rewrite to show more ones.

㉘ 316 = ■ tens and 6 = ■ tens and ■

㉙ 400 = ■ tens and 0 = ■ tens and ■

㉚ 503 = ■ tens and 3 = ■ tens and ■

Cumulative Review

Use after Lesson 20.

Write whether the answer is *odd* or *even*.

1. $7 + 7$
2. $8 + 3$
3. $40 + 50$
4. $12 + 12$
5. $9 + 3$
6. $4 + 11$

Write the standard name for these.

7. 5 tens and 4
8. 0 tens and 13
9. 5 tens and 14
10. 18 hundreds

Solve these problems.

11. Ryan took 48 pictures of his dog, Woofer. Nine of them did not come out. How many pictures of Woofer does Ryan have?
12. Hildy lives 45 miles from the beach. She drove there and back. How far did she drive?
13. Grant had 90¢. He spent some money on a comb. Now he has 14¢. How much did the comb cost?

Solve these problems. Watch the signs.

14. $$\begin{array}{r} 71 \\ -\ 36 \\ \hline \end{array}$$
15. $$\begin{array}{r} 50 \\ -\ 27 \\ \hline \end{array}$$
16. $$\begin{array}{r} 47 \\ +\ 34 \\ \hline \end{array}$$
17. $$\begin{array}{r} 34 \\ +\ 18 \\ \hline \end{array}$$
18. $$\begin{array}{r} 631 \\ -\ 346 \\ \hline \end{array}$$
19. $$\begin{array}{r} 328 \\ -\ 219 \\ \hline \end{array}$$
20. $$\begin{array}{r} 186 \\ +\ 347 \\ \hline \end{array}$$
21. $$\begin{array}{r} 259 \\ +\ 168 \\ \hline \end{array}$$

Solve.

22. $12 - 6 + 3 - 6 + 9 = \blacksquare$
23. $4 + 6 + 9 - 10 - 3 = \blacksquare$
24. $8 + 8 + 4 - 7 + 1 - 6 = \blacksquare$
25. $15 - 9 - 5 + 11 + 8 + 1 = \blacksquare$

Cumulative Review
Use after Lesson 23.

Solve these problems.

1 In Mr. Wright's class, there are 16 girls and 15 boys. How many students are in Mr. Wright's class?

2 Mr. Sanchez weighs 170 pounds. His son weighs 101 pounds. How much more does Mr. Sanchez weigh than his son?

451 children go to Hudson School. 389 children go to Mohawk School.

3 How many students go to the two schools all together?

4 How many more students go to Hudson School?

5 Which school has more library books?

Use the map to answer questions 6 and 7.

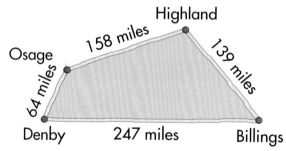

6 Julie drives a bus. Her daily route is from Billings to Denby and back. How many miles does she drive on her route?

7 Paul drives from Osage to Highland to Billings to Denby to Osage. How far is that?

Solve these problems. Watch the signs.

8   317
     + 534

9   866
     − 798

10   586
      + 391

11   235
      + 283

12   804
      − 347

13   912
      − 203

14   400
      − 155

15   715
      + 198

Cumulative Review
Use after Lesson 29.

Solve these problems. Watch the signs.

1	34 46 + 25	**2**	61 83 + 19	**3**	110 250 80 + 130	**4**	26 529 180 + 202

5	7462 − 3819	**6**	853 + 4307	**7**	1296 705 34 + 2183	**8**	6000 − 2468

Copy and complete the table. Show about how many years ago each famous person was born.

	Name	Year of Birth	Born This Many Years Ago
9	Cochise	1815	▪
10	Pablo Picasso	1881	▪
11	Duke Ellington	1899	▪
12	Anne Frank	1929	▪
13	Sadako Sasaki	1943	▪
14	Sally Ride	1951	▪

Use the number line to help solve these problems.
You may use a calculator.

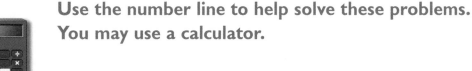

15 $10 - 4 - 4 - 4 =$ ▪   **16** $-6 + 10 =$ ▪

17 $7 - 3 - 3 - 3 - 3 =$ ▪   **18** $3 - 9 =$ ▪

19 $2 - 5 =$ ▪   **20** $-7 + 2 + 2 =$ ▪

Cumulative Review
Use after Lesson 33.

What is the right sign? Draw <, >, or =.

1 362 ● 326

2 714 ● 721

3 250 ● 250

4 100 ● 99

5 540 ● 54

6 2109 ● 3000

7 6 + 9 ● 7 + 8

8 30 + 60 ● 30 + 40

9 51 − 0 ● 55 − 0

10 2000 + 4000 ● 2000 + 4005

11 4 + 87 ● 87 + 34

12 147 − 10 ● 147 − 20

13 6382 + 213 ● 6328 + 213

14 297 − 97 ● 397 − 197

Round to the nearest ten.

15 33

16 87

17 55

18 26

Round to the nearest hundred.

19 738

20 850

21 382

22 949

Round to the nearest thousand.

23 4307

24 1296

25 1166

26 7500

Choose the correct answer.

27 10 + 20 + 50 = ■
 a. 80
 b. 800
 c. 8000

28 400 + 900 = ■
 a. 13
 b. 130
 c. 1300

29 9000 − 7000 = ■
 a. 20
 b. 200
 c. 2000

30 80 − 30 = ■
 a. 50
 b. 500
 c. 5000

Cumulative Review
Use after Lesson 36.

Find the perimeter.

1

2 cm

2 cm   2 cm

2 cm

2

3 cm   5 cm

4 cm

Solve.

3 Officer Shen patrols the park every day. How far does he walk to go once around the park?

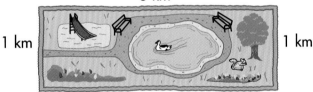

3 km

1 km   1 km

3 km

4 What shape is the park?

Write _T_ if the statement is true. Write _F_ if it is false.

5 $4 + 17 > 20$

6 $100 + 700 = 7000$

7 $200 + 3456 = 3654$

8 $7012 - 4 > 7008$

9 $1000 > 999 - 1$

10 $870 - 10 < 807$

11 $75 < 81 - 6$

12 $503 > 53 + 500$

Solve these problems. Watch the signs.

13	**14**	**15**	**16**
4003 − 3171	2850 + 4978	1083 + 8789	6745 − 2176

17	**18**	**19**	**20**
9872 − 3894	4625 + 4585	3366 + 5729	9173 − 8577

Cumulative Review
Use after Lesson 38.

Tell the time in three ways.

1

■ minutes after ■

■ minutes before ■

2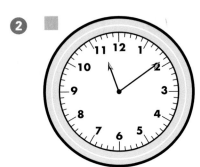

■ minutes after ■

■ minutes before ■

Solve.

3 The pool at the town park is a rectangle. It is 75 feet long and 50 feet wide. What is the perimeter of the pool?

4 Chandra wants to put ribbon around a square napkin that she made. Each side is 20 centimeters long. She has 24 centimeters of ribbon. How much more ribbon does Chandra need?

Rewrite to show more tens.

5 370 = ■ hundreds and ■ tens   **6** 420 = ■ hundreds and ■ tens

7 610 = ■ hundreds and ■ tens   **8** 880 = ■ hundreds and ■ tens

9 530 = ■ hundreds and ■ tens   **10** 770 = ■ hundreds and ■ tens

11 310 = ■ hundreds and ■ tens   **12** 950 = ■ hundreds and ■ tens

Round to the nearest ten.

13 4674   **14** 4289   **15** 4016   **16** 5667

Round to the nearest hundred.

17 5467   **18** 9014   **19** 3090   **20** 8409

Cumulative Review

Use after Lesson 42.

Find the area.

1

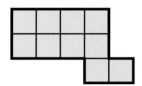

■ square centimeters

2

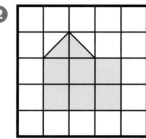

■ square centimeters

Solve.

3 Each ant has six legs. There are three ants. How many legs are there all together? 3 × 6 = ■

4 Each lion has four legs. There are four lions. How many legs are there all together? 4 × 4 = ■

Estimate the area of the blue part of each rectangle.

5 4 cm

2 cm

6

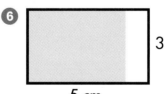

3 cm

5 cm

Fill in the missing numbers.

7 2, 4, ■, ■, ■, 12, ■, ■, ■, 20 . . .

8 3, 7, 11, ■, ■, 23, ■, ■, 35 . . .

9 4, 7, 10, ■, ■, 19, ■, ■, 28 . . .

Add or subtract.

10 6 + 5 = ■   **11** 7 − 0 = ■   **12** 13 − 9 = ■

13 8 + 6 = ■   **14** 5 + 8 = ■   **15** 10 − 6 = ■

Cumulative Review
Use after Lesson 46.

Solve these problems.

Five cars enter the park. Each car has two, three, or four people in it.

1 What is the least number of people that might be in the cars?

2 What is the greatest number of people that might be in the cars?

Multiply.

3 $4 \times 4 = \blacksquare$ **4** $3 \times 6 = \blacksquare$ **5** $4 \times 5 = \blacksquare$

6 $6 \times 6 = \blacksquare$ **7** $7 \times 3 = \blacksquare$ **8** $1 \times 9 = \blacksquare$

Copy and complete the chart about stickers.

	Number	Star 4¢	Cat 9¢	Bat 10¢	Car 6¢	Heart 5¢
9	1					
10	2					
11	3					
12	4					

13 How much will ten bats cost?

14 How much will four of each sticker cost all together?

15 How much will three stars and four hearts cost all together?

Solve these problems. Watch the signs.

16
$$\begin{array}{r} 823 \\ -\ 478 \\ \hline \end{array}$$
17
$$\begin{array}{r} 687 \\ +\ 294 \\ \hline \end{array}$$
18
$$\begin{array}{r} 108 \\ +\ 798 \\ \hline \end{array}$$
19
$$\begin{array}{r} 823 \\ -\ 478 \\ \hline \end{array}$$
20
$$\begin{array}{r} 531 \\ -\ 369 \\ \hline \end{array}$$

Cumulative Review
Use after Lesson 48.

Multiply.

1 100 × 10 = ■   **2** 384 × 10 = ■   **3** 5 × 100 = ■

4 111 × 100 = ■   **5** 24 × 1000 = ■   **6** 1000 × 76 = ■

7 10 × 1000 = ■   **8** 444 × 100 = ■   **9** 802 × 1000 = ■

Copy and complete the chart.

	Item	How Many	Unit Price	Total Price
10	Pencil	9	10¢	■
11	Eraser	3	8¢	■
12	Paper Clip	10	5¢	■
13	Fastener	5	7¢	■

Multiply.

14 7   **15** 3   **16** 5   **17** 2   **18** 9
    × 4   × 9   × 5   × 8   × 6

19 8   **20** 1   **21** 8   **22** 4   **23** 0
    × 9   × 3   × 4   × 5   × 2

Solve these problems.

24 Tina bought four pads of paper. Each pad has 100 sheets of paper. How many sheets of paper does Tina have?

25 Mekhi can make one origami bird in three minutes. How long would it take him to make five origami birds?

Cumulative Review
Use after Lesson 51.

Write the area in square centimeters.

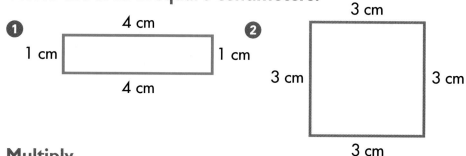

1 4 cm 1 cm 1 cm 4 cm

2 3 cm 3 cm 3 cm 3 cm

Multiply.

3 $7 \times 8 = \blacksquare$ **4** $0 \times 7 = \blacksquare$ **5** $8 \times 9 = \blacksquare$

6 $6 \times 10 = \blacksquare$ **7** $5 \times 8 = \blacksquare$ **8** $4 \times 6 = \blacksquare$

9 $7 \times 7 = \blacksquare$ **10** $9 \times 3 = \blacksquare$ **11** $6 \times 6 = \blacksquare$

CLIPS 18¢

CHALK 6¢ EACH

Name Tags HELLO my name is 8¢ each

TAPE 45¢

Solve these problems.

12 How much will seven name tags cost?

13 How much will two rolls of tape cost?

14 Fred has three dimes. Can he buy two paper clips?

15 Anya has a quarter. How many pieces of chalk can she buy?

Cumulative Review
Use after Lesson 66.

Solve these problems. Watch the signs.

1. $7 \times 8 = \blacksquare$
2. $4 \times 9 = \blacksquare$
3. $7 \times 3 = \blacksquare$
4. $45 \div 5 = \blacksquare$
5. $48 \div 6 = \blacksquare$
6. $24 \div 8 = \blacksquare$
7. $0 \times 6 = \blacksquare$
8. $32 \div 4 = \blacksquare$
9. $35 \div 7 = \blacksquare$
10. $49 \div 7 = \blacksquare$
11. $8 \times 8 = \blacksquare$
12. $81 \div 9 = \blacksquare$

Divide.

13. $9\overline{)36}$
14. $2\overline{)14}$
15. $8\overline{)32}$
16. $3\overline{)15}$
17. $4\overline{)20}$
18. $6\overline{)36}$
19. $5\overline{)40}$
20. $1\overline{)8}$

Solve.

21. If $9 \times 7 = 63$, then $63 \div 9 = \blacksquare$.
22. If $10 \times 8 = 80$, then $80 \div 8 = \blacksquare$.

Isaac uses three eggs to make a cake.

23. How many cakes can he make with 21 eggs?
24. How many eggs are needed to make five cakes?

Carly has 18 bones to divide equally among her four dogs.

25. How many bones should each dog get?
26. How many bones will be left over?
27. Rod drove from home to work and back. He drove a total of 20 miles. How far is it from his home to his work?

Solve these problems. Watch the signs.

28. $587 + 745$
29. $820 - 446$
30. $316 + 598$

Cumulative Review

Use after Lesson 75.

Solve these problems. Watch the signs.

① $70 \div 10 = \blacksquare$ ② $90 \div 9 = \blacksquare$ ③ $30 \div 10 = \blacksquare$

④ $8 \times 10 = \blacksquare$ ⑤ $10 \times 5 = \blacksquare$ ⑥ $7 \times 7 = \blacksquare$

⑦ $6 \times 8 = \blacksquare$ ⑧ $35 \div 7 = \blacksquare$ ⑨ $3 \div 3 = \blacksquare$

Find the value of y.

⑩ $y \longrightarrow \boxed{+9} \longrightarrow 13$ ⑪ $y \longrightarrow \boxed{\div 2} \longrightarrow 8$

$y = \blacksquare$ $y = \blacksquare$

Find a function rule for each set of numbers.

⑫ $0 \longrightarrow \boxed{?} \longrightarrow 0$ ⑬ $72 \longrightarrow \boxed{?} \longrightarrow 62$

$3 \longrightarrow \boxed{?} \longrightarrow 9$ $45 \longrightarrow \boxed{?} \longrightarrow 35$

$6 \longrightarrow \boxed{?} \longrightarrow 18$ $36 \longrightarrow \boxed{?} \longrightarrow 26$

Function rule is $\blacksquare$ Function rule is $\blacksquare$

Use inverse arrow operations to find the value of n.

⑭ $n \longrightarrow \boxed{-5} \longrightarrow m \longrightarrow \boxed{\div 2} \longrightarrow 4$

⑮ $36 \longleftarrow \boxed{\times 6} \longleftarrow m \longleftarrow \boxed{-5} \longleftarrow n$

Find the area.

⑯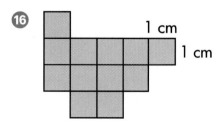

1 cm

1 cm

⑰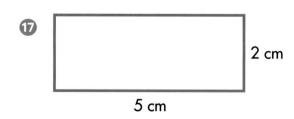

2 cm

5 cm

Multiply.

⑱ $365 \times 10 = \blacksquare$ ⑲ $80 \times 100 = \blacksquare$ ⑳ $1000 \times 209 = \blacksquare$

Cumulative Review
Use after Lesson 79.

Solve these problems. Watch the signs.

1
```
  9836
− 5438
```

2
```
  8000
− 3071
```

3
```
  6291
+ 1357
```

4
```
  5772
+ 2808
```

5
```
  684
  703
+ 145
```

6
```
  318
   72
+ 846
```

7
```
  10
×  6
```

8
```
   7
× 8
```

9 6 × ■ = 48

10 ■ × 9 = 63

11 5 × ■ = 5

12 9 ÷ ■ = 3

Solve these problems.

Morgan needs 27 masks for a party. The masks come in packages of five.

13 How many packages should Morgan buy?

14 Will he have extra masks?

15 Does he have enough money to buy them?

$$x \longrightarrow \boxed{÷7} \longrightarrow y$$

16 If $x = 42$, what is y?

17 If $x = 70$, what is y?

18 If $y = 7$, what is x?

19 If $y = 4$, what is x?

20 Kimiko's bedroom is a square. Each side is 9 feet long. What is the area of Kimiko's bedroom?

Cumulative Review
Use after Lesson 83.

Use the graph to answer the questions about the growth of a plant.

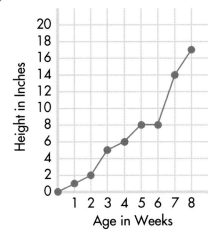

1 How tall was the plant after one week?

2 How many weeks did it take for the plant to grow to 6 inches?

3 Between which weeks did the plant not grow any taller?

4 How tall was the plant after seven weeks?

Give the temperature.

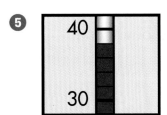

5 40
      30

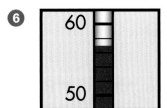

6 60
      50

What is the right sign? Draw <, >, or =.

7 7482 ● 7824

8 835 ● 853

9 111 ● 111

10 5 × 5 ● 6 × 4

11 2 × 9 ● 3 × 6

12 499 ● 500

Round to the nearest thousand.

13 6709

14 2183

15 1076

Cumulative Review
Use after Lesson 86.

Tell the time in three ways.

1 ■

■ minutes after ■

■ minutes before ■

Solve these problems.

2 1 km = ■ m

3 4000 g = ■ kg

4 3 m = ■ cm

5 1 foot = ■ inches

6 1 pound = ■ ounces

7 1 yard = ■ feet

Choose the number that seems most reasonable.
Watch the units.

8 A puppy weighs about ■ kilograms.

  a. 2000

  b. 200

  c. 2

9 A dictionary is about ■ inches thick.

  a. 300

  b. 30

  c. 3

10 A lighthouse is about ■ meters tall.

  a. 20

  b. 200

  c. 2000

Cumulative Review
Use after Lesson 88.

Estimate the length. Then use an inch ruler to check.

1

Solve these problems.

Kerri has 3 feet of red ribbon. She needs pieces that are 8 inches long.

2 How many 8-inch pieces of ribbon can she cut?

3 How long will the leftover piece of ribbon be?

A pineapple weighs 1 kilogram. A melon weighs 867 grams.

4 Which weighs more?

5 How much more?

Write whether the answer is *odd* or *even*.

6 9 + 9   **7** 6 + 5   **8** 30 + 20

Solve these problems. Watch the signs.

9 $7 \times 8 = \blacksquare$ **10** $16 - 7 = \blacksquare$

11 $15 \div 3 = \blacksquare$ **12** $3 + 8 = \blacksquare$

13 $6 \times 9 = \blacksquare$ **14** $90 \div 10 = \blacksquare$

What is the right sign? Draw <, >, or =.

15 $24 \div 3 \bullet 24 \div 8$ **16** $64 \div 8 \bullet 63 \div 7$

17 $5 \times 8 \bullet 4 \times 10$ **18** $1 \times 1 \bullet 8 \times 0$

19 $11 + 3 \bullet 7 + 8$ **20** $10 \div 5 \bullet 18 \div 9$

Cumulative Review
Use after Lesson 90.

Jared has two one-dollar bills and 18 dimes.

1 Does Jared have enough money to buy the batteries?

2 Does Jared have enough money to buy two baseballs?

3 Does he have enough money to buy one baseball and the batteries?

Solve these problems.

4 3 m = ■ dm

5 400 cm = ■ m

6 25 dm = ■ m and ■ dm

7 1 m and 25 cm = ■ cm

8 1.7 m = ■ m and ■ dm

9 ■ m and ■ cm = 1357 cm

Solve these problems.

10 300¢ = $■

11 ■¢ = $7

12 $2 and 54¢ = ■¢

13 $■ and ■¢ = 468¢

Give the length in decimeters and centimeters, and in just centimeters.

14

_____

15

_____

Cumulative Review
Use after Lesson 94.

Complete each statement.

1 There are ▦ hundredths in 3 tenths.

2 There are 70 hundredths in ▦ tenths.

What is the correct sign? Draw <, >, or =.

3 6.2 ● 6.09   **4** 1.42 ● 14.2   **5** 5.80 ● 5.8   **6** 7.38 ● 7.32

7 2.01 ● 2.10   **8** 0.4 ● 0.04   **9** 90.0 ● 9.00   **10** 0.1 ● 0.10

Add.

11
$$\begin{array}{r} 4.23 \\ +\ 6.9 \\ \hline \end{array}$$

12
$$\begin{array}{r} 6.8 \\ +\ 3.25 \\ \hline \end{array}$$

13
$$\begin{array}{r} 27.97 \\ +\ 34.06 \\ \hline \end{array}$$

14
$$\begin{array}{r} 94.5 \\ +\ 94.5 \\ \hline \end{array}$$

15 5.4 + 3.8 = ▦   **16** 6 + 8.4 = ▦

17 71.63 + 9.8 = ▦   **18** 428.04 + 77.7 = ▦

Subtract.

19
$$\begin{array}{r} 23.61 \\ -\ 8.03 \\ \hline \end{array}$$

20
$$\begin{array}{r} 30.00 \\ -\ 6.78 \\ \hline \end{array}$$

21
$$\begin{array}{r} 9.1 \\ -\ 0.7 \\ \hline \end{array}$$

22
$$\begin{array}{r} 12.5 \\ -\ 10.95 \\ \hline \end{array}$$

23 3.0 − 1.3 = ▦   **24** 7.7 − 2.01 = ▦

25 0.64 − 0.08 = ▦   **26** 12.3 − 9.87 = ▦

Solve these problems. Watch the signs.

27
$$\begin{array}{r} 7 \\ \times\ 6 \\ \hline \end{array}$$

28
$$\begin{array}{r} 10 \\ \times\ 5 \\ \hline \end{array}$$

29 $4\overline{)28}$

30 $9\overline{)54}$

Cumulative Review
Use after Lesson 96.

Solve these problems.

1 3.47
\+ 0.63

2 347
\+ 63

3 8.04
\- 3.7

4 50.1
\- 26.08

5 5010
\- 2608

6 0.54
\+ 29.3

7 47.61
\+ 8.89

8 40.02
\- 9.95

Solve these problems.

9 It takes 1.33 yards of fabric to make a vest. How many yards of fabric does it take to make four vests?

10 Kier had $10. He spent some money at the mall. He has $4.17 left. How much did Kier spend?

11 DeAnn is 1.18 meters tall. Lacey is 1.2 meters tall. Who is taller? How much taller?

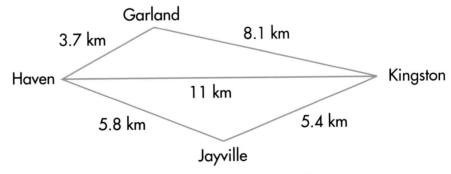

12 How far is it from Haven to Kingston if you go through Jayville?

13 How much shorter is it to go from Haven to Kingston directly?

Complete the pattern.

14 1.3, 1.6, 1.9, ■, ■, ■, 3.1

15 $3.75, $4.00, $4.25, ■, ■, ■, $5.25

Cumulative Review
Use after Lesson 107.

What fraction of each figure is shaded?

1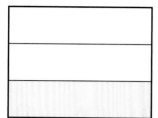

2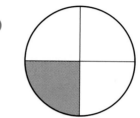

3 Which is more, $\frac{1}{2}$ of the bread or $\frac{1}{3}$ of the bread?

4 Which is more, $\frac{1}{4}$ of the bread or $\frac{1}{3}$ of the bread?

What is the right sign? Draw < or >.

5 4 ● $3\frac{1}{2}$ **6** 3 ● $3\frac{1}{2}$ **7** 3 ● $2\frac{1}{2}$ **8** $\frac{1}{2}$ ● 0

Solve.

9 $\frac{1}{2}$ of 12 is ■.

10 $\frac{1}{3}$ of 12 is ■.

11 $\frac{1}{2}$ of 18 is ■.

12 $\frac{1}{6}$ of 18 is ■.

What fraction is shaded?

13 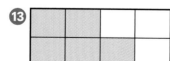 **14**   **15**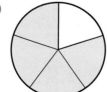

Cumulative Review
Use after Lesson 110.

Solve these problems. Draw pictures or use manipulatives to help you.

1 $\frac{1}{2}$ of 10 is ■.

2 $\frac{1}{4}$ of 24 is ■.

3 $\frac{1}{3}$ of 15 is ■.

4 $\frac{1}{8}$ of 16 is ■.

5 $\frac{2}{3}$ of 9 is ■.

6 $\frac{3}{10}$ of 20 is ■.

What fraction is shaded?

7 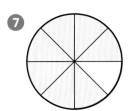   **8** 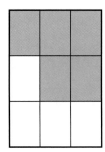   **9**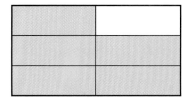

How many minutes?

10 $\frac{1}{2}$ of an hour = ■ minutes   **11** $\frac{2}{3}$ of an hour = ■ minutes

12 $\frac{2}{2}$ of an hour = ■ minutes   **13** $\frac{3}{4}$ of an hour = ■ minutes

Solve these problems. Watch the signs.

14 $5\overline{)35}$

15 $7\overline{)28}$

16
$$\begin{array}{r} 7 \\ \times\ 6 \\ \hline \end{array}$$

17
$$\begin{array}{r} 6 \\ \times\ 3 \\ \hline \end{array}$$

18 $3\overline{)15}$

19 $9\overline{)45}$

20
$$\begin{array}{r} 9 \\ \times\ 6 \\ \hline \end{array}$$

21 $8\overline{)64}$

Solve these problems. Watch the signs.

22
$$\begin{array}{r} \$45.63 \\ +\ \ \ 9.87 \\ \hline \end{array}$$

23
$$\begin{array}{r} 0.24 \\ -\ 0.1 \\ \hline \end{array}$$

24
$$\begin{array}{r} 4.6 \\ -\ 1.85 \\ \hline \end{array}$$

25
$$\begin{array}{r} 13.25 \\ +\ 28.09 \\ \hline \end{array}$$

Cumulative Review
Use after Lesson 112.

Find the next three numbers in each series.

① 3, 8, 13, ■, ■, ■

② 3, 6, 12, 24, ■, ■, ■

③ 0, 4, 3, 7, 6, ■, ■, ■

Solve these problems. Watch the signs.

④ 48 ÷ 6 = ■   **⑤** 0 × 7 = ■   **⑥** 18 − 9 = ■

⑦ 36 ÷ 4 = ■   **⑧** 7 × 6 = ■   **⑨** 5 + 8 = ■

⑩ 9 ÷ 9 = ■   **⑪** 5 × 1 = ■   **⑫** 6 − 0 = ■

What is the right sign? Draw <, >, or =.

⑬ 3.45 ● 3.54   **⑭** 6.7 ● 6.70   **⑮** 1.2 ● 1.02

⑯ 49.8 ● 50   **⑰** 8.04 ● 8.1   **⑱** 12.21 ● 12.2

Solve these problems.

⑲ 436 cm = ■ m   **⑳** ■ cm = 1.98 m

㉑ 783¢ = $■   **㉒** $8.06 = ■¢

㉓ Ursula paid $32 for four tapes. How much does one tape cost?

What fraction is shaded?

㉔ 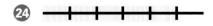   **㉕**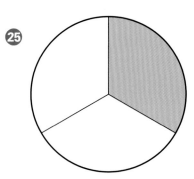

Cumulative Review

Use after Lesson 120.

How many cubes?

1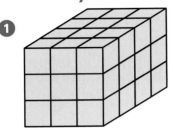

2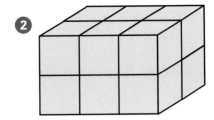

Solve.

3 1 L = ▩ mL

4 ▩ L = 4000 mL

5 9 L = ▩ mL

6 ▩ L = 6000 mL

Write the name of the unit that makes sense. Write *milliliters* **or** *liters.*

7

About 300 ▩ of cocoa

8

About 4 ▩ of cider

Solve these problems.

9 1 quart = ▩ pints

10 4 pints = ▩ gallons

11 $\frac{1}{4}$ gallon = ▩ cups

12 1 gallon = ▩ cups

Which unit makes more sense?

13

About 1 (quart, cup)

14

About $\frac{1}{2}$ (gallon, pint)

Cumulative Review
Use after Lesson 122.

Write the Arabic numeral for each Roman numeral.

1 XIV   **2** CLXV   **3** CCCLIX   **4** LIV

Write the Roman numeral for each Arabic numeral.

5 39   **6** 24   **7** 191   **8** 68

Solve these problems. Watch the signs.

9 2
   × 7

10 5)‾15‾

11 9)‾36‾

12 8
   × 3

13 5
   × 6

14 4)‾24‾

15 9
   × 8

16 8)‾48‾

17 3)‾18‾

18 0
   × 3

gumdrops 7¢ each

lollipops 10¢ each

mints 4¢ each

Solve these problems.

19 How much will five lollipops cost?

20 How much will seven mints and three gumdrops cost?

21 How much will three gumdrops, two lollipops, and five mints cost?

Solve these problems. Watch the signs.

22   7952
   + 8928

23   70,000
   − 34,567

24   316
   − 197

25   463,751
   + 507,812

Cumulative Review
Use after Lesson 127.

Show where these two lines will meet.

1

Tell how many line segments. Tell how many angles.

2

3

4

____ segments

____ angles

____ segments

____ angles

____ segments

____ angles

Write the name of each figure.

5

6

7

Solve.

8 Diameter *EF* is ■ centimeters long.

9 Diameter *CB* is ■ centimeters long.

10 Radius *AD* is ■ centimeters long.

11 Radius *AF* is ■ centimeters long.

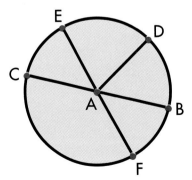

Solve these problems. Watch the signs.

12 5 × 3 = ■

13 42 ÷ 6 = ■

14 6 × 6 = ■

15 18 ÷ 6 = ■

16 8 × 8 = ■

17 49 ÷ 7 = ■

18 35 ÷ 7 = ■

19 21 ÷ 3 = ■

20 7 × 7 = ■

Cumulative Review
Use after Lesson 136.

Which triangles are congruent?

1

Draw the line of symmetry.

2

3

Name the solid figure.

4

5

6

Multiply.

7 24
   × 3

8 37
   × 4

9 19
   × 2

10 67
   × 1

Solve.

11 $\frac{1}{2}$ of 14

12 $\frac{1}{4}$ of 32

13 $\frac{1}{5}$ of 50

14 $\frac{7}{10}$ of 20

Cumulative Review
Use after Lesson 139.

Solve these problems.

1 A school bus can hold 48 people. How many people can eight buses hold?

2 It costs $18 to rent a computer for one day. How much will it cost to rent the computer for three days?

Multiply.

3
$$\begin{array}{r} 352 \\ \times\ \ 6 \\ \hline \end{array}$$

4
$$\begin{array}{r} 416 \\ \times\ \ 5 \\ \hline \end{array}$$

5
$$\begin{array}{r} 372 \\ \times\ \ 4 \\ \hline \end{array}$$

6
$$\begin{array}{r} 108 \\ \times\ \ 5 \\ \hline \end{array}$$

7
$$\begin{array}{r} 607 \\ \times\ \ 8 \\ \hline \end{array}$$

8
$$\begin{array}{r} 301 \\ \times\ \ 9 \\ \hline \end{array}$$

9
$$\begin{array}{r} 639 \\ \times\ \ 1 \\ \hline \end{array}$$

10
$$\begin{array}{r} 745 \\ \times\ \ 7 \\ \hline \end{array}$$

What is the right sign? Draw <, >, or =.

11 $\frac{1}{2} \bullet \frac{1}{3}$

12 $\frac{2}{3} \bullet \frac{1}{4}$

13 $\frac{3}{10} \bullet \frac{1}{2}$

14 $\frac{4}{8} \bullet \frac{1}{2}$

Divide.

15 $6\overline{)36}$

16 $3\overline{)12}$

17 $5\overline{)20}$

18 $2\overline{)12}$

19 $9\overline{)72}$

20 $4\overline{)28}$

21 $7\overline{)42}$

22 $8\overline{)56}$

Round to the nearest ten.

23 68

24 20

25 16

26 82

Solve.

27 $\frac{1}{2}$ of 14

28 $\frac{1}{4}$ of 32

29 $\frac{1}{5}$ of 50

30 $\frac{7}{10}$ of 20

Cumulative Review
Use after Lesson 141.

What is the right sign? Draw <, >, or =.

1. 0.3 + 0.10 ● 0.03
2. 0.1 ● 0.10 + 0
3. 0.07 ● 0.6 − 0.4
4. 0.04 ● 0.3 + 0.1
5. 0.2 − 0.12 ● 0.08
6. 1.5 − 1.2 ● 0.15

Copy the chart. Write the missing amounts.

	Activity	Hours Each Day	Days Each Year	Hours Each Year
7	Bike riding	2	365	■
8	Sleeping	9	365	■
9	Brushing the dog	1	175	■
10	Doing homework	3	140	■

Solve these problems.

11. David's heart beats 72 times in a minute. How many times does it beat in eight minutes?

12. A small bag of chips costs 49¢. How much will five bags cost?

13. Mr. Ruiz earns $450 each week. How much money does he earn in six weeks?

14. If one third of a pound of shrimp costs $2.33, how much will 1 pound of shrimp cost?

Multiply.

15.   35
    × 6

16.   46
    × 7

17.   30
    × 9

18.   126
    × 4

How many?

19. 10^2

20. 2^5

Cumulative Review
Use after Lesson 147.

Multiply.

① 77
  × 25

② 64
  × 30

③ 58
  × 51

④ 79
  × 46

⑤ 2.14
  ×   5

⑥ 8.03
  ×   7

⑦ 5.9
  × 8

⑧ 6.37
  ×   9

Solve these problems.

⑨ There are 48 cans of tuna in each case. How many cans are in 25 cases?

⑩ Selina has 25 quarters. Is that more or less than $10?

⑪ The cupboard is 1 meter high. Pasta boxes are 27 cm high. Can Jack stack four pasta boxes in the cupboard?

⑫ There are 24 hours in one day. July has 31 days. How many hours are there in July?

⑬ One book costs $6.89. How much do seven books cost?

⑭ Each table is 1.35 meters long. How many meters long are four tables placed end to end?

What is the right sign? Draw <, >, or =.

⑮ 40×60 ● 24×10

⑯ 57×93 ● 93×57

⑰ 3×5.91 ● 3×59.1

⑱ 40×20 ● 8×100

In each problem, two answers are clearly wrong and one is correct. Choose the correct answer.

⑲ $31.2 + 47.4 =$ **a.** 786
  b. 16.2
  c. 78.6

⑳ $7548 - 3486 =$ **a.** 3186
  b. 4062
  c. 8888

Cumulative Review
Use after Lesson 151.

Count up. Fill in the missing numbers.

① 9999	10,000	■	■	10,003
② 909,998	■	■	910,001	■
③ 999,999	■	1,000,001	■	■

Copy and fill in the charts.

Distance in Meters	Distance in Centimeters
④ 10	■
⑤ 100	■
⑥ 1000	■

Amount in Dimes	Amount in Dollars
⑦ 100	■
⑧ 1000	■
⑨ 10,000	■

Add.

⑩ 76,543
+ 26,891

⑪ 83,961
+ 28,074

⑫ 5,302,178
+ 9,478,273

⑬ 15,003,859
+ 38,825,006

⑭ 9,003,425
+ 4,469,168

⑮ 18,123,654
+ 11,974,065

Cumulative Review
Use after Lesson 152.

Multiply.

① 8
  × 3

② 4
  × 9

③ 6
  × 5

④ 1
  × 8

⑤ 7
  × 7

Divide.

⑥ 6)30 **⑦** 5)45 **⑧** 9)63 **⑨** 4)16 **⑩** 8)48

Solve these problems. Watch the signs.

⑪ 5.24
  + 69.4

⑫ 6.7
  − 0.81

⑬ 8.1
  − 6.92

⑭ 21.05
  + 7.85

⑮ 11.7
  − 3.8

What fraction is shaded?

⑯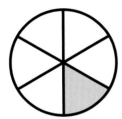

⑰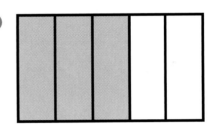

What is the right sign? Draw <, >, or =.

⑱ 1.06 ● 1.6

⑲ 35.7 ● 35.70

⑳ 5 × 6 ● 7 × 5

㉑ 60 × 70 ● 42 × 10

㉒ 0.3 ● 0.03 + 0.27

㉓ 14 × 24 ● 11 × 24

Solve these problems.

㉔ Ruby built a block with centimeter cubes. It was five cubes wide, three cubes high, and four cubes deep. How many cubes did Ruby use?

㉕ A theater has 36 rows. Each row has 54 seats. How many seats are there in the theater?

GLOSSARY

A

addend A number that is added to another number to make a sum. For example:

$$35 \text{ --- addend} \qquad 7 + 8 = 15 \text{ --- sum}$$
$$+ \ 48 \text{ --- addend} \qquad \qquad \qquad \text{--- addend}$$
$$\overline{83} \text{ --- sum} \qquad \qquad \qquad \text{--- addend}$$

algorithm A step-by-step way to solve a certain type of problem.

approximation An answer to a mathematical problem that is not precise but is close enough for the purpose. Sometimes an approximate answer is more useful than a precise answer. (See *estimate*.)

area The number of square units inside a figure. The area of this rectangle is 6 square centimeters:

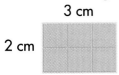

3 cm

2 cm

arrow operation A way to show an action of a function machine. In $7 \longrightarrow \boxed{\times 8} \longrightarrow 56$, 7 goes in and is multiplied by 8 to give 56. The function rule in this case is ×8. In the operation $6 \longleftarrow \boxed{-5} \longrightarrow 11$, 11 goes in and 5 is subtracted from it to give 6. The function rule in this case is −5.

average A number that can sometimes be used to describe a group of numbers. To find the average of a set of numbers, add the numbers and divide the sum by how many numbers were added. The average of 5, 6, 6, 8, and 10 is 7 (5 + 6 + 6 + 8 + 10 = 35, and 35 ÷ 5 = 7). (Also called *mean*.)

axes (of a graph) The two zero lines of a graph that give the coordinates of points. The horizontal axis is the *x*-axis. The vertical axis is the *y*-axis.

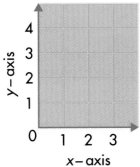

B

balance 1. The amount of money remaining in an account. 2. A double-pan balance is an instrument used to measure weight.

bound A number that an answer must be greater than or less than. For example, 36 × 21 must be less than 40 × 30, or 1200. So 1200 is an upper bound. The answer to 36 × 21 must be greater than 30 × 20, or 600. So 600 is a lower bound.

C

circle A figure (in a plane) in which all points are the same distance from a point called the *center*. In this figure, for example, points *A*, *B*, and *C* are the same distance from point *O*, the center of the circle:

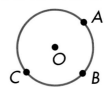

common multiple A number that is a multiple of two or more numbers.

composite function A function with two or more operations.

For example:

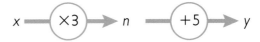

composite number A whole number having factors other than 1 and itself.

congruent Figures that are the same size and shape; that is, they fit perfectly when placed on top of each other. These triangles are congruent:

These triangles are not congruent:

coordinates Numbers that give the position of a point on a graph. In the figure shown, for example, the

cylinder   **fraction**

coordinates of point *A* are (2, 3). 2 is the *x*-coordinate. 3 is the *y*-coordinate.

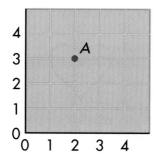

cylinder A space figure with two faces that are circles.

 D

decimal point A dot used to separate the ones digit from the tenths digit.

denominator The part of a fraction written below the line. The part written above the line is called the *numerator*. The denominator tells how many equal parts something is divided into; the numerator tells how many of those parts are being referred to. In the fraction $\frac{3}{4}$ the denominator (4) indicates that something is divided into four equal parts. The numerator (3) says to consider three of those parts.

diameter A line segment, going through the center of a circle, that starts at one point on the circle and ends at the opposite point on the circle. (Also, the length of that line segment.) *AB* is a diameter of this circle.

difference The amount by which one number is greater or less than another. For example:

$$\begin{array}{r} 43 \\ -\ 16 \\ \hline 27 \end{array}$$ — minuend
— subtrahend
— difference

$10 - 7 = 3$ — difference
— subtrahend
— minuend

digit Any of the numbers 0, 1, 2, 3, 4, 5, 6, 7, 8, and 9. The two digits in 15 are 1 and 5.

dividend A number that is divided by a divisor. For example:

$6 \div 3 = 2$ — quotient
— divisor
— dividend

$$8\overline{)347}$$ — quotient
— dividend

$$\begin{array}{r} 32 \\ \hline 27 \\ 24 \\ \hline 3 \end{array}$$

divisor A number that a dividend is divided by. (See *dividend*.)

 E

edge The segment where two faces of a space figure meet.

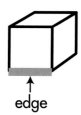

edge

equilateral triangle A triangle with all three sides the same length. For example:

equivalent fractions Fractions that have the same value. For example, $\frac{2}{6}$, $\frac{4}{12}$, and $\frac{1}{3}$ are equivalent fractions.

estimate A judgment about the size or quantity of something. (Also, to make such a judgment.) Sometimes it is more useful to make an estimate than to measure or count precisely. (See *approximation*.)

even number Any multiple of 2. The numbers 0, 2, 4, 6, 8, and so on are even numbers.

 F

face A flat surface of a space figure.

factor A number that is multiplied by another number. (See *multiplicand*.)

fraction Examples of fractions are $\frac{1}{2}$, $\frac{3}{4}$, and $\frac{7}{8}$. The fraction $\frac{3}{4}$ means that something is divided into four equal parts and that we are considering three of those parts. (See *denominator* and *numerator*.)

function machine A machine (sometimes imaginary) that does the same thing to every number that is put into it. (See *arrow operation*.)

function rule See *arrow operation*.

half line See *ray*.

heptagon A polygon with seven sides.

hexagon A polygon with six sides.

hundredth If a whole is divided into 100 equal parts, each part is one hundredth of the whole.

improper fraction A fraction whose numerator is greater than or equal to its denominator.

inequality A statement that tells which of two numbers is greater. For example, 4 > 3 is read "4 is greater than 3," and 3 + 6 < 10 is read "3 plus 6 is less than 10."

intersecting lines Lines that meet. In this figure, lines *AB* and *CD* intersect at point *E*:

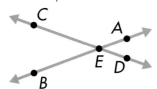

inverse operation An operation that undoes the results of another operation. Multiplication and division are inverse operations; addition and subtraction are inverse operations.

is the inverse of

is the inverse of

isosceles triangle A triangle with two equal sides. These are isosceles triangles:

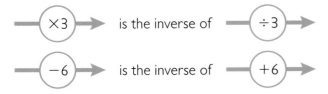

line of symmetry A line on which a figure can be folded into two congruent parts.

line segment A part of a line with two endpoints. For example, *AB* is a line segment; points *A* and *B* are its endpoints.

A   B

mean See *average*.

median The middle number in a group of numbers when they are listed in order from least to greatest. If there are two numbers in the middle, their average is the median. The median of 2, 3, 4, 5, and 6 is 4.

minuend A number from which another number is subtracted. (See *difference*.)

mixed number A number made up of a whole number and a fraction. The numbers $1\frac{1}{2}$, $2\frac{3}{4}$, and $7\frac{7}{8}$ are mixed numbers.

mode The number that occurs most often in a set of numbers. The mode of 1, 2, 3, 1, 4, and 1 is 1.

multiple A number that is some whole number of times another number. 12 is a multiple of 3 because 3 × 4 = 12.

multiplicand A number that is multiplied by another number, the multiplier. For example:

$$
\begin{array}{ll}
5 & \text{— multiplicand} \\
\times\,3 & \text{— multiplier} \\
\hline
15 & \text{— product}
\end{array}
$$

$$3 \times 5 = 15 \text{ — product}$$

multiplicand

multiplier

The multiplier and multiplicand are also called the factors of the product.

multiplier See *multiplicand*.

numerator The part of a fraction written above the line. (See *denominator*.)

octagon

octagon A polygon with eight sides.

odd number A whole number that is not a multiple of 2. All whole numbers that are not even are odd. The numbers 1, 3, 5, 7, 9, 11, and so on are odd numbers.

ordered pair Two numbers written so that one is considered before the other. Coordinates of points are written as ordered pairs, with the *x*-coordinate written first, then the *y*-coordinate. For example: (3, 4). (See *coordinates*.)

parallel lines Lines in a plane that do not intersect. Lines *AB* and *CD* are parallel:

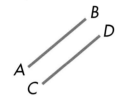

Lines *EF* and *GH* are not parallel:

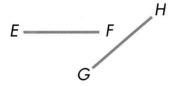

parallelogram A quadrilateral with opposite sides parallel and congruent.

parentheses A pair of symbols ( ) used to show in which order operations should be done. For example, (3 × 5) + 7 says to multiply 5 by 3 and then add 7. 3 × (5 + 7) says to add 5 and 7 and then multiply by 3.

partial product The product that comes from multiplying the multiplicand by one of the digits of the multiplier. For example:

```
    36        This partial product comes from
  × 12        multiplying 36 by 2 ones.
   ───
    72        This partial product comes from
    36        multiplying 36 by 1 ten.
   ───
   432        The product comes from
              adding the partial products.
```

pentagon A polygon with five sides.

perimeter The distance around a figure. The perimeter of this rectangle is 6 cm:

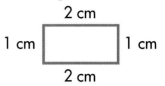

2 cm
1 cm   1 cm
2 cm

perpendicular lines Lines that intersect at right angles. These lines are perpendicular:

So are these:

But these are not:

place value The value of a digit in a number. The value of 7 in 27 is 7 ones; in 74 its value is 70, or 7 tens; and in 726 its value is 700, or 7 hundreds.

polygon A certain kind of figure with straight sides. These figures are polygons:

These are not:

Here are the names of some common polygons and the number of their sides:

Number of Sides	Name
3	triangle
4	quadrilateral
5	pentagon—a regular pentagon has five equal sides:

6   hexagon—a regular hexagon has six equal sides:

8   octagon—a regular octagon has eight equal sides:

prime number A whole number (other than 1) divisible only by 1 and itself.

prism A space figure with two parallel, congruent faces, called bases. These are prisms:

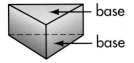

probability How likely it is that something will happen. The probability that a certain thing will happen is a fraction. The denominator is the total number of possible things that can happen, and the numerator is the number of ways this particular thing can happen. The probability that an ordinary coin will land on heads when it is flipped is about $\frac{1}{2}$.

product The result of multiplying two numbers together. (See *multiplicand*.)

profit In a business, the money that is left after all expenses have been paid.

pyramid A space figure formed by connecting points of a polygon to a point not in the plane of the polygon. These are pyramids:

quadrilateral A polygon with four sides.

quotient The result (other than the remainder) of dividing one number by another number. (See *dividend*.)

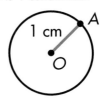

radius A line segment that goes from the center of a circle to a point on the circle. (Also, the length of such a segment.) *OA* is a radius of the circle shown here. The radius of this circle is 1 centimeter.

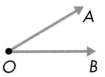

ray A set of points that has one endpoint and extends without end in one direction. In the figure below, *OA* and *OB* are rays.

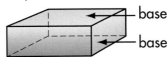

rectangle A quadrilateral in which all four angles are right angles.

reflection A change in the location of a figure when it is flipped over a line.

regroup To rename a number to make adding and subtracting easier.

Example of regrouping in subtraction:

$$\begin{array}{r} \overset{1\ \ 15}{\cancel{2}\cancel{5}} \\ -\ 17 \\ \hline 8 \end{array}$$

(To subtract in the ones column, 2 tens and 5 is regrouped as 1 ten and 15.)

Example of regrouping in addition:

$$\begin{array}{r} \overset{1}{2}96 \\ +\ 442 \\ \hline 738 \end{array}$$

(After the tens column is added, 13 tens is regrouped as 1 hundred and 3 tens.)

relation signs The three basic relation signs are > (greater than), < (less than), and = (equal to). (See *inequality*.)

remainder A number less than the divisor that remains after the dividend has been divided by the divisor as many times as possible. For example, when you divide 25 by 4, the quotient is 6 with a remainder of 1:

right angle An angle that forms a square corner. These are right angles:

These are not:

rotation A change in the location of a figure when it is turned in a circle around a point.

rounding Changing a number to another number that is easier to work with and that is close enough for the purpose. (See *approximation*.)

sphere A space figure with all points the same distance from a point called the *center*.

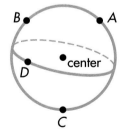

square A quadrilateral with four equal sides and four equal angles.

subtrahend A number that is subtracted from another number. (See *difference*.)

sum The result of adding two or more numbers. (See *addend*.)

symmetrical figure A figure that can be divided in half so that each half looks exactly like the other. (See *line of symmetry*.)

tenth If a whole is divided into ten equal parts, each part is one tenth of the whole.

translation A change in the location of a figure when it is placed on top of another figure.

trapezoid A quadrilateral with exactly one pair of parallel sides. This is a trapezoid:

triangle A polygon that has three sides.

unit cost The cost of one item or one specified amount of an item. If 20 pencils cost 40¢, then the unit cost is 2¢ for each pencil. If dog food costs $9 for 3 kilograms, then the unit cost is $3 per kilogram.

vertex 1. The point where two rays meet. 2. The point of intersection of two sides of a polygon. 3. The point of intersection of three edges of a space figure.

volume The number of cubic units that fit inside a space figure.

whole number The numbers that we use to show how many (0, 1, 2, 3, and so on). The number 3 is a whole number, but $3\frac{1}{2}$ and 4.5 are not whole numbers.

zero The number that tells how many things there are when there aren't any. Any number times 0 is 0 and any number plus 0 is that number: $0 \times 3 = 0$ and $0 + 3 = 3$.